PROLEGOMENA
TO THE METAPHYSICS OF ISLAM

AN EXPOSITION OF THE FUNDAMENTAL ELEMENTS OF THE WORLDVIEW OF ISLĀM

Syed Muhammad Naquib al-Attas
Founder-Director
International Institute of Islamic Thought and Civilization
and
Holder
Distinguished al-Ghazali Chair of Islamic Thought

INTERNATIONAL INSTITUTE OF ISLAMIC THOUGHT AND CIVILIZATION
(ISTAC)
KUALA LUMPUR
2001

Table of Contents

Diagrams

Preface

The conception and conceptualization of knowledge and the sciences, as well as the adaptation of methods and theories, are in each civilization formulated within the framework of its own metaphysical system forming its worldview. Each metaphysical system, and thus also the worldview it projects, is not the same for every other civilization; it differs from one another in accordance with differences in the interpretation of what is taken to be ultimately true and real. If knowledge and the sciences that grow from it are not aligned to the statements and general conclusions of revealed Truth, then what is taken to be true may not always be truly so, nor what is taken to be real to be really so; and such interpretation must therefore undergo recurrent corrective revision necessitating what is called 'paradigm shifts' which involve also changes in the worldview and the metaphysical system that projects it. We do not agree with those who take the position that reality and truth, and values derived from them, are separate, and that they articulate their meanings within the paradigms of relativity and plurality having equal validity.

Since we maintain that knowledge is not entirely a property of the human mind, and that the sciences derived from it are not the products solely of unaided human reason and sense experience possessing an objectivity that preclude value judgement, but that knowledge and the sciences need guidance and verification from the statements and general conclusions of revealed Truth, it is incumbent upon scholars and the learned among us who are entrusted to teach and to educate to acquaint themselves with a clear understanding of the metaphysics of Islam and of the permanently established constituent elements of the worldview derived from it. This is because that metaphysics is not only established upon reason and experience as reflected in the intellectual and religious tradition of Islām, but also upon the articulation of the revealed religion itself about the nature of reality and of truth in verification of the Revelation. The book that now lies between your hands sets forth preliminary discourses on the nature of the metaphysics of Islām.

With the exception of chapter I, which was written twenty years ago in the month of Ramaḍān, the other six chapters were written and completed during the months of the years 1989 (III); 1990 (IV, V and VI); 1993 (II); and 1994 (VII). In chapter II, which is a commentary of the explanation on happiness given in chapter I, I have introduced a new theory of my own on the meaning and origin of tragedy. The whole book, as I have explained in the Epilogue, leads ultimately to an interpretation of the hidden meaning of the Quranic passages on the Creation in Six Days.

These chapters were originally published as separate monographs in limited quantities at the request of the academic staff of ISTAC and others. They requested that I elaborate commentaries on each monograph, in the form of lectures at ISTAC which became known as the Saturday Night Lectures. These lectures, begun in 1992, were attended by all professors, visiting professors, research fellows, and students of ISTAC, as well as by professors and academic staff from other institutions of higher learning, and by professionals and senior officials from government departments, institutes, and ministries. I wish to thank them all for their sincere support, especially to Associate Professor Dr. Wan Mohd. Nor Wan Daud, my Acting Deputy Director, for his constant cooperation and encouragement, and to Research Fellow Muhammad Zainiy Uthman, who helped me in preparing the General Index to the book.

Syed Muhammad Naquib al-Attas
5 September, 1995/9 Rabī'al-Ākhir 1416
KUALA LUMPUR

Preface to the Second Edition

Prolegomena to the Metaphysics of Islām, published by the International Institute of Islamic Thought and Civilization (ISTAC) in 1995, is now reissued by the Institute without alteration. Since its first publication several parts of the book have been translated into various languages. The *Introduction* to the book has been translated into Persian; Chapter I into Arabic, Persian, Turkish, Bosnian, Urdu, Malayalam, Japanese, Korean, Indonesian; Chapter II into Arabic, Turkish, German, Italian, Bosnian, Malay; Chapter III into Persian, Turkish, Bosnian, German, Indonesian; and Chapters V, VI, and VII into Persian. The entire book has recently been translated into Russian under the auspices of the Institute of Islamic Civilization, Moscow, in collaboration with members of the Russian Academy of Science, whose Institute of Philosophy invited me to speak at a Special Presentation of my ideas expressed in the book, and accompanied by my Deputy Professor Dr. Wan Mohd. Nor, to the Academy in Moscow in May 2001.

I wish to thank the International Institute of Islamic Thought and Civilization (ISTAC) for reissuing the book in its present form, and to renew my thanks to Professor Dr. Wan Mohd. Nor Wan Daud, Deputy Director of the Institute, and to Associate Professor Dr. Muhammad Zainiy Uthman, Academic Librarian of the Institute for their constant support of my work. In this second printing of the book, I wish also to thank a new member of our academic staff, Associate Professor Dr. Mohamed Ajmal Abdul Razak, General Editor of Publications of the Institute, who read the proof of the book throughout its printing.

Syed Muhammad Naquib al-Attas
5 September 2001/17 Jumad al-Ākhir 1422
KUALA LUMPUR

بسم الله الرحمن الرحيم

الحمد لله رب العالمين

والصلاة والسلام على اشرف الأنبياء والمرسلين

INTRODUCTION

From the perspective of Islām, a 'worldview' is not merely the mind's view of the physical world and of man's historical, social, political and cultural involvement in it as reflected, for example, in the current Arabic expression of the idea formulated in the phrase *naẓrat al-islām li al-kawn*. It is incorrect to refer to the worldview of Islām as a *naẓrat al-islām li al-kawn*. This is because, unlike what is conveyed by *naẓrat*, the worldview of Islām is not based upon philosophical speculation formulated mainly from observation of the data of sensible experience, of what is visible to the eye; nor is it restricted to *kawn*, which is the world of sensible experience, the world of created things. If such expressions are now in use in Arabic in contemporary Muslim thought, it only demonstrates that we are already being unduly influenced by the modern, secular Western scientific conception of the world that is restricted to the world of sense and sensible experience. Islām does not concede to the dichotomy of the sacred and the profane; the worldview of Islām encompasses both *al-dunyā* and *al-ākhirah*, in which the *dunyā*-aspect *must* be related in a profound and inseparable way to the *ākhirah*-aspect, and in which the *ākhirah*-aspect has ultimate and final significance. The *dunyā*-aspect is seen as a *preparation* for the *ākhirah*-aspect. Everything in Islām is ultimately focussed on the *ākhirah*-aspect without thereby implying any attitude of neglect or being unmindful of the *dunyā*-aspect. Reality is not what is often 'defined' in modern Arabic dictionaries as *wāqi'iyyah*, whose use, particularly in its grammatical form *wāqi'iy*, is now in vogue. Reality is *ḥaqīqah*, which significantly is now seldom used due to the preoccupation with *wāqi'iyyah* which only points to factual occurrences. A factual occurrence is only one aspect in many of *ḥaqīqah*, whose ambit encompasses *all* of reality. Moreover, a factual occurrence may be an actualization of something false (*i.e. bāṭil*); whereas reality is the actualization always of something true (*i.e. ḥaqq*). What is meant by 'worldview', according to the perspective of Islām, is then the *vision of reality and truth* that appears before our mind's eye revealing what existence is all about; for it is the world of existence in its totality that Islām is projecting. Thus by 'worldview' we must mean *ru'yat al-islām li al-wujūd.*

The Islamic vision of reality and truth, which is a metaphysical survey of the visible as well as the invisible worlds including the perspective of life as a whole, is not a worldview that is formed merely by the gathering together of various cultural objects, values and phenomena into artificial coherence.[1] Nor is it one that is formed gradually through a historical and developmental process of philosophical speculation and scientific discovery, which must of necessity be left vague and open-ended for future change and alteration in line with paradigms that change in correspondence with changing circumstances. It is not a worldview that undergoes a dialectical process of transformation repeated through the ages, from thesis to antithesis then synthesis, with elements of each of these stages in the process being assimilated into the other, such as a worldview based upon a system of thought that was originally god centered, then gradually became god-world centered, and is now world centered and perhaps shifting again to form a new thesis in the dialectical process. Such a worldview changes in line with ideological ages characterized by a predominance of the influence of particular and opposing systems of thought advocating different interpretations of worldview and value systems like that which have occurred and will continue to occur in the

---

1. I mean by 'artifical coherence', a coherence that is not natural in the sense we mean as *fiṭrah.* Such coherence projected as a worldview must necessarily be subject to change with the change of circumstances.

history of the cultural, religious and intellectual tradition of the West. There have not been in the history of the cultural, religious and intellectual tradition of Islām distinct ages characterized by a preponderance of a system of thought based upon materialism or idealism, supported by attendant methodological approaches and positions like empiricism, rationalism, realism, nominalism, pragmatism, positivism, logical positivism, criticism, oscillating between centuries and emerging one after another right down to our time. The representatives of Islamic thought — theologians, philosophers, metaphysicians — have all and individually applied various methods in their investigations without preponderating on any one particular method. They combined in their investigations, and at the same time in their persons, the empirical and the rational, the deductive and the inductive methods and affirmed no dichotomy between the subjective[2] and the objective, so that they all affected what I would call the *tawḥīd* method of knowledge. Nor have there been in Islām historical periods that can be characterized as 'classical', then 'medieval', then 'modern' and now purportedly shifting again to 'post-modern'; nor critical events between the medieval and the modern experienced as a 'renaissance' and an 'enlightenment'. Proponents of shifts in systems of thought involving changes in the fundamental elements of the worldview and value system may say that all forms of cultures must experience such shifts, otherwise in the process of interaction with changing circumstances they exhaust

---

2. By 'subjective' I mean not the popular understanding of the word. The human soul is creative; by means of perception, imagination, and intelligence it participates in the 'creation' and interpretation of the worlds of sense and sensible experience, of images, and of intelligible forms. 'Subjective' here is something not opposed to what is objective, but complementary to it.

themselves and become uncreative and petrified. But this is true only in the experience and consciousness of civilizations whose systems of thought and value have been derived from cultural and philosophical elements aided by the science of their times. Islām is not a form of culture, and its system of thought projecting its vision of reality and truth and the system of value derived from it are not merely derived from cultural and philosophical elements aided by science, but one whose original source is Revelation, confirmed by religion, affirmed by intellectual and intuitive principles. Islām ascribes to itself the truth of being a truly revealed religion, perfected from the very beginning, requiring no historical explanation and evaluation in terms of the place it occupied and the role it played within a process of development. All the essentials of the religion: the name, the faith and practice, the rituals, the creed and system of belief were given by Revelation and interpreted and demonstrated by the Prophet in his words and model actions, not from cultural tradition which necessarily must flow in the stream of historicism. The religion of Islām was conscious of its own identity from the time of its revelation. When it appeared on the stage of world history Islām was already 'mature', needing no process of 'growing up' to maturity. *Revealed* religion can only be that which knows itself from the very beginning; and that self-knowledge comes from the Revelation itself, not from history. The so called 'development' in the religious traditions of mankind cannot be applied to Islām, for what is assumed to be a developmental process is in the case of Islām only a process of interpretation and elaboration which must of necessity occur in alternating generations of believers of different nations, and which refer back to the unchanging Source.[3] As such the worldview of Islām is characterized by an authenticity and a finality that points to what

---

3. Cf. al-Attas, *Islām and Secularism*, Kuala Lumpur, 1978, ch.II.

is ultimate, and it projects a view of reality and truth that encompasses existence and life altogether in total perspective whose fundamental elements are permanently established. These are, to mention the most salient ones, the nature of God; of Revelation (*i.e.* the Qur'ān); of His creation; of man and the psychology of the human soul; of knowledge; of religion; of freedom; of values and virtues; of happiness — all of which, together with the key terms and concepts that they unfold, have profound bearing upon our ideas about change, development, and progress. I propose here in this Introduction to give a gist only of some of these fundamental elements of the worldview of Islām. A comprehensive statement of their nature is already set forth in the chapters of this book. It is these fundamental elements of our worldview that we maintain to be permanently established that modernity is challenging, seeing that the shifting systems of thought that have brought modernity forth from the womb of history were fathered by the forces of secularization as a philosophical ideology. But as a matter of fact modernity or postmodernity has itself no coherent vision to offer that could be described as a worldview. If we could strike even a superficial similitude between a worldview and a picture depicted in a jigsaw puzzle, then the jigsaw of modernity is not only far from depicting any coherent picture, but also the very pieces to form such a picture do not fit. This is not to mention postmodernity, which is already undoing all the pieces. No true worldview can come into focus when a grandscale ontological system to project it is denied, and when there is a separation between truth and reality and between truth and values. These fundamental elements act as integrating principles that place all our systems of meaning and standards of life and values in coherent order as a unified system forming the worldview; and the supreme principle of true reality that is articulated by these fundamental elements is focussed on knowledge of the nature of God as revealed in the Qur'ān.

The nature of God as revealed in Islām is derived from

Revelation. We do not mean by Revelation the sudden visions great poets and artists claim for themselves; nor the apostolic inspiration of the writers of sacred scripture; nor the illuminative intuition of the sages and people of discernment. We mean by it the speech of God concerning Himself, His creation, the relation between them, and the way to salvation communicated to His chosen Prophet and Messenger, not by sound or letter, yet comprising all that He has represented in words, then conveyed by the Prophet to mankind in a linguistic form *new in nature* yet comprehensible, without confusion with the Prophet's own subjectivity and cognitive imagination. This Revelation is final, and it not only confirms the truth of preceding revelations in their original forms, but includes their substance, separating the truth from cultural creations and ethnic inventions.

Since we affirm the Qur'ān to be the speech of God revealed in a new form of Arabic, the description of His nature therein is therefore the description of Himself by Himself in His own words according to that linguistic form. It follows from this that the Arabic of the Qur'ān, its interpretation in the Tradition, and its authentic and authoritative usage throughout the ages establishes the validity of that language to a degree of eminence in serving to describe reality and truth.[4] In this sense and unlike the situation prevailing in modernist and postmodernist thought, we maintain that it is not the concern of Islām to be unduly involved in the semantics of languages in general that philosophers of language find problematic as to their adequacy to approximate or correspond with true reality. The conception of the nature of God that is derived from Revelation is also established upon the foundations of reason and intuition, and in some cases upon empirical intuition, as a result of man's

---

4. For further details, see my *The Concept of Education in Islām*, Kuala Lumpur, 1980, pp.1-13.

experience and consciousness of Him and of His creation.

The nature of God understood in Islām is not the same as the conceptions of God understood in the various religious traditions of the world; nor is it the same as the conceptions of God understood in Greek and Hellenistic philosophical tradition; nor as the conceptions of God understood in Western philosophical or scientific tradition; nor in that of Occidental and Oriental mystical traditions. The apparent similarities that may be found between their various conceptions of God with the nature of God understood in Islām cannot be interpreted as evidence of identity of the One Universal God in their various conceptions of the nature of God; for each and every one of them serves and belongs to a different conceptual system, which necessarily renders the conception as a whole or the super system to be dissimilar with one another. Nor is there a 'transcendent unity of religions', if by 'unity' is meant 'oneness' or 'sameness'; and if by 'unity' is not meant 'oneness' or 'sameness', then there is plurality or dissimilarity of religions even at the level of transcendence. If it is conceded that there is plurality or dissimilarity at that level, and that by 'unity' is meant 'interconnectedness of parts that constitute a whole', so that the unity is the interconnection of the plurality or dissimilarity of religions as of parts constituting a whole, then it follows that at the level of ordinary existence, in which mankind is subject to the limitations of humanity and the material universe, any one religion is incomplete in itself, is in itself inadequate to realize its purpose, and can only realize its purpose, which is true submission to the One Universal God without associating Him with any partner, rival, or like, at the level of transcendence. But religion is meant to realize its purpose precisely at the level of existence in which mankind is subject to the limitations of humanity and the material universe, and not when mankind is not subject to these limitations as the term 'transcendent' conveys. If 'transcendent' is meant to refer to an ontological condition not included under any of the ten categories, God is, strictly speaking, not the God of religion (*i.e. ilāh*) in the sense that there could be such a thing as a 'unity' of *religions* at that level. At that level God is recognized as *rabb,* not as *ilāh*; and recognizing Him as *rabb* does not necessarily imply oneness or sameness in the proper acknowledgement of the truth that is recognized, since Iblīs also recognized God as *rabb* and yet did not properly acknowledge Him. Indeed, all of Adam's progeny have already recognized Him as *rabb* at that level. But mankind's recognition of Him as such is not *true* unless followed by proper acknowledgement at the level in which He is known as *ilāh.* And proper acknowledgement at the level in which He is known as *ilāh* consists in not associating Him with any partner, rival, or like, and in submitting to Him in the manner and form approved by Him and shown by His sent Prophets. If 'transcendent' is meant to refer to a psychological condition at the level of experience and consciousness which 'excels' or 'surpasses' that of the masses among mankind, then the 'unity' that is experienced and made conscious of at the level of transcendence is not of religions, but of religious experience and consciousness, which is arrived at by the relatively few individuals only among mankind. But religion is meant to realize its purpose for the generality of mankind; and mankind as a whole can never be at the level of transcendence for there to be a unity of religions at that level. Then if it is denied that the unity at that level is the interconnection of the plurality or dissimilarity of religions *as of parts constituting a whole,* rather that every one of the religions at the level of ordinary existence is not a part of a whole, but is a whole in itself — then the 'unity' that is meant is 'oneness' or 'sameness' not really of religions, but of the God of religions at the level of transcendence (*i.e.* esoteric), implying thereby that at the level of ordinary existence (*i.e.* exoteric), and despite the plurality and diversity of religions, each religion is adequate and valid in its own limited way, each authentic and conveying limited though equal truth. The notion of a plurality of truth of equal validity in the plurality and diversity of religions is perhaps aligned to the statements and general conclusions of modern philosophy and science arising from the discovery of a plurality and diversity of laws governing the universe having equal validity each in its own cosmological system. The trend to align modern scientific discovery concerning the systems of the universe with corresponding statements applied to human society, cultural traditions, and values is one of the characteristic features of modernity. The position of those who advocate the theory of the transcendent unity of religions is based upon the assumption that all religions, or the major religions of mankind, are *revealed* religions. They assume that the universality and transcendence of esoterism validates their theory, which they 'discovered' after having acquainted themselves with the metaphysics of Islām. In their understanding of this metaphysics of the transcendent unity of existence, they further assume that the transcendent unity of religions is already implied. There is grave error in all their assumptions, and the phrase 'transcendent unity of religions' is misleading and perhaps meant to be so for motives other than the truth. Their claim to belief in the transcendent unity of religions is something suggested to them inductively by the imagination and is derived from intellectual speculation and not from actual experience. If this is denied, and their claim is derived from the experience of others, then again we say that the sense of 'unity' experienced is not of religions, but of varying degrees of individual religious experience which does not of necessity lead to the assumption that the religions of individuals who experienced such 'unity', have truth of equal validity as *revealed* religions at the level of ordinary existence. Moreover, as already pointed out, the God of that experience is recognized as the *rabb,* not the *ilāh* of revealed religion. And recognizing Him as the *rabb* does not necessarily mean that acknowledging Him in true submission follows from that recognition, for rebellion, arrogance, and falsehood have their origin in that very realm of transcendence. There is only one revealed religion. It was the religion conveyed by all the earlier Prophets, who were sent to preach the message of the revelation *to their own people* in accordance with the wisdom and justice of the Divine plan to prepare the peoples of the world for reception of the religion in its ultimate and consummate form as a Universal Religion at the hands of the last Prophet, who was sent to convey the message of the revelation not only to his own people, but to mankind as a whole. The essential message of the revelation was always the same: to recognize and acknowledge and worship the One True and Real God (*ilāh*) alone, without associating Him with any partner, rival, or equal, nor attributing a likeness to Him; and to confirm the truth preached by the earlier Prophets as well as to confirm the final truth brought by the last Prophet as it was confirmed by all the Prophets sent before him. With the exception of the people of this last Prophet, through whom the revealed religion achieved utmost perfection whose original purity is preserved to this day, most of the peoples to whom the earlier Prophets were sent deliberately renounced the guidance preferring instead cultural creations and ethnic inventions of their own, claiming these as 'religions' in imitation of revealed religion. There is only one genuine revealed religion, and its name is given as *Islām*, and the people who follow this religion are praised by God as the best among mankind. As for some among the peoples who preferred to follow their own and diverse forms of belief and practice described as 'religions', their realization of the Truth is their rediscovery, by means of guidance and sincerity of heart, of what is already clearly manifest in Islām even at the level of ordinary existence. Only Islām acknowledges and affirms the Unity of God absolutely without having to arrive at the level of transcendence to do so; without confusing such acknowledgement and affirmation with traditional forms of belief and practice described as 'religions'; without confounding such acknowledgement and affirmation with cultural creations and ethnic inventions interpreted in imitation of revealed religion. Therefore Islām does not admit of any error in the understanding of the Revelation, and in this sense Islām is not merely a *form* — it is the *essence* itself of religion (*dīn*). We do not admit in the case of Islām of a horizontal dividing line separating the exoteric from the esoteric understanding of the Truth in religion. We maintain rather a vertical line of continuity from the exoteric to the esoteric; a vertical line of continuity which we identify as the Straight Path of *islām-īmān-iḥsān* without there being any inconsistency in the three stages of the spiritual ascent such that the Reality or transcendent Truth that is recognized and acknowledged is in our case accessible to many. It is futile to attempt to camouflage error in the religions, in their respective understanding and interpretation of their scriptures which they believe reflect the original revelation, by resorting to the characteristics and peculiarities of different forms of ethnicity and symbolism, and then to explain away the symbolism by means of a contrived and deceptive hermeneutic such that error appears as truth. Religion consists not only of affirmation of the Unity of God (*al-tawḥīd*), but also of the *manner* and *form* in which we verify that affirmation as shown by His last Prophet, who confirmed, perfected and consolidated the manner and form of affirmation and verification of Prophets before him. This manner and form of verification is the manner and form of submission to God. The test of *true affirmation* of the Unity of God, then, is the *form of submission* to that God. It is only because the form of submission enacted by the religion that affirms the Unity of God is *true to the verification of such affirmation* that that particular religion is called *Islām*. Islām, then, is not merely a verbal noun signifying 'submission'; it is also *the name of a particular religion* descriptive of true submission, as well as *the definition of religion*: submission to God. Now the manner and form of submission enacted in religion is definitely influenced by the conception of God in the religion. It is therefore the conception of God in the religion that is crucial to the correct articulation of the form of true submission; and this conception must be adequate in serving to describe the true nature of God, which can only be derived from Revelation, not from ethnic or cultural tradition, nor from an amalgamation of ethnic and cultural tradition with sacred scripture, nor from philosophical speculation aided by the discoveries of science.

The conception of the nature of God in Islām is the consummation of what was revealed to the Prophets according to the Qur'ān. He is one God; living, self-subsistent, eternal and abiding. Existence is His very essence. He is one in essence; no division in His essence, whether in the imagination, in actuality, or in supposition is possible. He is not a locus of qualities, nor is a thing portioned and divisible into parts, nor is He a thing compounded of constituent elements. His oneness is absolute, with an absoluteness unlike the absoluteness of the natural universal, for while being thus absolute He is yet individuated in a manner of individuation that does not impair the purity of His absoluteness nor the sanctity of His oneness. He is transcendent, with a transcendence that does not make it incompatible for Him to be at once omnipresent, so that He is also immanent, yet not in the sense understood as belonging to any of the paradigms of pantheism. He possesses real and eternal attributes which are qualities and perfections which He ascribes to Himself; they are not other than His essence, and yet they are also distinct from His essence and from one another without their reality and distinctness being separate entities subsisting apart from His essence as a plurality of eternals; rather they coalesce with His essence as an unimaginable unity. His unity is then the unity of essence, attributes, and acts, for He is living and powerful, knowing, willing, hearing and seeing, and speaking through His attributes of life and power, knowledge, will, hearing and sight, and speech; and the opposite of these are all impossible in Him.

He is unlike the Aristotelian First Mover, for He is always in act as a free agent engaged in perpetual creative activity not involving change in Him or transformation and becoming. He is far too exalted for the Platonic and

Aristotelian dualism of form and matter to be applied to His creative activity; nor can His creating and His creation be described in terms of the Plotinian metaphysics of emanation. His creating is the bringing forth of ideal realities that preexist in His knowledge into external existence by His power and His will; and these realities are entities that he causes to become manifest in the interior condition of His being. His creating is a single act repeated in an eternal process, whereas the contents of the process which are His creation are noneternal, being originated in new yet similar guises in discrete durations of existence for as long as He wills.

It is through Revelation, in which God has described Himself, His creative activity and His creation, and not through Greek or Hellenistic philosophical tradition, neither even through philosophy nor through science, that Islām interprets the world together with all its parts in terms of events that occur within a perpetual process of a new creation. This interpretation entails the affirmation of realities and their double nature consisting of complementary opposites; their existential condition of permanence and change; their involvement in a continual process of annihilation and renewal by similars; their absolute beginning in past time and their absolute end in future time. There are limitations to time and space; and both are the result of the creative act that brings the cosmos into existence. Change is not in the phenomenal things, as that would imply the persistence of existence in the things making them substrata for change to take place, but at the ontological level of their realities which contain within themselves all their future states. Change is then the successive actualization, by means of the creative act, of potentialities inherent in the realities of things which as they unfold their contents in correspondence with the creative command preserve their identities through time. The dual condition of the realities involving permanence on the one hand and change on the other presupposes a third ontological category in the interior condition of Being between external existence and non-existence. This is the realm of ideal realities subsisting as permanently established entities in the consciousness of God, and they are none other than the forms and aspects of the names and attributes of God considered in their aspect of difference from Him.

Islām affirms the possibility of knowledge; that knowledge of the realities of things and their ultimate nature can be established with certainty by means of our external and internal senses and faculties, reason and intuition, and true reports of scientific or religious nature, transmitted by their authentic authorities. Islām has never accepted, nor has ever been affected by ethical and epistemological relativism that made man the measure of all things, nor has it ever created the situation for the riṣe of skepticism, agnosticism, and subjectivism, all of which in one way or another describe aspects of the secularizing process which have contributed to the birth of modernism and postmodernism.

Knowledge is both the arrival of meaning in the soul as well as the soul's arrival at meaning. In this definition we affirm that the soul is not merely a passive recipient like the *tabula rasa,* but is also an active one in the sense of setting itself in readiness to receive what it wants to receive, and so to consciously strive for the arrival at meaning. Meaning is arrived at when the proper place of anything in a system is clarified to the understanding. The notion of 'proper place' already implies the existence of 'relation' obtaining between things which altogether describe a system, and it is such relation or network of relations that determines our recognition of the thing's proper place within the system. By 'place' is meant here that which occurs not only in the spatio-temporal order of existence, but also in the imaginal, intelligible, and transcendental orders of existence. Since objects of knowledge from the point of view of human cognition are without limit, and since our external and internal senses and faculties of imagination and cognition all have limited powers and potentials, each created to convey and conserve information concerning that for which it was appointed, reason demands that there is a limit of truth for every object of knowledge, beyond which or falling short of which the truth about the object as it and its potentials should be known becomes false. Knowledge of this limit of truth in every object of knowledge is either attained by way of common sense if the object is already something obvious to the understanding, or it is achieved through wisdom, either practical or theoretical as the case may be, when the object is something obscure to the understanding. The apparent and obvious meanings of the objects of knowledge have to do with their respective places within the system of relations; and their 'proper' places become apparent to our understanding when the limits of their significance are recognized. This then is the position of truth: that there are limits to the meaning of things in the way they are meant to be known, and their proper places are profoundly bound up with the limits of their significance. *True* knowledge is then knowledge that recognizes the limit of truth in its every object.

Our real challenge is the problem of the corruption of knowledge. This has come about due to our own state of confusion as well as influences coming from the philosophy, science, and ideology of modern Western culture and civilization. Intellectual confusion emerged as a result of changes and restriction in the meaning of key terms that project the worldview derived from Revelation. The repercussions arising from this intellectual confusion manifest themselves in moral and cultural dislocation, which is symptomatic of the degeneration of religious knowledge, faith, and values. The changes and restrictions in the meanings of such key terms occur due to the spread of secularization as a philosophical program, which holds sway over hearts and minds enmeshed in the crisis of truth and the crisis of identity. These crises, in turn, have become actualized as a result of a secularized system of education that causes deviations, if not severance, from historical roots that have been firmly established by our wise and illustrious predecessors upon foundations vitalized by religion. One must see that the kind of problem confronting us is of such a profound nature as to embrace all the fundamental elements of our worldview that cannot simply be resolved by legalistic and political means. Law and order can only find their places when recognition of *truth* as distinguished from falsehood, and *real* as distinguished from illusory, is affirmed and confirmed by action in acknowledgement of the recognition. This is achieved by means of right knowledge and right method of disseminating it. So let us not dissipate our energies in attempting to find the way out by groping in the labyrinths of legalism, but concentrate them instead by grappling the main problem, which is bound up intimately with the correct understanding and appreciation of religion and the worldview projected by it, because that directly concerns man, his knowledge and purpose in life, his ultimate destiny.

The process of acquisition of knowledge is not called 'education' unless the knowledge that is acquired includes moral purpose that activates in the one who acquires it what I call *adab*. *Adab* is right action that springs from self-discipline founded upon knowledge whose source is wisdom. For the sake of convenience I shall translate *adab* simply as 'right action'. There is an intrinsic connection between meaning and knowledge. I define 'meaning' as the *recognition of the place of anything in a system, which occurs when the relation a thing has with others in the system becomes clarified and understood.* 'Place' refers to right or proper place in the system; and 'system' here refers to the Quranic conceptual system as formulated into a worldview by tradition and articulated by religion. Knowledge as we have already defined is the *arrival of meaning in the soul,* and the *soul's arrival at meaning,* and this is the *recognition of the proper places of things in the order of creation, such that it leads to the recognition of the proper place of God in the order of being and existence.* But knowledge as such does not become an education unless the recognition of proper places is actualized by acknowledgement — that is, by confirmation and affirmation in the self — of the reality and truth of what is recognized. Acknowledgement necessitates action that is proper to recognition. *Adab,* or right action, consists of such acknowledgement. Education, then, is the absorption of *adab* in the self. The actualization of *adab* in individual selves composing society as a collective entity reflects the condition of justice; and justice itself is a reflection of wisdom, which is the light that is lit from the lamp of prophecy that enables the recipient to discover the right and proper place for a thing or a being to be. The *condition* of being in the proper place is what I have called justice; and *adab* is that cognitive action by which we *actualize* the condition of being in the proper place. So *adab* in the sense I am defining here, is also a reflection of wisdom; and with respect to society *adab* is the just order within it. *Adab,* concisely defined, is the spectacle of justice (*'adl*) as it is reflected by wisdom (*ḥikmah*).

In order to explain what I mean by *adab* and to appreciate my definition of it, let us consider, for example, one's self. The human self or soul has two aspects: the one predisposed to praiseworthy acts, intelligent by nature, loyal to its covenant with God; the other inclined to evil deeds, bestial by nature, heedless of its covenant with God. The former we call the rational soul (*al-nafs al-nāṭiqah*), the latter the carnal or animal soul (*al-nafs al-ḥayawāniyyah*). When the rational soul subdues the animal soul and renders it under control, then one has put the animal soul in its proper place and the rational soul also in its proper place. In this way, and in relation to one's self, one is putting one's self in one's proper place. This is *adab* toward one's self. Then in relation to one's family and its various members; when one's attitude and behaviour toward one's parents and elders display sincere acts of humility, love, respect, care, charity; this shows one knows one's proper place in relation to them by putting them in their proper places. This is *adab* toward family. And similarly, such attitude and behaviour, when extended to teachers, friends, community, leaders, manifest knowledge of one's proper place in relation to them; and this knowledge entails requisite acts in order to *actualize adab* toward them all. Again, when one puts words in their proper places so that their true meanings become intelligible, and sentences and verses in like manner such that prose and poetry become literature, then that is *adab* toward language. Further, when one puts trees and stones, mountains, rivers, valleys and lakes, animals and their habitat in their proper places, then that is *adab* toward nature and the environment. The same applies to one's home when one arranges furniture and puts things in their proper places therein until harmony is achieved — all such activity is *adab* towards home and furniture. And we cite also putting colours, shapes, and sounds in their proper places producing pleasing effects — that is *adab* toward art and music. Knowledge too, and its many branches and disciplines, some of which have more important bearing upon our life and destiny than others; if one grades them according to various levels and priorities and classifies the various sciences in relation to their priorities putting each one of them in its proper place, then that is *adab* toward knowledge. It should already become clear that my interpretation of the meaning of *adab* reveals that *adab* implies knowledge; it is knowledge derived from wisdom (*hikmah*); it manifests the purpose of seeking knowledge; it is also internal and external activity of the soul that springs from ethical and moral values and virtues; its fount of origin is not philosophy nor science, but revealed truth that flows from religion.

From the above definitions of some of the major key concepts in Islām, which all converge upon the concept of knowledge, it becomes clear that their meanings are closely interrelated, in particular their meanings which all focus upon the notion of 'proper place' which points to a certain 'order' in the system and one's relation to that order. The order is in the form of hierarchy which pervades the created order of being and existence, both external existence and mental existence. The hierarchy I mean, when applied to the human order, is not to be misunderstood as the kind of hierarchy created by man and articulated into a social structure such as a system of caste, or a graded priestly organization, or any kind of social stratification according to class. It is not something to be organized into a social structure; it is rather something to be organized *in the mind* and actualized *in the attitude and the behaviour.* The organization in the mind is not formulated by the human criteria of power, wealth, and lineage, but by the Quranic criteria of knowledge, intelligence, and virtue. When the mind recognizes the reality that knowledge and being are ordered according to their various levels and degrees, and when the attitude and the behaviour acknowledges by action what the mind recognizes, then this conformity of the acknowledgement with the recognition, by which the self assumes its proper place in coincidence with the act of acknowledgement, is none other than *adab.* But when the mind displaces the levels and degrees of knowledge and being, disrupting the order in the legitimate hierarchy, then this is due to the corruption of knowledge. Such corruption is reflected in the confusion of justice, so that the notion of 'proper places' no longer applies in the mind or externally, and the disintegration of *adab* takes place.

The disintegration of *adab,* which is the effect of the corruption of knowledge, creates the situation whereby false leaders in all spheres of life emerge; for it not only implies the corruption of knowledge, but it also means the loss of the capacity and ability to recognize and acknowledge true leaders. Because of the intellectual anarchy that characterizes this situation, the common people become determiners of intellectual decisions and are raised to the level of authority on matters of knowledge. Authentic definitions become undone, and in their stead we are left with platitudes and vague slogans disguised as profound concepts. The inability to define; to identify and isolate problems, and hence to provide for right solutions; the creation of pseudo-problems; the reduction of problems to mere political, socio-economic and legal factors become evident. It is not surprising if such a situation provides a fertile breeding ground for the emergence of deviationists and extremists of many kinds who make ignorance their capital.

Language reflects ontology. Introducing key concepts foreign to a language involves not merely the translating of words, but more profoundly the translating of symbolic forms belonging to the super system of a foreign worldview not compatible with the worldview projected by the language into which such concepts are introduced. Those responsible for introducing them and advocating their currency are the scholars, academics, journalists, critics, politicians and amateurs not firmly grounded upon knowledge of the essentials of religion and its vision of reality and truth. One of the main causes for the emergence of intellectual confusion and anarchy is the changes and restrictions which they have effected in the meanings of key terms that project the worldview of Islām which is derived from Revelation. The major factor that influenced their thinking is undoubtedly the introduction of the concept *secular* and its implications into our language and our universe of discourse, which Muslims as a whole have yet to perceive from its proper perspective.

The early latinized Western Church monopolized learning and coined the term 'secular' (*saeculum*) to refer to people who are unable to read and write, who are therefore not learned in the arts and sciences, especially in law and medicine, who are then generally called the 'laity': the non-professional, not expert. Due to the preoccupation of such people with mundane matters, the term also conveys a general meaning of 'being concerned with the affairs of the world'; of being 'not sacred', 'not monastic', 'not ecclesiastical'; of being something 'temporal', something 'profane'. Hence we find this term being translated by Christian Arabs into Christian Arabic as '*almāniy*', meaning: *laysa min arbāb al-fann aw al-ḥirfah*; and 'secularity' as *al-ihtimām bi umūr al-dunyā*, or *al-ihtimām bi al-ʿālamiyyāt*; and 'to secularize' as *ḥawwal ilā gharaḍ ʿālamiy ay dunyawiy*. This translation of the term and its various grammatical forms, in the sense understood by the Western Christian Church and its Christian Arab translators, has been allowed to gain currency in contemporary mainstream Islamic Arabic, despite the clear fact that it has no relevance whatsoever to Islām and to the Muslim *ummah.* There is no equivalent in Islām to the concept *secular,* especially when there is no equivalent to 'church' or 'clergy', and when Islām does not concede that there is a dichotomy of the sacred and the profane which naturally brings about a demeaning of the profane world. If the nearest equivalent were to be found in Islām to the concept *secular,* then it would be that which is connoted by the Quranic concept of *al-ḥayāt al-dunyā*: 'the worldly life'. The word *dunyā,* derived from *danā,* conveys the meaning of something being 'brought near'. This something that is being 'brought near', according to my interpretation, is the world together with all its parts; for it is the world that is being brought *near,* that is, being *brought near to the experience and consciousness of man.* Hence the world is called *dunyā.* By virtue of the fact that what is being brought near — that is, the world and the life in it — surround us as it were and overwhelm us, they are bound to distract from consciousness of our final destination, which is beyond this world and this life, which is what comes *after,* that is, *al-ākhirah.* Since it comes at the *end, al-ākhirah* is felt as *far,* and this accentuates the distraction created by what is *near.* The Holy Qur'ān says that the Hereafter is better than the life of this world; it is more abiding, everlasting. But the Holy Qur'ān does not derogate the world itself; or dissuade from contemplation and reflection and interpretation of it and its wonders; rather it extols the world of creation and urges us to contemplate and reflect upon it and its wonders in order that we might be able to interpret and derive their practical and beneficial purpose. The Holy Qur'ān only warns of the distracting and ephemeral nature of life in the world. The warning emphasis in the concept of *al-ḥayat al-dunyā* is the *life* in it, not the *world,* so that the world and nature are not demeaned as implied in the concept *secular.* That is why I said that *al-ḥayat al-dunyā* is the nearest equivalent to the concept *secular,* because in actual fact there is no real equivalent concept in the worldview of Islām projected by the Holy Qur'ān. Moreover, since the world is that which is 'brought near', and since the world and nature are signs or *āyāt* of God, it is the signs of God that are brought near to our experience and consciousness; and it would be blasphemous, to say the least, to derogate the world and nature knowing them in their true character and purpose. It is God's manifestation of His infinite mercy and loving kindness that He caused His signs to be brought near to us, the better for us to understand their intended meanings. There can be no excuse, therefore, for those who, struck by awe of the signs, worship them instead of God to whom they point; or those who, seeking God, yet demean and abjure His signs because they see tempting evil in them and not in themselves; or again those who, denying God, appropriate His signs for their own materialistic ends and change them in pursuit of illusory 'development'. The world cannot develop as it is already perfect according to its own *fiṭrah;* only life in the world can develop. There is a final end to the world just as there is a final end to life in the world. Development of life in the world is that which leads to success in that which comes after it, for there is no meaning to 'development' unless it is aligned to a *final objective.*

The Latin term *saeculum* in its original sense relates to the doctrinal formulations of the Western Christian religious tradition. The true meanings couched in it, however, gradually asserted their intentions in the experience and consciousness of Western man extending over a period of more than seven centuries of his intellectual and scientific development until their full implications have now become actualized. Whereas originally the term 'secular', from *saeculum,* conveyed a spatio-temporal connotation, as can be understood from the way it was used, the order of precedence in the formulation of the dual meaning has now undergone a change emphasizing the *temporal* rather than the *spatial* aspect. The original spatio-temporal connotation is derived historically out of the experience and consciousness born of the fusion of the Graeco-Roman and Judaic traditions in Western Christianity. It is this 'fusion' of the mutually conflicting elements of the Hellenic and Hebrew worldviews which have deliberately been incorporated into Christianity that modern Christian theologians and intellectuals recognize as problematic, in that the former views existence as basically *spatial* and the latter as basically *temporal*. The arising confusion of worldviews becomes the root of their epistemological and hence also theological problems. Since the world has only in modern times been more and more understood and recognized by them as historical, the emphasis on the temporal aspect of it has become more meaningful and has conveyed a special significance to them. For this reason they exert themselves in efforts emphasizing what they conceive to be the Hebrew vision of existence, which they think is more congenial with the spirit of 'the times', and denouncing the Hellenic as a grave and basic mistake. So they now say that the concept *secular* conveys a markedly dual connotation of *time* and *location*; the time referring to the 'now' or 'present' sense of it, and the location to the 'world' or 'worldly' sense of it. Thus *saeculum* is interpreted to mean basically 'this age' or the 'present time'; and this age or the present time refers to events in this world, and it also then means 'contemporary events'. The emphasis of meaning is set on a particular time or period in the world viewed as a *historical process*. The concept *secular* refers to the *condition* of this world at this particular time or period or age. Already here we discern the germ of meaning that easily develops itself naturally and logically into the existential context of an ever-changing world in which there occurs the relativity of human values. And this natural and logical development of the concept *secular* is now taking place in contemporary, modern Western civilization, which is propagating it throughout the world.

We must see, in view of the fact that secularization is

not merely confined to the Western world, that their experience of it and their attitude toward it is most instructive for Muslims. We must be made aware that secularization, in the way in which it is also happening in the Muslim world, does effect our beliefs and way of life, even if not in the same way it does the beliefs and way of life of Western man; because problems arising out of secularization, though not quite the same as those besetting the West, have certainly caused much confusion in our midst. It is not surprising that these problems are caused due to the introduction of Western ways of thinking, and judging, and believing emulated by some modernist as well as traditionalist Muslim scholars and intellectuals who have been unduly influenced by the modern West and overawed by its scientific and technological achievements, who by virtue of the fact that they could so readily be thus influenced betray their lack of true understanding and full grasp of both the worldviews of Islām and of the modern West and the essential beliefs and modes of thought that project them. They have, because of their influential positions in Muslim society, become conscious or unconscious disseminators of unnecessary confusion that is founded upon a crisis of identity. The situation in our midst can indeed be seen as critical when we consider the fact that Muslims are generally unaware of what the secularizing process implies. It is therefore essential that we obtain a clear understanding of it from those who know and are conscious of it, who believe and welcome it, who teach and advocate it to the world.

Secularization is defined as "the deliverance of man first from religious then from metaphysical control over his reason and his language"[5] It is the setting free of the world from religious and semi-religious understandings of itself; the

5. This definition was formulated by the Dutch theologian, Cornelis van Peursen, who occupied the chair of philosophy

dispelling of all closed worldviews, the breaking of all supernatural myths and sacred symbols; the "defatalization" of history; the discovery by man that he has been left with the world on his hands, that he can no longer blame Fortune or the Furies for what he does with it; it is man turning his attention away from the worlds beyond and toward this world and this time.

Secularization encompasses not only the political and social aspects of life, but also inevitably the cultural, for it denotes "the disappearance of religious determination of the symbols of cultural integration". It implies an irreversible historical process in which culture and society are "delivered from tutelage to religious control and closed metaphysical worldviews". It is considered a "liberating development", and the end product of secularization is historical relativism. Hence according to them history is a process of secularization. The integral components in the dimensions of secularization are the "disenchantment of nature", the "desacralization of politics', and the "deconsecration of values". By the disenchantment of nature — a term and concept borrowed from the German sociologist Max Weber[6] — they mean as he means, the "freeing of nature from its religious overtones", which means to deprive nature of spiritual meaning so that man can act upon it as he

---

at the University of Leiden. It was given in a report on a conference held at the Ecumenical Institute of Bossey, Switzerland, in September 1959. See also the work of the Harvard theologian Harvey Cox, *The Secular City,* New York, 1965, p.2; and for what follows, pp.2-17; 20-23; 30-36; 109 *et passim.* A fuller treatment of secularization as a philosophical program is given in my *Islām and Secularism,* Kuala Lumpur, 1978, chs.I and II.

6. The phrase 'disenchantment of the world' was used by Friedrich Schiller and quoted by Weber. Another term which

pleases and make use of it according to his needs and plans, and hence create historical change and 'development'. By the desacralization of politics they mean the "abolition of sacral legitimation of political power and authority", which is the prerequisite of political change and hence also social change allowing for the emergence of the historical process. By the deconsecration of values they mean the "rendering transient and relative all cultural creations and every value system" which for them include religion and worldviews having ultimate and final significance, so that in this way history, the future, is open to change, and man is free to create the change and immerse himself in the 'evolutionary' process. This attitude toward values demands an awareness on the part of secular man of the relativity of his own views and beliefs; he must live with the realization that the rules and ethical codes of conduct which guide his own life will change with the times and generations. This attitude demands what they call 'maturity'; and hence secularization is also a process of 'evolution' of the consciousness of man from the 'infantile' to the 'mature' states, and is defined as the "removal of juvenile dependence from every level of society"; the process of "maturing and assuming responsibility"; the "removal of religious and metaphysical supports and putting man on his own". They further say that this recurring change of values is also the recurrent phenomenon of "conversion" which occurs "at the intersection of the action of history on man and the action of man on history", which they call "responsibility", the acceptance of "adult accountability". Thus as already mentioned, they visualise the con-

---

Weber used in this connection is 'rationalization'. See Weber's *Essays in Sociology,* New York, 1958; see also his *Sociology of Religion,* Boston, 1964; chs.III and V of the former; and for Weber's concept of rationalization, see Talcott Parson's explanation of it in the Introduction to the latter work, pp.xxxi-xxxiii.

temporary experience of secularization as part of the evolutionary process of human history; as part of the irreversible process of 'coming of age', of 'growing up' to 'maturity' when they will have to 'put away childish things' and learn to have 'the courage to be'.

If the full implications of the foregoing brief exposition of the meaning of secularization is understood, it will become obvious that the twentieth century Christian Arabic usage and accepted translation of the term 'secular' as *'almāniy* merely reflects its meaning as formulated by the latinized Western Christianity of the thirteenth century. Even though the modern translators vaguely refer to the term 'secular' as meaning also *jīliy* or *qarniy*, yet they were completely unaware of the way in which the concept couched in the term 'secular' has evolved during the last seven centuries in the experience and consciousness of Western man, causing the rise of contemporary problems never encountered before. Their description of secularity as *al-ihtimām bi umūr al-dunyā*, or as *al-ihtimām bi al-'ālamiyyāt* is not quite correct, because to be preoccupied with the affairs of the world, or with worldly things, is according to us not necessarily to be opposed to religion; whereas secularity understood in the modern sense is necessarily opposed to religion. Similarly, to secularize is not quite the same as *ḥawwal ilā gharaḍ 'ālamī ay dunyawī*, because to change in accordance with what is good in the pursuit of worldly ends is according to us not necessarily to change in opposition to religion. Secularization in the modern sense described above, and which is actually happening, is a process which is definitely opposed to religion; it is a *philosophical program* or an *ideology* that seeks to destroy the very foundations of religion. *'Almāniyyah*, then, cannot be a description of 'secularism'; as it seems to me nearer the truth to describe it as *wāqi 'iyyah* in view of its close conceptual connection with the philosophical ideology of positivism. Be that as it may, since the dual connotation of *place* and *time* is fundamental to the concept of *saeculum*, which conveys already the germ of meaning that evolves naturally and logically into its present, contagious fullness; and since the place and the time refer to *here* and *now* respectively, it would be more precise to describe 'secularism' literally by some compound word such as *hunālāniyyah*, from *hunā* and *al-ān*. For the 'here-and-nowness' elicited by *hunālāniyyah* clearly projects a conception of the world and of life in it that rejects other worlds beyond; that repudiates the past except insofar as it confirms the present; that affirms an open future; that altogether denies religion and worldviews having ultimate and final significance. But better still to emulate the method of discerning scholars, savants, and sages among our early predecessors who were very much aware of the paramount importance of language and its profound connection with reason; who were meticulous in the correct usage of language and the pursuit of authentic meaning; who exercised great care not to confuse Islamic terms and concepts with those that do not correspond and cohere with the worldview of Islām; who were not inclined to hasty and negligent arabization of alien terms and concepts opposed to our religion and our vision of reality and truth. Many of the Greek terms and concepts were transcribed in their original forms so as to render their foreign origin immediately recognizable such that their proper places become known. So it would be better if the term 'secular' were just transcribed into Arabic spelled *sīn-yā'-kāf-lām-rā'*, with *kasrah* to *sīn*; *ḍammah* to *kāf*; and *fatḥah* to *lām*. In this way we would know at once that the term and the concept is not Islamic Arabic. To arabize such terms and concepts is to introduce confusion in our minds, because that will give the impression that they are natural to Islām and would encourage Muslims not only to think in those terms and concepts, but to actualize such thought that are alien and opposed to Islām into concrete reality.

I strongly believe with sound reason that the arabization and introduction of the ambivalent concept of *'almāniyyah* into mainstream contemporary Arabic is largely responsible for insinuating into the Muslim mind the dichotomous separation of the sacred and the profane, creating therein the socio-political notion of an unbridgeable gap separating what it considers to be a 'theocratic state' from a 'secular state'. There is confusion in the Muslim mind in misunderstanding the Muslim 'secular' state by setting it in contrast with the 'theocratic' state. But since Islām does not involve itself in the dichotomy between the sacred and the profane, how then can it set in contrast the theocratic state with the secular state? An Islamic state is neither wholly theocratic nor wholly secular. A Muslim state calling itself or is called by others 'secular', does not necessarily have to divest nature of spiritual meaning; does not necessarily have to deny religious values and virtues in politics and human affairs; does not necessarily have to oppose religious truth and religious education in the way that the philosophical and scientific process which I call 'secularization' necessarily does involve the divesting of spiritual meaning from the world of creation; the denial of religious values and virtues from politics and human affairs; and the relativization of all values and of truth in the human mind and conduct. It is this confusion in the Muslim mind that is causing the emergence in our midst of social and political upheavals and disunity. Unity has two aspects: the outward, external unity manifested in society as communal and national solidarity; and the inward, internal unity of ideas and mind revealed in intellectual and spiritual coherence that encompasses realms beyond communal and national boundaries. Understanding of our identity as Muslims pertains to the second aspect, which is fundamental to the realization of the first. The coherence of this second aspect depends upon the soundness and integrity of concepts connoted in language, the instrument of reason which influences the reasoning of its users. If the soundness and integrity of concepts in language is confused, then this is due to a confusion in 'worldview' caused by the corruption of knowledge.

In the languages of Muslim peoples, including Arabic, there is a basic vocabulary consisting of key terms which govern the interpretation of the Islamic vision of reality and truth, and which project the worldview of Islām in correct perspective. Because the words that comprise this basic vocabulary have their origins in the Holy Qur'ān these words are naturally in Arabic, and are deployed uniformly in all Muslim languages, reflecting the intellectual and spiritual unity of the Muslims throughout the world. The Islamic basic vocabulary is composed of key terms and concepts related to one another meaningfully, and altogether determining the conceptual structure of reality and existence projected by them. The *islamization* of language, which is a fundamental element in conversion to Islām, is none other than this infusion of the Islamic basic vocabulary into the languages of Muslim peoples. In this way, each language of a Muslim people with every other has in common this Islamic basic vocabulary as its own basic vocabulary; and as such all languages of Muslim peoples indeed belong to the same family of Islamic languages. What I wish to introduce here is the concept of Islamic language — that there is such a thing as *Islamic language.* Because language that can be categorized as Islamic does exist by virtue of the common Islamic vocabulary inherent in each of them, the key terms and concepts in the basic vocabulary of each of them ought indeed to convey the *same meanings,* since they all are involved in the same conceptual and semantic network. If, for example, we find today that the focus word *'ilm,* which is a major key term in the basic vocabulary of all Islamic languages, conveys different connotations in each member of the family of Islamic languages, then this regrettable fact is not caused by what is vaguely termed as 'social change', but by ignorance and error, which is productive of the confusion that *causes* social change. To say that restriction of meaning, or alteration of meaning, such that the original intention is no longer conveyed, affecting key terms in the basic vocabulary of Islām, is due to social change, and to acquiesce to such restriction and alteration of meaning as the exponents of modern linguistics teach, is to imply the legitimacy of authority invested in the common people, in society, to effect semantic change. This kind of teaching, which has in fact been propagated in the name of 'scientific' knowledge, is misleading and dangerous and must not be tolerated, for Islām does not accept 'society' as authoritative in matters of knowledge, or invest it with authority to bring about changes that will lead Muslims astray. Society, insofar as knowledge and the understanding of Islām and its worldview are concerned, has no authority; on the contrary, society is generally ignorant and needs proper education and constant guidance by the learned and the wise within it so as to ensure its salvation. This means that the learned and the wise among Muslims must exercise constant vigilance in detecting erroneous usage in language which impinges upon semantic change in major key concepts in order to prevent the occurrence of general confusion and error in the understanding of Islām and of its vision of reality and truth.

Many major key terms in the Islamic basic vocabulary of the languages of Muslim peoples have now been displaced and made to serve absurdly in alien fields of meaning in a kind of regression towards non-Islamic worldviews; a phenomenon which I call the *deislamization* of language. Ignorance and confusion, making possible the infusion of alien concepts, have also let loose the forces of narrow national sentiment and ideologization of ethnic and cultural traditions. Words conveying meanings which focus upon fundamental truths peculiar to Islām, such as among others, 'knowledge' (*'ilm*), 'justice' (*'adl*), right action (*adab*), 'education' (*ta'dīb*), have been tampered with, so that 'knowledge' becomes restricted to 'jurisprudence', or to that which is based only on restricted forms of reason and sense experience; 'justice' to mean unqualified equality, or mere procedure; 'right action' to mean hypocritical etiquette; and 'education' to mean the kind of training leading to ends derived from philosophic and secular rationalism. If even a few of such focus words were restricted in their meanings, or were made to convey meanings which are not authentic and authoritative — by which I mean whose intentions no longer reflect those understood by authorities among the early Muslims — then this would inevitably create confusion and error in the minds of Muslims and disrupt intellectual and spiritual unity among them. Moreover, it would render sciences once considered praiseworthy to become blameworthy. I am not here suggesting something that may be construed as not allowing language to develop, to unfold itself according to its potential powers of tracing the rich tapestry of life as it unfolds, to evolve with ideas as they evolve, to grasp reality-truth as it manifests itself in the fleeting passage of time. I am only suggesting that the basic vocabulary in the Islamic language can only develop from its roots, and not severed from them, nor can they develop from roots stunted in restriction. Secular and materialistic value systems have their initial locus in minds, then there translated into linguistic symbols, and afterwards become manifest in the external world in urban areas whence they spread like a raging contagion to the rural masses. Failure to apply language correctly and to convey correct meaning implies unawareness of proper perspective of the true and real situation, which involves understanding not only the language, but the worldview projected by it. Widespread intellectual secularization due to ignorance of Islām as the true revealed religion, its manifestation as civilization, and its vision of reality and truth as worldview has tended to confuse many of our scholars and intellectuals and their followers into imitating the shifting slogans of modernity, effecting changes and restrictions in the meanings of key terms that reflect our system of values. Meanings reflecting reality and truth whose transparency was known to our experience and consciousness have now begun to become opaque in minds fused with the formulations of modernity. Fundamental elements of our worldview and the system of values they convey, involving the meanings of 'virtue', 'freedom', and 'happiness', are also affected.

Since we maintain that virtue (*faḍīlah*) is an activity of

the soul, and that man has a dual nature, the animal and the rational, the realization of virtues in the self requires discernment of reality and truth accompanied by action in conformity with that discernment involving subordination of the bodily and appetitive faculties of the animal soul, to the practical and theoretical faculties of the rational soul such that a stable state of soul, commended by intellect and by religion, is attained. This exercise of subordinating the faculties of the animal soul to those of the rational soul requires freedom.

The activity that is called 'freedom' is in *ikhtiyār*, which is an act, not in *ḥurriyyah*, which is a condition. The act that is meant in *ikhtiyār* is that of making a choice, not between many alternatives but between two alternatives: the good or the bad. Because *ikhtiyār* is bound in meaning with *khayr*, meaning 'good', being derived from the same root *khāra* (*khayara*), the choice that is meant in *ikhtiyār* is the choice of what is good, better, or best between the two alternatives. This point is most important as it is aligned to the philosophical question of freedom. A choice of what is bad of two alternatives is therefore not a choice that can be called *ikhtiyār*, in fact it is not a choice, rather it is an act of injustice (*ẓulm*) done to oneself. Freedom is to act as one's real and true nature demands — that is, as one's *ḥaqq* and one's *fiṭrah* demands — and so only the exercise of that choice which is of what is good can properly be called a 'free choice'. A choice for the better is therefore an act of freedom, and it is also an act of justice (*'adl*) done to oneself. It presupposes knowledge of good and evil, of virtues and vices; whereas a choice for the worse is not a choice as it is grounded upon ignorance urged on by the instigation of the soul that inclines toward the blameworthy aspects of the animal powers; it is then also not an exercise of freedom because freedom means precisely being free of domination by the powers of the soul that incites to evil. *Ikhtiyār* is the cognitive act of choosing for the better of two alternatives in accordance with virtues that culminate in justice to oneself and which is, as such, an exercise of freedom. The doing of what is good is accomplished by means of virtues. In Islām all virtues, including those considered as principal virtues such as wisdom, temperance, courage, and justice and their subdivisions, are religious virtues since they are derived from the Qur'ān and from the exemplary life of the Prophet. The source of these principal virtues and their subdivisions is true faith or *īmān*, which is the verification by deed what tongue and heart affirm as real and true of God's Revelation and His commands and prohibitions. *Īmān* already implies consciousness of God and remembrance of Him that brings about a condition of tranquility in the soul; it is *freedom* from worry resulting from doubt; *freedom* from disquietude and from fear that refers to ultimate destiny; it is inward security that comes about when the soul is submissive to God; and being submissive to God is *freedom*, which causes to arise in the soul the consciousness of peace called *islām*. These inner activities of the soul implies a prior consciousness in the soul of the truth that comes from divine guidance; and this consciousness is that of *certainty* of the truth (*yaqīn*). From this it is clear that happiness, which is the goal of virtuous activity leading to the state of stability of soul, is not something that relates only to this world; is not something that consists of only feelings and emotions that vary in degree from moment to moment; is not something only psychological and biological, which is shared also by animals. Nor is happiness an end in itself which somehow cannot be experienced consciously as something enduring, something permanent in the course of our worldly existence.

The tradition of Western thought takes the position that there are two conceptions of happiness: the ancient which goes back to Aristotle; and the modern which gradually emerged in Western history as a result of the process of secularization. The Aristotelian conception maintains that happiness relates only to this world; that it is an end in itself; and that it is a state that undergoes changes and variations in degrees from moment to moment; or it is something that cannot be consciously experienced from moment to moment and can be judged as having been attained only when one's worldly life, if virtuously lived and attended by good fortune, has come to an end. The modern conception agrees with the Aristotelian conception that happiness relates only to this world and that it is an end in itself, but whereas for the former the end is considered in terms of a standard for proper conduct, the latter considers it to be terminal psychological states having no relation with moral codes. It is the modern conception of happiness that is acknowledged to be prevalent in the West today. We do not agree with the Aristotelian position that virtue and happiness relate only to this world, and that consequently happiness as a permanent condition experienced consciously in the course of our worldly life is unattainable. We do not restrict our understanding of happiness only to the domain of temporal, secular life, for in accord with our worldview we affirm that the relation of happiness to the hereafter has an intimate and a profound bearing upon its relation to worldly life, and that since in the former case it is a spiritual and permanent condition there is, even in its temporal and secular involvement, an element of happiness that we experience and are conscious of which when once attained is permanent. As for the modern conception of happiness, it is not much different in essence from the ones known and practiced in ancient times by pagan societies.

Happiness (*i.e.* we mean *sa'ādah*) as known in the experience and consciousness of those who are truly submissive to God and follow His guidance is not an end in itself because the highest good in this life is love of God. Enduring happiness in life refers not to the physical entity in man, not to the animal soul and body of man; nor is it a state of mind, or feeling that undergoes terminal states, nor pleasure nor amusement. It has to do with certainty (*yaqīn*) of the ultimate Truth and fulfillment of action in conformity with that certainty. And certainty is a permanent state of consciousness natural to what is permanent in man and perceived by his spiritual organ of cognition which is the heart (*qalb*). It is peace and security and tranquility of the heart (*ṭuma'nīnah*); it is knowledge (*ma'rifah*) and knowledge is true faith (*īmān*). It is knowledge of God as He described Himself in genuine Revelation; it is also knowing one's rightful and hence proper place in the realm of creation and one's proper relationship with the Creator accompanied by requisite action (*'ibādah*) in conformity with that knowledge such that the condition which results is that of justice (*'adl*). It is only through such knowledge that love of God can be attained in earthly life.

From this interpretation of the meaning and experience of happiness in Islām we derive conclusion that happiness in this life is not an end in itself; that the end of happiness is love of God; that in worldly life two levels of happiness can be discerned. The first level is psychological, temporal and terminal states which may be described as feelings or emotions, and which is attained when needs and wants are achieved by means of right conduct in accord with the virtues. The second level is spiritual, permanent, consciously experienced, becoming the substratum of worldly life which is affirmed to be probationary, the testing of conduct and virtuous activity being by good fortune or ill. This second level, when attained, occurs concurrently with the first, except that wants are diminished and needs are satisfied. This second level of happiness is a preparation for a third level in the hereafter of which the highest state is the Vision of God. There is no change in this meaning and experience of happiness in the consciousness of genuine believers throughout the ages.

In the foregoing pages I have set forth in bare summary some of the fundamental, permanently established elements, together with the key concepts that they unfold, that act as integrating principles placing all our systems of meaning and standards of life and values in coherent order as a unified supersystem forming the worldview of Islām. These fundamental elements and the key concepts pertinent to them have profound bearing, we said earlier, upon our ideas about change, development, and progress. Even though diversity and change can and do indeed occur within the ambience of this worldview, such as the diversity in the schools of jurisprudence, theology, philosophy and metaphysics, and in the traditions, cultures and languages; and the change in meeting the tides of changing fortune in the course of history, yet the diversity and the change have never affected the character and role of these fundamental elements themselves, so that what is projected as a worldview by the supersystem remains intact. This is so because the diversity and the change have taken their rise within the bounds of cognitive restraint deliberated by a knowing community conscious of its identity, ensuring thereby no involvement of change nor encroachment of confusion in the key concepts that serve the fundamental elements of the worldview. The worldview resides in the minds of genuine Muslims. The discerning ones among them know that Islām is not an *ideal*—it is a *reality*; and that whatever may be demanded of them by the challenges of the age in which they live must be met without confusing that worldview with alien elements. They know that the advances in science and technology and their being put to adequate use in everyday life do not necessarily have to involve confusion in their vision of reality and truth. Technology is not the same as science; and acceptance of useful and relevant technology does not necessarily have to involve acceptance also of the implications in the science that gave it birth. Confusion arises only as a result of inadequate knowledge of Islām and of the worldview projected by it, as well as ignorance of the nature of the confronting intellectual, religious, and ideological challenges, and of the implications inherent in the statements and general conclusions of modern secular philosophy and science.

Change, *development*, and *progress*, in their true senses ultimately mean for us a conscious and deliberate movement towards genuine Islām at a time when we encounter challenges, as we do now, that seek to encroach on our values and virtues, our modes of conduct, our thought and faith, our way of life. Our present engagement is with the challenges of an alien worldview surreptitiously introduced into Muslim thought and belief by confused modernist Muslim scholars, intellectuals, academics, writers and their followers, as well as by religious deviationists and extremists of many sorts. They have wittingly or unwittingly come under the spell of modern secular Western philosophy and science, its technology and ideology which have disseminated a global contagion of secularization as a philosophical program. We are not unaware of the fact that not *all* of Western science and technology are necessarily objectionable to religion; but this does not mean that we have to uncritically accept the scientific and philosophical theories that go along with the science and the technology, and the science and the technology themselves, without first understanding their implications and testing the validity of the values that accompany the theories. Islām possesses within itself the source of its claim to truth and does not need scientific and philosophical theories to justify such a claim. Moreover, it is not the concern of Islām to fear scientific discoveries that could contradict the validity of its truth. We know that no science is free of value; and to accept its presuppositions and general conclusions without being guided by genuine knowledge of our worldview — which entails knowledge also of our history, our thought and civilization, our identity — which will enable us to render correct judgements as to their validity and relevance or otherwise to our life, the change that would result in our way of life would simply be a change congenial to what is alien to our worldview. And we would neither call such change a 'development' nor a 'progress'. Development consists not in 'activating and making visible and concrete what is latent in biological man' because man is not merely a biological entity: humanity is something much more than rationality and animality. Progress is neither 'becoming' or 'coming-into-being', nor movement towards that which is coming-into-being and never becomes 'being'; for the notion of 'something aimed at', or the 'goal' inherent in the concept of progress can only convey real and true meaning when it refers to that which is understood as something permanently established, as already *being*. Hence what is already clarified in the mind and permanently established therein *and* externally, already in the state of being, cannot suffer change, nor be subject to constant slipping from the grasp of achievement, nor constantly receding beyond attainment. The term 'progress' refers to a *definite direction* that is aligned to a *final purpose* that is meant to be achieved in worldly life. If the direction sought is still vague, still coming-into-being as it were, and the purpose aligned to it is not final, then how can involvement in it truly mean progress? People who grope in the dark cannot be referred to as progressing, and they who say such people are progressing have merely uttered a lie against the true meaning and purpose of progress.

The concepts of 'change', 'development', and 'progress' presuppose situations in which we find ourselves confused by a commixture of the true and the false, of the real and the illusory, and become captive in the ambit of ambiguity. In such ambivalent situations, our positive action in the exercise of freedom to choose for the better, to accept what is good and relevant to our needs, to deliberate correctly in our judgement of needs, all the while maintaining our endeavour to return to the straight path and direct our steps in agreement with it — such endeavour, which entails change, is development; and such return, which consists in development, is progress.

I

ISLĀM: THE CONCEPT OF RELIGION AND THE FOUNDATION OF ETHICS AND MORALITY

The concept couched in the term *dīn,* which is generally understood to mean *religion,* is not the same as the concept *religion* as interpreted and understood throughout Western religious history. When we speak of Islām and refer to it in English as a 'religion', we mean and understand by it the *dīn,* in which all the basic connotations inherent in the term *dīn* [1] are conceived as gathered into a single unity of coherent meaning as reflected in the Holy Qur'ān and in the Arabic language to which it belongs.

The word *dīn* derived from the Arabic root DYN has many primary significations which although seemingly contrary to one another are yet all conceptually interconnected, so that the ultimate meaning derived from them all presents itself as a clarified unity of the whole. By 'the whole' I mean that which is described as the Religion of Islām, which contains within itself all the relevant possibilities of meaning inherent in the concept of *dīn.* Since we are dealing with an Islamic concept which is translated into actual reality intimately and profoundly lived in human experience, the

---

1 In this chapter my interpretation of the basic connotations inherent in the term *dīn* is based on Ibn Manẓūr's standard classic, the *Lisān al-'Arab* (Beyrouth, 1968, 15v.), hereafter cited as *LA*. For what is stated in this page and the next, see vol. 13: 166, col. 2–171, col. 2. The formulation and the conceptualization of the meaning of religion (*dīn*), as well as the explanation of the key concepts in meaningful order are, however, my own.

apparent contrariness in its basic meanings is indeed not due to vagueness; it is, rather, due to the contrariness inherent in human nature itself, which they faithfully reflect. And their power to reflect human nature faithfully is itself clear demonstration of their lucidity and veracity and authenticity in conveying truth.

The primary significations of the term *dīn* can be reduced to four: (1) *indebtedness;* (2) *submissiveness;* (3) *judicious power;* (4) *natural inclination* or *tendency.* In what presently follows, I shall attempt to explain them briefly and place them in their relevant contexts, drawing forth the coherent ultimate meaning intended, which denotes the faith, beliefs and practices and teachings adhered to by the Muslims individually and collectively as a Community, and manifesting itself altogether as an objective whole as the Religion called *Islām.*

The verb *dāna* which derives from *dīn* conveys the meaning of *being indebted,* including various other meanings connected with *debts,* some of them contraries. In the state in which one finds oneself being in debt, that is to say, a *dā'in* it follows that one subjects oneself, in the sense of *yielding* and *obeying,* to law and ordinances governing debts, and also, in a way, to the creditor, who is likewise designated as a *dā'in.* [2] There is also conveyed in the situation described the fact that one in debt is under *obligation,* or *dayn.* Being in debt and under obligation naturally involves *judgement: daynūnah,* and *conviction: idānah,* as the case may be. All the above significations including their contraries inherent in *dāna* are practicable possibilities only in organized societies involved in commercial life in *towns* and *cities,* denoted by

---

2 *Dā'in* refers both to *debtor* as well as *creditor,* and this apparent contrariness in meaning can indeed be resolved if we transpose both these meanings to refer to the two natures of man, that is, the rational soul and the animal or carnal soul. See below pp. 57–60.

mudun or madā'in. A town or city, a *madīnah,* has a *judge, ruler,* or *governor,* a *dayyān.* Thus already here, in the various applications of the verb *dāna* alone, we see rising before our mind's eye a picture of civilized living; of societal life of law and order and justice and authority.[3] It is, conceptually at least, connected intimately with another verb *maddana*[4] which means: to *build* or to *found cities:* to *civilize,* to *refine* and

---

3 It is I think extremely important to discern both the intimate and profoundly significant connection between the concept of *dīn* and that of *madīnah* which derives from it, and the role of the believers individually in relation to the former and collectively in relation to the latter. Considerable relevance must be seen in the significance of the change of name of the town once known as Yathrib to *al-Madīnah: the City*—or more precisely, *Madīnatu'l-Nabiy: the City of the Prophet*—which occurred soon after the Holy Prophet (may God bless and give him Peace!) made his historic Flight (*hijrah*) and settled there. The first Community of Believers was formed there at the time, and it was that Flight that marked the New Era in the history of mankind. We must see the fact that al-Madīnah was so called and named because it was there that true *dīn* became realized for mankind. There the believers enslaved themselves under the authority and jurisdiction of the Holy Prophet, its *dayyān;* there the realization of the debt to God took definite form, and the approved manner and method of its repayment began to unfold. The City of the Prophet signified the place where true *dīn* was enacted under his authority and jurisdiction. We may further see that the City became, for the Community, the epitome of the socio-political order of Islām; and for the individual believer it became, by analogy, the symbol of the believer's body and physical being in which the rational soul, in emulation of him who may God bless and give Peace!, exercises authority and just government. For further relevant interpretations, see below, pp. 43–52; 53–59; 60–68; 72–74; 75–80; 83–84.

4 *LA,* vol. 13 :402, col. 2–403, col. 1.

to *humanize;* from which is derived another term: *tamaddun,* meaning *civilization* and *refinement* in *social culture.* Thus we derive from the primary signification of being in a state of debt other correlated significations, such as: to *abase oneself;* to *serve* (a master), *to become enslaved;* and from another such signification of *judge, ruler* and *governor* is derived meanings which denote the *becoming mighty, powerful* and *strong;* a *master,* one *elevated in rank,* and *glorious;* and yet further, the meanings: *judgement, requital or reckoning* (at some appointed time). Now the very notion of law and order and justice and authority and social cultural refinement inherent in all these significations derived from the concept *dīn* must surely presuppose the existence of a *mode* or *manner of acting* consistent with what is reflected in the law, the order, the justice, the authority and social cultural refinement, a mode or manner of acting, or a *state of being* considered as *normal* in relation to them; so that this *state of being* is a state that is *customary* or *habitual.* From here, then, we can see the logic behind the derivation of the other primary signification of the concept *dīn* as *custom, habit, disposition* or *natural tendency.* At this juncture it becomes increasingly clear that the concept *dīn* in its most basic form indeed reflects in true testimony the natural tendency of man to form societies and obey laws and seek just government. The idea of a *kingdom,* a *cosmopolis,* inherent in the concept *dīn* that rises before our vision is most important in helping us attain a more profound understanding of it, and needs be reiterated here, for we shall have recourse to it again when we deal with the religious and spiritual aspects of man's existential experience.

I have thus far explained only in cursory manner the basic concept of *dīn,* reducing the various connotations to four primary significations and showing their mutual actual and conceptual connections, in the context of human 'secular' relations. In the religious context, that of the relationship between man and God, and what God approves of man's relations with his fellow-men, the primary significations, while maintaining their basic meanings, nevertheless undergo profound synthesis and intensification at once true to the experience described and to the description of the Religion of Islām as the objective faith, beliefs and practices and teachings experienced and lived by each and every member of the Muslim Community as well as by the Community as a whole.

How can the concept of *being indebted* be explained in the religious and spiritual context?—one may ask; what is the nature of the debt?, and to whom is the debt owed? We answer that man is indebted to God, his Creator and Provider, for bringing him into existence and maintaining him in his existence. Man was once nothing and did not exist, and now he is.

> 'Man We did create from a quintessence of clay;
> Then We placed him as a drop of sperm in a place of rest, firmly fixed;
> Then We made the sperm into a clot of congealed blood; then of that clot We made a lump; then We made out of that lump bones and clothed the bones with flesh; then We developed out of it another creature. So blessed be God, the Best to create!' [5]

The man who ponders seriously his origin will realize that a few decades ago he did not exist, and the whole of mankind now existing neither existed nor knew of their possible present existence. The same truth applies to all ages of man from the beginning of his existence in time. So naturally he who ponders thus sincerely knows intuitively that his sense of being indebted for his creation and existence cannot really be directed to his parents, for he knows equally well that his parents too are subject to the same process by the same

---

5 *Al-Mu'minūn* (23):12–14.

Creator and Provider. Man does not himself cause his own growth and development from the state of a clot of congealed blood to the one that now stands mature and perfect. He knows that even in his mature and perfect state he is not able to create for himself his sense of sight or hearing or other—and let alone move himself in conscious growth and development in his helpless embryonic stage. Then again:

> 'When thy Lord drew forth from the Children of Ādam—from their loins—their descendents, and made them testify concerning themselves (saying): "Am I not your Lord?"—they said: "Yea! we do testify !"[6]

The rightly guided man realizes that his very self, his soul, has already acknowledged God as his Lord, even before his existence as a man, so that such a man recognizes his Creator and Cherisher and Sustainer. The nature of the debt of creation and existence is so tremendously total that man, the moment he is created and given existence, is *already* in a state of utter loss, for he possesses really nothing himself, seeing that everything about him and in him and from him is what the Creator owns Who owns everything. And this is the purport of the words in the Holy Qur'ān:

> 'Verily man is in loss (*khusr*)...[7]

Seeing that he owns absolutely nothing to 'repay' his debt, *except his own consciousness* of the fact *that he is himself the very substance* of the debt, so must he 'repay' with himself, so must he 'return' himself to Him Who owns him absolutely. He is himself the debt to be returned to the Owner, and 'returning the debt' means to *give himself up in service,* or *khidmah,* to his Lord and Master; to *abase himself* before Him

---

6 *Al-A'rāf* (7):172.

7 *Al-'Aṣri* (103):2.

and so the rightly guided man sincerely and consciously *enslaves himself* for the sake of God in order to fulfill His commands and prohibitions and ordinances, and thus to live out the dictates of His law. The concept of 'return' alluded to above is also evident in the conceptual structure of *dīn,* for it can and does indeed mean, as I will elaborate in due course, a 'return to man's inherent nature', the concept 'nature' referring to the spiritual and not altogether the physical aspect of man's being.[8] It must also be pointed out that in the words of the Holy Qur'ān:

> 'By the heaven that hath rain',[9]

the word interpreted as 'rain' is *raj',* which means literally 'return'.[10] It is interpreted as rain because God *returns* it time and again, and it refers to *good return* in the sense of *benefit, profit,* and *gain. Raj'* is therefore used synonymously in

---

8 The concept of return is also expressed in the meaning of the term *'uwwida* in the sense of returning to the past, that is, to tradition. Hence the signification of *dīn* as custom or habit. In this sense it means return to the tradition of the Prophet Ibrāhīm (upon whom be Peace!). In this connection please see above p. 44 and below, pp. 51–55. It must be pointed out that by 'tradition' here is not meant the kind of tradition that originated and evolved in human history and culture and had its source in the human mind. It is, rather, what God has revealed and commanded and taught His Prophets and Messengers, so that although they appeared in successive and yet unconnected periods in history, they conveyed and acted as if what they conveyed and acted upon had been embodied in the continuity of a tradition.

9 *Al-Êāriq* (86):II; *LA,* vol. 8:120, col. 2.

10 There is a close connection between the concept here described and the application of the verb *raja'a* in its various forms in the Holy Qur'ān with reference to man's return to God.

this sense with *rabaḥ,* meaning gain,[11] which is the opposite or contrary of *khusr,* loss, to which reference has already been made above. Now it is appropriate to mention here that one of the basic meanings of *dīn* which has not been explained above is *recurrent rain,* rain that returns again and again; and hence we perceive that *dīn* here, like such a rain, alludes to benefit and gain (*rabaḥ*). When we say that in order to 'repay' his debt man must 'return' himself to God, his Owner, his 'returning himself' is, like the returning rain, a gain unto him.[12] And this is the meaning of the saying:

> 'He who enslaves himself gains'[13] (*rabiḥa* whose infinitive noun is: *rabaḥ*).

The expression 'enslaves himself' (*dāna nafsahu*) means 'gives himself up' (in service), and hence also 'returns himself' (to his Owner) as explained.[14] The same meaning is expressed in the words of the Holy Prophet:

> "The intelligent one is he who enslaves himself (*dāna nafsahu*) and works for that which shall be after death." [15]

'That which shall be after death' is that which shall be

---

[11] *LA,* vol. 2:442, col. 2–445, col. 1.

[12] True *dīn* brings life to a body otherwise dead just as 'the rain which God sends down from the skies, and the life which He gives therewith to an earth that is dead.' See *Al-Baqarah* (2):164.

[13] *LA,* vol. 13 :167, col. 1.

[14] It clearly refers to the man who, having consciously realized that he is himself the subject of his own debt to His Creator and Sustainer and Cherisher, enslaves himself to his self and hence 'returns' himself to his true Lord.

[15] *LA,* vol. 13:169, col. 2.

reckoned good, the requital, the good return. This good return is like the returning rain which brings benefit to the earth by bringing life to it and by causing goodly growth beneficial to life to grow from it. In like manner that rain gives life to the earth which would otherwise be dead, so does *dīn* give life to man, without which man would be as one who is, as it were, also 'dead'. This is aptly symbolized by God's words in the Holy Qur'ān, where He says:

> '...In the rain which God sends down from the skies, and the life which He gives therewith to an earth that is dead...' [16]

By 'returning himself' to his Lord and Master, by loyally and truly following and obeying God's commands and prohibitions and ordinances and law, the man thus acting will be requited and will receive his good return multiplied many times over, as God says in the Holy Qur'ān:

> 'Who is he who will loan (*yuqriḍu*) to God a beautiful loan (*qarḍan ḥasanan*) which God will double to his credit and multiply many times?'[17]

Notice here that the verb used to signify 'loan' (*yuqriḍu*), from *qaraḍa, qarḍ* has not the same connotation as that which is termed as 'debt' (*dayn*), for the latter term is applicable to man only. The 'loan' here meant is 'the return of that which is owned 'originally' by the One Who now asks for it, and which is to be returned to Him.' Man is God's property and his existence is only 'lent' him for a time. On the other hand the expression 'goodly loan' (*qarḍan ḥasanan*) as applied to man has a metaphorical significance, in that it is his 'service to God', his 'good works' that is

---

16 *Al-Baqarah* (2):164.
17 *Al-Baqarah* (2) :245.

meant, for these can indeed be said to *belong* to him, and for the offering of which he will be requited in abundance. God is the Requiter, the Supreme Judge: *al-dayyān*. He is the King, *mālik*, of the Day of Judgement and Requital, *yawm al-dīn*, also called the Day of Reckoning, *yawm al-ḥisāb*.[18] The fact that God is referred to as King, and everything else as the Kingdom over which He exercises absolute power and authority, *malakūt*, shows again that man is His *mamlūk*, His *slave*. *So dīn* in the religious context also refers to the state of being a slave. [19] We referred a while ago to man's 'returning himself' as meaning 'giving himself up in service' (*khidmah*) to God. We now say that in effect what is truly meant is not 'service' in the sense of *any* service, or the kind offered to another man or human institution. The concept of *khidmah* implies that the one who gives such service is 'free', is not a bondman, but is 'his own master' in respect of himself. The concept *mamlūk*, however, conveys the implicit fact of ownership by the one who takes his service. The *mamlūk* is possessed by the *mālik*. So we do not say of one who serves God that he is a *khādim*, meaning servant, but that he is God's *'ābid*, and he is in truth God's *'abd*, meaning also servant or slave, which term has the connotation of 'being owned' by Him Whom he serves. In the religious context, therefore, *'abd* is the correct term of reference to one who, in the realization that he is indebted absolutely to God, abases himself in service to Him; and hence the act of service appropriate for him is called *'ibādah* and the service is *'ibādāt*, which refers to all conscious and willing acts of service for the sake

---

18 *Dīn* also means correct reckoning: *ḥisāb al-ṣaḥīḥ*. It is the apportioning of the precisely correct measure to a number or thing so that it fits into its proper place: *'adad al-mustawā*. This somewhat mathematical meaning conveys the sense of there being a system or law governing all and maintaining all in perfect equilibrium. See *LA*, vol. 13:169, col. 1.

19 *LA*, vol. 13:170, col. 1.

of God alone and approved by Him, including such as are prescribed worship. By worshipping God in such manner of service the man is fulfilling the purpose for his creation and existence, as God says in the Holy Qur'ān:

> 'I have only created the Jinn and Man that they may serve Me' (*ya'budūni*).[20]

When we say that such a man is fulfilling the purpose for his creation and existence, it is obvious that that man's obligation to serve God is felt by him as *normal* because it comes as a *natural inclination* on the man's part to do so. This natural tendency in the man to serve and worship God is also referred to as *dīn,* as we have observed in the beginning in connection with its connotation as *custom, habit,* and *disposition.* However, here in the religious context it has a more specific signification of the *natural state of being* called *fiṭrah.* In fact *dīn* does also mean *fiṭrah.*[21] *Fiṭrah* is the pattern according to which God has created all things. It is God's manner of creating, *sunnat Allāh,* and everything fits each into its pattern created for it and set in its proper place. It is the law of God. Submission to it brings harmony, for it means realization of what is inherent in one's true nature; opposition to it brings discord, for it means realization of what is extraneous to one's true nature. It is *cosmos as* opposed to *chaos;* justice as opposed to injustice. When God said: "Am I not your Lord?", and man's true self, testifying for itself, answered: "Yea !" in acknowledgement of the truth of God's lordship, it has sealed a covenant with God. Thus when man is manifested as man in this wordly life he will, if rightly guided, remember his covenant and act accordingly as outlined above, so that his worship, his acts of piety, his

---

20 *Al-Dhāriyāt* (51):56

21 *LA,* vol. 5:58, cols. 1 & 2; see also *Al-Rūm* (30):30.

life and death is lived out for the sake of God alone. One of the meanings of *fiṭrah* as *dīn* refers to the realization of this covenant by man.[22] Submission in the sense described above means conscious, *willing* submission, and this submission does not entail loss of 'freedom' for him, since freedom in fact means *to act as his true nature demands.* The man who submits to God in this way is living out the *dīn.*

Submission, we say again, refers to conscious and willing submission, for were it neither conscious nor willing it cannot then mean *real* submission. The concept of submission is perhaps common to all religions, just as belief or faith is the core of all religions, but we maintain that not all religions enact real submission. Neither is the submission meant the kind that is momentary or erratic, for real submission is a continuous act lived throughout the entire span of one's ethical life; nor is it the kind that operates only within the realm of the heart without manifesting itself outwardly in the action of the body as works performed in obedience to God's law. Submission to God's will means also obedience to His law. The word denoting this sense of submission is *aslama,* as is evident in the Holy Qur'ān where God says:

> 'Who can be better in religion (*dīn*) than one who submits (*aslama*) his face (*i.e.,* his whole self) to God. . . ?'[23]

The *dīn* referred to is none other than Islām. There are, no doubt, other *forms* of *dīn,* but the one in which is enacted total submission (*istislām*) to God alone is the best, and this one is the only *dīn* acceptable to God, as He says in the Holy Qur'ān:

> 'If anyone desires a religion (*dīn*) other than

[22] *LA,* vol. 5:56, col. 2, 57, col. 1.
[23] *Al-Nisā'* (4) :125

> Islām (*al-Islām*), never will it be accepted of him...'[24]

and again:

> 'Verily the Religion (*al-dīn*) in the sight of God is Islām (*al-Islām*)'[25]

According to the Holy Qur'ān, man cannot escape being in the state of living a *dīn* since all submit (*aslama*) to God's will. Hence the term *dīn* is also used, albeit metaphorically, to denote religions other than Islām. However, what makes Islām different from the other religions is that the submission according to Islām is *sincere* and *total* submission to God's will, and this is enacted *willingly* as absolute obedience to the law revealed by Him. This idea is implicitly expressed in the Holy Qur'ān, for example, in the following passage:

> 'Do they seek for other than the religion (*dīn*) of God? while all creatures in the heavens and on earth have, willing or unwilling, submitted (*aslama*) to His Will, and to Him shall they all be returned.'[26]

The form in which submission is enacted or expressed is the form of the *dīn*, and it is here that diversity occurs between one *dīn* and another.[27] This form, which is the man-

---

24 *Āli 'Imrān* (3) :85

25 *Āli 'Imrān* (3) :19.

26 *Āli 'Imrān* (3): 83.

27 This of course does not imply that the diversity between religions is only a matter of form, for the difference in the form indeed implies a difference in the conception of God, His Essence and Names and Attributes and Acts—a difference in the conception expressed in Islām as *tawḥīd:* the Unity of God.

ner of institution of belief and faith, the manner of expression of the law, the manner of religious attitude and ethical and moral conduct—the manner in which submission to God is enacted in our life, is expressed by the concept *millah.* Islām follows the *millah* of the Prophet Ibrāhīm (Abraham), which is also the *millah* of the other Prophets after him (Peace be upon them all !). Their *millah* altogether is considered to be the *form* of the right religion *dīn al-qayyim,* because of all other *milal,* their *millah* alone inclined perfectly, *ḥanīfan,* towards the true Religion (*al-Islām*). They thus anticipated Islām in religious faith and belief and law and practice and hence are called also Muslims, even though the Religion of Islām as such reached its perfect crystallization only in the form externalized by the Holy Prophet. Other religions have *evolved* their own systems or forms of submission based upon their own cultural traditions which do not necessarily derive from the *millah* of the Prophet Ibrāhīm and yet some others, such as the religion of the *Ahlu'l-Kitāb*—People of the Book—have evolved a mixture of their own cultural traditions with traditions based upon Revelation. It is to these various systems or forms of submission that, to return to the passage just quoted, the "unwilling" type of submission refers.[28]

---

28 In a sense, the words of God in the Holy Qur'ān:
—'Let there be no compulsion in religion' (*Al-Baqarah* (2):256)—corroborates what has been explained above in that in *true* religion there should be no compulsion: not only in the sense that, in the act of subjugating to religion and submitting to it, one must not compel others to submit; but in the sense that even with oneself, one must subjugate and submit oneself wholeheartedly and willingly, and love and enjoy the submission. Unwilling submission betrays arrogance, disobedience and rebellion, and is tantamount to misbelief, which is one of the forms of unbelief (*kufr*). It is a mistake to think belief in One God alone is sufficient in true religion, and that such

The concept of *dīn* in the sense of true obedience and real submission such as is here described in brief outline is manifested in living reality in the Religion of Islām. It is in Islām that true and perfect *dīn* is realized, for in Islām alone is its self-expression fulfilled completely. Islām emulates the pattern or form according to which God governs His Kingdom; it is an imitation of the cosmic order manifested here in this worldly life as a social as well as political order. The social order of Islām encompasses all aspects of man's physical and material and spiritual existence in a way which, here and now, does justice to the individual as well as the society; and to the individual as a physical being as well as the individual as spirit, so that a Muslim is at once himself and his Community, and his Community is also he, since every other single member strives, like him, to realize the same purpose in life and to achieve the same goal. The social order of Islām is the Kingdom of God on earth, for in

---

belief guarantees security and salvation. Iblīs (Satan), who believes in the One True God and knows and acknowledges Him as his Creator, Cherisher and Sustainer, his *rabb,* is nevertheless a misbeliever (*kāfir*). Although Iblīs submits to God, yet he submits grudgingly and insolently, and his *kufr* is due to arrogance, disobedience and rebellion. His is the most notorious example of unwilling submission. Unwilling submission, then, is not the mark of true belief, and a *kāfir* might therefore be also one who, though professing belief in One God, does not submit in real submission, but prefers instead to submit in his own obstinate way—a way, or manner, or form neither approved nor revealed and commanded by God. Real submission is that which has been perfected by the Holy Prophet as the model for mankind, for that is the manner of submission of all the Prophets and Messengers before him, and the form approved, revealed, and commanded by God. Thus, the fundamental core of true religion, then, is not the *belief,* but rather, more fundamentally, the *submission;* for the submission confirms and affirms the belief to be true and genuine.

that order God, and not man, is *still* the King, the Supreme Sovereign Whose will and law and ordinances and commands and prohibitions hold absolute sway. Man is only His vicegerent or *khalīfah,* who is given the trust of government, the *amānah,* to rule according to God's will and His pleasure. When we say "rule", we do not simply mean to refer to the socio-political sense of 'ruling', for we mean by it also, indeed far more fundamentally so, the rule of one's self by itself, since the trust refers to responsibility and freedom of the self to do justice to itself. Of this last statement we shall have recourse to elaborate presently, since what is meant reveals the very principle of Islamic ethics and morality. Islām, we say again, is a social order, but in that order every individual, each according to his latent capacity and power bestowed upon him by God to fulfill and realize his responsibility and freedom, strives to achieve and realize the ideal for himself in the Way [29] manifested by the Revealed Law[30] obeyed by all members of the Community. Thus then, just as every Muslim is a *khalīfah* of God on earth, so is every Muslim also His slave, His *'abd,* striving by himself to perfect his service and devotion, his *'ibādah,* in the manner approved by God, his Absolute Master. And since every individual in this social order is answerable to God alone, so even in that social order each individual is personally directing his true and real loyalty, *ṭā'ah,* to God alone, his Real King.

We have already said that the concept *dīn* reflects the idea of a kingdom—a cosmopolis. Commerce and trade are the life blood of the cosmopolis, and such activity together with its various implications is indeed inherent in the concept *dīn* as we have thus far described. It is no wonder then

---

[29] By 'the Way' I mean what refers *to iḥsān,* or perfection in virtue.

[30] The Revealed Law, or *sharī'ah,* is the law of God.

that in the Holy Qur'ān worldly life is depicted so persistently in the apt metaphors of commercial enterprise. In the cosmopolis or kingdom reflected in the concept *dīn,* there is depicted the bustling activities of the traffic of trade. Man is inexorably engaged in the trade: *al-tijārah,* in which he is himself the subject as well as object of his trade. He is his own capital, and his loss and gain depend upon his own sense of responsibility and exercise of freedom. He carries out the trust of buying and selling, of *bay'ah,* and bartering: *ishtarā,* and it is his self that he buys or sells or barters; and depending upon his own inclination towards the exercise of his will and deeds his trade will either prosper: *rabiḥa'l-tijārah,* or suffer loss: *mā rabiḥa'l-tijārah.* In the situation that rises before our vision we must see that the man so engaged realizes the utter seriousness of the trading venture he has willingly undertaken.[31] He is not simply an animal that eats and drinks and sleeps and disports after sensual pleasure[32]—no savage nor barbarian he who thus transcends himself in the realization of his weighty responsibility and consciousness of his freedom to fulfil and redeem himself of the burden of existence. It is of such as he who barters his self for his true self that God refers when He says in the Holy Qur'ān:

> 'Verily God has purchased of the Believers their selves'—. [33]

The concept *dīn* with reference to the man of Islām[34] presupposes the emergence in him of the higher type of man capable of lofty aspirations towards self-improvement—the self-improvement that is no less than the actualization of

---

31 See *Al-Aḥzāb* (33):72.

32 See *Al-A'rāf* (7) 179.

33 *Al-Tawbah* (9) :111.

34 The man of Islām, *i.e.,* the Muslim.

his latent power and capacity to become a perfect man. The man of Islām as a city dweller, a cosmopolitan, living a civilized life according to clearly defined foundations of social order and codes of conduct is he to whom obedience to Divine Law, endeavour towards realizing true justice and striving after right knowledge are cardinal virtues. The motive of conduct of such a man is eternal blessedness, entrance into a state of supreme peace which he might even here perchance foretaste, but which shall be vouchsafed to him when he enters the threshold of that other City and becomes a dweller, a citizen of that other Kingdom wherein his ultimate bliss shall be the beholding of the Glorious Countenance of the King.

While Islām is the epitome of the Divine cosmic order, the man of Islām who is conscious of his destiny realizes that he is himself, as physical being, also an epitome of the cosmos, a microcosmic representation, *'ālam saghīr,* of the macrocosmos, *al-'ālam al-kabīr.* Hence in the manner that Islām is like a kingdom, a social order, so the man of Islām knows that he is a kingdom in miniature, for in him, as in all mankind, is manifested the Attributes of the Creator, without the reverse being the case, since "God created man in His Own Image." Now man is both body and soul, he is at once physical being and spirit, and his soul governs his body as God governs the Universe. The human soul also has two aspects analogous to his dual nature: the higher, rational soul: *al-nafs al-nāṭiqah;* and the lower, animal or carnal soul: *al-nafs al-ḥayawāniyyah.* Within the conceptual framework of the concept *dīn* applied here as a subjective, personal, individual affair, man's rational soul is king and must exert its power and rule over the animal soul which is subject to it and which must be rendered submissive to it. The effective power and rule exercised by the rational soul over the animal soul, and the subjugation and total submission of the latter to the former can indeed be interpreted as *dīn,* or as *islām* in the subjective, personal, individual sense of the relationship thus established. In this context it is the animal soul that enslaves itself in submission and service and so 'returns' itself to the power and authority of the rational soul. When the Holy Prophet said:

"Die before ye die."—

it is the same as saying: "Return before ye *actually* return"; and this refers to the subjugation of one's self by one's real self, one's animal soul by one's rational soul; and it is pertaining to knowledge of this self that he means when he says:

"He who knows his self knows his Lord".

Further, when God proclaimed His lordship to Ādam's progeny it is the rational soul of man that He addressed, so that every soul has heard the "Am I not your Lord?" and answered "Yea !" and testified thus unto itself. So the man of Islām who is rightly guided acts accordingly as befits the true servant of God, His *'abd.* We referred earlier to the purpose for man's creation and existence, saying that it is to serve God; and we said that the act of service on the man's part is called *'ibādah* and the service as such *'ibādāt,* which refers to all conscious and willing acts of service for the sake of God alone and approved by Him, including such as are prescribed worship. In point of fact, we now say further that to the man of Islām his whole ethical life is one continuous *'ibādah,* for Islām itself is a complete way of life. When the man has, by means of *'ibādāt,* succeeded in curbing his animal and carnal passions and has thereby rendered submissive his animal soul, making it subject to the rational soul, the man thus described has attained to *freedom* in that he has fulfilled the purpose for his creation and existence; he has achieved supreme peace[35] and his soul is pacified, being set at liberty,

---

[35] When we also say that Islām means 'Peace', we refer in fact to the *consequence* of the submission denoted by the verb *aslama.*

as it were, free from the fetters of inexorable fate and the noisy strife and hell of human vices. His rational soul in this spiritual station is called in the Holy Qur'ān the 'pacified' or 'tranquil' soul: *al-nafs al-muṭma' innah.* This is the soul that 'returns' itself willingly to its Lord, and to it will God address His words:

> "O thou soul at peace! Return thou to thy Lord,—well-pleased (thyself) and well-pleasing unto Him ! Enter thou, then, among My servants! Yea, enter thou My Garden [36]

This is the soul of the servant who has fulfilled in constant affirmation his covenant with his Lord, and since none *knows* his Lord better than the true and loyal servant, who by reason of such service gains *intimacy* with his Lord and Master, so *'ibādah* means, in its final, advanced stages, knowledge: *ma'rifah.*[37]

---

36 *Al Fajr* (89) :27-30

37 We do not in the least imply here that when *'ibādah* becomes identified with *ma'rifah,* the former as *work* or *service* (*'amal*) including prayer (*ṣalāt*)—*i.e.* the prescribed (*farḍ*), the confirmed practice of the Prophet (*sunnah*), the supererogatory (*nawāfil*)—is no longer incumbent on the one who attains to the latter, or that for such a one prayer means simply intellectual contemplation, as some philosophers thought. *Ma'rifah* as 'knowledge' is both right cognition ('*ilm*) and right feeling or spiritual mood (*ḥāl*); and the former, which marks the final stages of the spiritual 'stations' (*maqāmāt*), precedes the latter, which marks the beginning of the spiritual 'states' (*aḥwāl*). So *ma'rifah* marks the spiritual transition-point between the spiritual station and the spiritual state. As such, and since it is knowledge that comes from God to the heart (*qalb*) and depends entirely upon Him, it is not necessarily a permanent condition unless continually secured and fortified by *'ibādah.* He who discerns knows that it is absurd in the case of one who

I have traced in bare outline the fundamental core of the Religion of Islām and have shown in a general way which can, albeit, be elaborated to its minutest logical details its all-encompassing nature which pervades the life of the individual as well as the society. I have said that Islām is the subjective, personal religion of the individual as well as the objective pervading self-same religion of the Community—that it operates as the same religion in the individual as a single entity as well as the society composed collectively of such entities.[38] It is implicit in our exposition that Islām is both belief and faith (*īmān*) as well as submission in service (*islām*); it is both assent of the heart (*qalb*) and mind (*'aql*) confirmed by the tongue (*lisān*) as well as deed and work

---

receives knowledge from God about God (*i.e.* the *'ārif*) to transform thereby his *'ibādah* solely into contemplation, for the *'ārif* is acutely aware of the fact that he becomes one at least partly due to his *'ibādah*, which is the means by which he approaches his Lord.

38 There is in truth no such thing as subjective Islām and objective Islām in the sense that the former implies less of its reality and truth than the latter, to the extent that the former is regarded as less valid and less authentic than the latter; or that the latter is other than the former as one independent reality and truth while the former is the many interpretations of the experience of the latter. We maintain that what is experienced as Islām by every individual Muslim subjectively is the same as Islām as it objectively is, and we use the terms 'subjective' and 'objective' here to distinguish rather than to differentiate the one from the other. The distinction between the two pertains to the level of understanding and the degree of insight and practice existing between one Muslim and another. The distinction thus refers to the *iḥsān*-aspect of Islamic experience. In spite of the naturally different levels of understanding and degrees of insight and practice existing between one Muslim and another yet all are Muslims and there is only one Islām, and what is common to them all is the same Islām.

(*'amal*);[39] it is the harmonious relationship established between both the soul and the body; it is obedience and loyalty (*ṭā'ah*) both to God as well as to the Holy prophet; it is accepting wholeheartedly the truth of the Testimony (*kalimah shahādah*) that there is no God but Allāh, and that Muḥammed is the Messenger of Allāh—Islām is the unity of all these, together with what they entail, in belief and in practice, in the person of the Muslim as well as in the Community as a whole. There can be no separation, nor division, nor dichotomy between the harmoniously integrated parts of the unity thus established, so that there can be, for Islām, no true believer nor faithful one (*Mu'min*) without such a one being also submissive in service (*Muslim*); no real assent of heart and mind confirmed by tongue without deed and work; no genuine obedience and loyalty to God without obedience and loyalty to His Messenger; nor can there be true acceptance of the Testimony that there is no God but Allāh without also accepting Muḥammad as His Messenger, who in fact first made manifest the Formula of Unity (*kalimah al-tawḥīd*). I have also pointed out the fundamental nature of the Quranic revelation of the soul's covenant with God in respect of His lordship and the concept of *dīn* as reflecting the cosmos, as God's government of the realm of creation, and I have drawn a comparison in respect of that concept of *dīn* and the concept of the macrocosm and its analogous relationship with man as a microcosm in which his rational soul governs his animal soul and body as God governs His Kingdom. The soul's covenant with God and the nature of the relationship revealed in that covenant indeed occupies a central position in the concept of *dīn* and is *the* fundamental basis of Islām, as I will reveal yet further. The covenant was made to all souls of Ādam's progeny and God addressed them both collectively as well as

---

39 *I.e.*, *'ibādah* and acts *of 'ibādāt.*

individually, so that it was a covenant made at once by every individual soul as well as all of them collectively to acknowledge God as their Lord. To acknowledge God as Lord (*rabb*) means to acknowledge Him as Absolute King (syn. *mālik*), Possessor and Owner (syn. *ṣāḥib*), Ruler, Governor, Master, Creator, Cherisher, Sustainer—since all these meanings denote the connotations inherent in the concept of *Lord*. All souls have the same status in relation to their Lord: that of being subject, possessed, owned, ruled, governed, enslaved, created, cherished and sustained. And since the covenant pertained at once to the individual soul as well as to the souls collectively, so we see that here when manifested as man within the fold of Islām the same souls are united in their endeavour to fulfill the covenant collectively as society and Community (*ummah*) as well as individually in such wise that Islām is, as we have said, both personal and subjective as well as social and communal and objective;[40] it is the harmonious blending of both the individual as well as the society. That which unites one Muslim individual to another in a wondrous and unique bond of brotherhood which transcends the restricting limitations of race and nation and space and time and is much stronger than even the familial bond of kinship is none other than this covenant, for those souls that here as man abide by that covenant recognize each other as brothers, as kindred souls. They were akin to one another in yonder place and here they are brethren who love one another for God's sake. Though one be in the East and the other in the West, yet they feel joy and comfort in each other's talk, and one who lives in a later generation than the other is instructed and consoled by the words of his brother. They were brothers involved in the same destiny long before they appeared as earthly brothers, and they were true kith and kin before they were born in earthly kinship. So here we

---

40 See above, note 38.

see that the same covenant is the very basis of Islamic brotherhood (*ukhuwwah*). It is this real feeling of brotherhood among Muslims based upon such firm spiritual foundation which no earthly power can rend asunder that unite the individual to the society in Islām without the individual having to suffer loss of individuality and personality, nor the society its polity and authority.

In the Islamic political and social organization—be it in one form or another—the same covenant becomes their very foundation. The man of Islām is not bound by the social contract, nor does he espouse the doctrine of the Social Contract. Indeed, though he lives and works within the bounds of social polity and authority and contributes his share towards the social good, and though he behaves *as if* a social contract were in force, his is, nevertheless, an *individual contract* reflecting the covenant his soul has sealed with God; for the covenant is in reality made for *each* and *every individual* soul. The purpose and end of ethics in Islām is ultimately for the individual; what the man of Islām does here he does in the way he believes to be good only because God and His Messenger say so and he trusts that his actions will find favour with God. Neither the state nor the society are for him real and true objects of his loyalty and obedience, for to him they are not the prerogatives of state and society to the extent that such conduct is due to them as their right; and if he in an Islamic state and society lives and strives for the good of the state and the society, it is only because the society composed of individual men of Islām and the state organized by them set the same Islamic end and purpose as their goal—otherwise he is obliged to oppose the state and strive to correct the errant society and remind them of their true aim in life. We know that in the ultimate analysis man's quest for 'happiness'—as they say in philosophy in connection with ethics—is always for the individual self. It is not the 'happiness' of the collective entity that matters so much more than individual happiness; and every man in reality must indeed think and act for his own salvation, for no other man can be made responsible for his actions since every man bears his own burden of responsibility.[41] 'Happiness', as I will elaborate in the next chapter, is related to a permanent condition in the rational soul; to knowledge and faith; to right conduct and to the attainment of a condition known as 'justice' (*'adl*)

In Islām—because for it religion encompasses life in its entirety—all virtue is religious; it has to do with the freedom of the rational soul, which freedom means the power to do justice to itself; and this in turn refers to exercise of its rule and supremacy and guidance and maintenance over the animal soul and body. The power to do justice to itself alludes to its constant affirmation and fulfilment of the covenant it has sealed with God. *Justice* in Islām is not a concept referring to a state of affairs which can operate only within a two-person-relation or dual-party-relation situation, such as: between one man and another; or between the society and the state; or between the ruler and the ruled; or between the king and his subjects. To the question: "Can one be unjust to one's self?" other religions or philosophies have not given a consistent clear-cut answer. Indeed in Western civilization, for example, though it is true that a man who commits suicide may be considered as committing an unjust act; but this is considered as such insofar only because his suicide deprives the state of the services of a useful citizen, so that his injustice is not to himself, but to the state and society. We have several times alluded to the concept that justice means a harmonious condition or state of affairs whereby every thing is in its right and proper place—such as the cosmos; or similarly, a state of equilibrium, whether it refers to things or living beings. With respect to man, we say that justice means basically a condition and situation whereby he is in his right and proper place. 'Place'

---

41 See *Al-An'ām* (6) :164.

here refers not only to his total situation in relation to others, but also to his condition in relation to his self. So the concept of justice in Islām does not only refer to relational situations of harmony and equilibrium existing between one person and another, or between the society and the state, or between the ruler and the ruled, or between the king and his subjects, but far more profoundly and fundamentally so it refers in a primary way to the harmonious and rightly-balanced relationship existing between the man and his self, and in a secondary way only to such as exists between him and another or others, between him and his fellow men and ruler and king and state and society. Thus to the question: "Can one be unjust to one's self?" we answer in the affirmative, and add further that justice and injustice indeed *begins* and *ends* with the self. The Holy Qur'ān repeatedly stresses the point that man, when he does wrong, is being unjust (*ẓālim*) to himself, and that injustice (*ẓulm*) is a condition wrought by man upon his self.[42] To understand this we have to refer once again to the soul's covenant with God and to the belief that man has a dual nature in respect of his soul and body. The real man can only in fact be his rational soul. If in his existence as a human being he allows his animal or carnal soul to get the better of him and consequently commits acts prohibited by God and displeasing to Him, or if he denies belief in God altogether, then he has thereby repudiated his own affirmation of God's Lordship which he as rational soul has covenanted with God. He does violence to his own covenant, his individual contract with God. So just as in the case of one who violates his own contract brings calamity upon himself, in the same way he who does wrong or evil, who disobeys or denies God, violates the contract his soul has made with God, thereby being unjust to his soul. He has also thereby 'lied'—*kadhaba,* another apt Quranic

---

[42] See *Al-Nisā'* (4) :123; *Yūnus* (10) :44.

expression—against his own self (soul). It is important in the light of this brief explanation to understand why the belief in the resurrection of bodies is fundamental in Islām, for the soul reconstituted with its former body will not be able to deny what its body had done, for its very eyes, tongue, hands and feet or limbs—the organs of ethical and moral conduct—will testify against its acts of injustice to itself.[43] Though in Islām injustice ostensibly applies between man and God, and between man and man, and between man and his self, in reality, however, injustice is ultimately applicable—even in the two former cases—to man's self alone; in the Islamic worldview and spiritual vision, whether a man disbelieves or disobeys God, or whether he does wrong to another man, it is really to his own self that he does wrong. Injustice, being the opposite of justice, is the putting a thing in a place not its own; it is to misplace a thing; it is to misuse or to wrong; it is to exceed or fall short of the mean or limit; it is to suffer loss; it is deviation from the right course; it is disbelief of what is true, or lying about what is true knowing it to be true. Thus when a man does an act of injustice, it means that he has wronged his own soul, for he has put his soul in a place not its own; he has misused it; he

---

43 Analogically, the legal concept of *habeas corpus* (you must have the body) as a fundamental procedure of justice that is definitely borrowed from the idea of resurrection in revealed religion, is perhaps only a mere imperfect reflection of the awesome and irrefutable Procedure to come. That the soul is capable of denial of acts of injustice is implied in *Al-A'rāf* (7):172–173; and in these verses must be seen clear evidence of the soul's capacity (*wus'*) to exercise a power (*quwwah*) of inclination towards right or wrong resulting in its acquisition or earning (*kasaba, iktasaba*) of good or evil. In the Islamic concept of justice and injustice outlined above, the fact that the witness to a man's actions, good or bad, is his own self is of great significance. See also *Al-Nūr* (24) :24.

has made it to exceed or fall short of its real nature; he has caused it to deviate from what is right and to repudiate the truth and to suffer loss. All that he has thus done—in one way or another—entails a violation of his covenant with God. It is clear from what we say about injustice that justice implies *knowledge* of the right and proper place for a thing or a being to be; of right as against wrong; of the mean or limit; of spiritual gain as against loss; of truth as against falsity and falsehood. This is why knowledge (*al-'ilm: ma'rifah: 'ilm*) occupies a most important position in Islām, where in the Holy Qur'ān alone we find more than eight hundred references to knowledge. And even in the case of knowledge, man has to do justice to it, that is, to know its limit of usefulness and not to exceed or fall short of it; to know its various orders of priority in relation to its usefulness to one's self; to know where to stop and to know what can be gained and what cannot, what is true knowledge and what is learned guess and theory—in sum, to put every datum of knowledge in its right place in relation to the knowing one in such wise that what is known produces harmony in the one who knows. To know how to put what knowledge in which place is wisdom (*ḥikmah*). Otherwise, knowledge without order and seeking it without discipline does lead to confusion and hence to injustice to one's self.[44]

Knowledge, as we understand it, is of two kinds: that given by God to man; and that acquired by man by means of his own effort of rational enquiry based upon experience and observation. The first kind can only be received by man through his acts of worship and devotion, his acts of service

---

44 'Order' and 'discipline' here do hot refer to the kind of order and discipline in the systematic deployment of knowledge found in modern universities and schools, but to the ordering of knowledge by the self that seeks to know, and to the disciplining of the self of itself to that ordering (see below pp. 72–74).

to God (*ibādāt*) which, depending upon God's grace and his own latent spiritual power and capacity created by God to receive it, the man receives by direct insight or spiritual savouring (*dhawq*) and unveiling to his spiritual vision (*kashf*). This knowledge (*ma'rifah*) pertains to his self or soul, and such knowledge—as we have touched upon cursorily in our comparison of the analogous relationship obtained between the macrocosm and the microcosm—gives insight into knowledge of God, and for that reason is the highest knowledge. Since such knowledge ultimately depends upon God's grace and because it entails deeds and works of service to God as prerequisites to its possible attainment, it follows that for it knowledge of the prerequisites becomes necessary, and this includes knowledge of the essentials of Islām (*arkān al-islām* and *arkān al-īmān*), their meanings and purpose and correct understanding and implementation in everyday life and practice: every Muslim must have knowledge of these prerequisites, must understand the basic essentials of Islām and the Unity of God (*tawḥīd*), and practise the knowledge (*al-'ilm*) in deeds and works of service to God so that every man of Islām is in fact already in the initial stage of that first knowledge; he is set ready on the Straight Path (*ṣirāṭ al-mustaqīm*) leading to God. His further progress on the pilgrim's path depends upon his own performance and sincerity of purpose, so that some serve God as though they see Him, and others serve Him as though He sees them; and the pilgrim's progress to the former way from the latter is what constitutes the highest virtue (*iḥsān*). The second kind of knowledge (*'ilm*) is acquired through, reason, experience and observation; it is discursive and deductive and it refers to objects of pragmatical value. As an illustration of the distinction between the two kinds of knowledge we might suppose a man and his neighbour who has just moved in to his neighbourhood. At first he knows his new neighbour only by acquaintance; he might know the other's general appearance and be able to recognize him when meeting in the street; he might learn his name, his marital status, the number of his children and many other such details of information which he can obtain by observation. Then he might, through inquiries from others he knows and private investigation, discover his neighbour's occupation and place of work and appointment, and he might even find out, through further discreet investigation, how much he earns. He might go on investigating in this way without coming into direct contact with his neighbour and accumulate other data about him, and yet his knowledge of him would still be on the level of acquaintance and not of intimacy; for no matter how many more details he might add on to the knowledge about his neighbour thus acquired, there will be many more important personal details which he will never be able to know, such as the other's loves and fears and hopes and beliefs, his thoughts on life and death, his secret thoughts and feelings, his good qualities and other details such as these. Now let us suppose that he decides to know the man directly and introduces himself to him; he visits him often and eats and drinks and sports with him. Then after long years of faithful friendship and sincere companionship and devotion he might perchance receive by direct and spontaneous revelation from his friend and companion some of the many personal details and secret thoughts and feelings that are now in a flash revealed in a way which he will not be able to obtain in a lifetime of investigation and observation and research. Even this knowledge, given as a result of intimacy is never complete, for we know that no matter how close the intimate relationship between the man and his friend—or brother, or wife and children, or parents, or lover—there will always be for him that veil of mystery that ever envelopes the one to be known like an infinite series of Chinese spherical ivory carving within carving, only to be unveiled for him by direct revelation from the other. And the other too will know by contemplating his self the infinite nature of that self that ever eludes his cognitive quest, so that even *he* is not able to reveal except only that which he knows. Every man is like an island set in a fathomless sea enveloped by darkness, and the loneliness his self knows is so utterly absolute because even he knows not his self completely. From this illustration we may derive certain basic conditions analogous to the first kind of knowledge. First, the desire by the one who gives knowledge about himself to be known. Second, the giving of such knowledge pertains to the same level of being, and this is because communication of ideas and feelings is possible and can be understood. Third, to be allowed to approach and know him, the one who seeks to know must abide by rules of propriety and codes of conduct and behaviour acceptable to the one who desires to be known. Fourth, his giving knowledge about himself is based on trust after a considerable period of testing of the other's sincerity and loyalty and devotion and capacity to receive—a period in which is established a firm bond of intimacy between the two. In like manner and even more so, then, is the case with knowledge given by God. In respect of the first condition, He says in the Holy Qur'ān that He has created man only that man may serve Him, and service in its profoundest sense ultimately means knowledge (*ma'rifah*), so that His purpose of creation is for the creature to *know* Him, as He says in a Holy Tradition (*Ḥadīth Qudsiyy*):

> "I was a Hidden Treasure, and I desired to be known, so I created Creation that I might be known."

Thus God reveals Himself to the rational soul, which possesses organs of spiritual communication and cognition such as the heart (*al-qalb*), which knows Him; the spirit (*al-rūḥ*), which loves Him; and the secret or inmost ground of the soul (*al-sirr*), which contemplates Him. Though the rational soul is not of the same level of being as God, there is yet in it that spark of Divine origin which makes it possible for it to receive communication from above and to have cognition of what is received; and from this we derive analogy for the second condition. In the case of the third condition, we say that man approaches God by sincere submission to His will and absolute obedience to His law; by conscious realization in himself of His commands and prohibitions and ordinances, and by performance of acts of devotion and supererogatory worship approved by Him and pleasing to Him, until such a man attains to the station in which His trust and friendship may be conferred upon him by means of knowledge given as a gift of grace to him for whom He has created the capacity to receive corresponding to the knowledge given. Thus His words in a Holy Tradition:

> "My servant ceases not to draw nigh unto Me by supererogatory worship until I love him; and when I love him I am his ear, so that he hears by Me, and his eye, so that he sees by Me, and his tongue, so that he speaks by Me, and his hand, so that he takes by Me."

As to the fourth condition of trust, it is part of the third, and this is in itself already clear. We see then that such knowledge, by virtue of its very nature, imparts truth and certainty of a higher order than that obtained in knowledge of the second kind; and because of this, and of the fact that it pertains to the soul or self of man and its fulfilment of the covenant made with God, knowledge of its prerequisites, which is in fact based on this given knowledge, is inextricably bound up with Islamic ethics and morality. By means of such knowledge and the practice it entails we guide and govern ourselves in daily conduct and set our values in life and ourselves aright. The first knowledge unveils the mystery of Being and Existence and reveals the true relationship between man's self and his Lord, and since for man such knowledge pertains to the ultimate purpose for knowing, it follows that knowledge of its prerequisites becomes the basis and essential foundation for knowledge of the second kind, for knowledge of the latter alone, without the guiding spirit of the former, cannot truly lead man in his life, but only confuses and confounds him and enmeshes him in the labyrinth of endless and purposeless seeking. We also perceive that there is a limit for man even to the first and highest knowledge; whereas no such limit obtains in the second kind, so that the possibility of perpetual wandering spurred on by intellectual deception and self-delusion in constant doubt and curiosity is always real. The individual man has no time to waste in his momentary sojourn on earth, and the rightly guided one knows that his individual quest for knowledge of the second kind must needs be limited to his own practical needs and suited to his nature and capacity, so that he may set both the knowledge and himself in their right places in relation to his real self and thus maintain a condition of justice. For this reason and in order to achieve justice as the end, Islām distinguishes the quest for the two kinds of knowledge, making the one for the attainment of knowledge of the prerequisites of the first obligatory to all Muslims (*farḍ 'ayn*), and that of the other obligatory to some Muslims only (*farḍ kifāyah*), and the obligation for the latter can indeed be transferred to the former category in the case of those who deem themselves duty bound to seek it for their self improvement. The division in the obligatory quest for knowledge into two categories is itself a procedure of doing justice to knowledge and to the man who seeks it, for *all* of the knowledge of the prerequisites of the first knowledge is good for man, whereas *not all* of the knowledge of the second kind is good for him; for the man who seeks that latter knowledge, which would bear considerable influence in determining his secular role and position as a citizen, might not necessarily be a *good* man. In Western civilization generally, because its conception of justice is based on secular foundations, it follows that its conception of knowledge is also based upon similar foundations, or complementary foundations emphasizing man as a physical entity and a rational animal being, to the extent that it admits of what we have referred to as the second kind of knowledge as the only valid 'knowledge' possible. Consequently, the purpose of seeking knowledge from the lower to the higher levels is, for Western civilization, to produce in the seeker a good citizen. Islām, however, differs in this in that for it the purpose of seeking knowledge is to produce in the seeker a good man. We maintain that it is more fundamental to produce a good man than to produce a good citizen, for the good man will no doubt also be a good citizen, but the good citizen will not necessarily also be a good man. In a sense we say that Islām too maintains that the purpose of seeking knowledge is to produce in the seeker a good citizen, only that we mean by 'citizen' a Citizen of that other Kingdom, so that he acts as such even here and now as a good man. The concept of a 'good man' in Islām connotes not only that he must be 'good' in the general social sense understood, but that he must also first be good to his self, and not be unjust to it in the way we have explained,[45] for if he were unjust to his self, how can he really be just to others? Thus we see that, already in this most fundamental concept in life—the concept of knowledge—Islām is at variance with Western civilization, in that for Islām (a) knowledge includes faith and true belief (*īmān*); and that (b) the purpose for seeking knowledge is to inculcate goodness or justice in man as man and individual self, and not merely in man as citizen or as integral part of society: it is man's value as a real man, as spirit, that is stressed, rather than his value as a physical entity measured in terms of the pragmatic or utilitarian sense of his usefulness to state and society and the world.

I have been describing what constitutes the very core of the Religion of Islām, and in this description have explained in brief but simple and succinct manner the fun-

---

[45] The concept of a "good man" is defined as a man of *adab* according to my definition of *adab* set forth in my *The Concept of Education in Islām*, Kuala Lumpur, 1980. See also the *Introduction* to this book.

damental concept of *dīn* and of faith and belief in Islām. I have touched upon the Islamic worldview and have stressed the paramount importance of the Quranic concept of man's covenant with God, showing how this covenant is of an essential nature; it is the starting point in the Islamic concept of religion, and is the dominant element in all other Islamic concepts bound up with it, such as those of freedom and responsibility, of justice, of knowledge, of virtue, of brotherhood; of the role and character of the individual and the society and of their mutual identity in the framework of the state and of collective life. I have in this description also emphasized the role of the individual, and of the individual the self, or soul, and its journey of return to God. It now behoves me to describe in outline the Islamic vision of Reality, which is no other than the metaphysical core of Islām which determines its worldview. Islām focusses its religious and metaphysical vision (*shuhūd*) of Reality and its worldview on Being, and distinguishes between Existence (*wujūd*) and Existent (*mawjūd*); between Unity (*waḥdah*) and Multiplicity (*kathrah*); between Subsistence (*baqāʾ*) and Evanescence (*fanāʾ*). This vision of Reality is based upon revealed knowledge through religious experience, and embraces both the objective, metaphysical and ontological reality as well as the subjective, intuitive and psychological experience of that reality. Phenomenologically Islām, in confirmation of its vision of Reality, affirms 'being' rather than 'becoming' or 'coming-into-being', for the Object of its vision is clear, established, permanent and unchanging. This confirmation and affirmation is absolute because it springs from the certainty (*yaqīn*) of revealed knowledge; and since its Object is clear and established and permanent and unchanging, so likewise is Islām, together with its way of life and method of practice and values, an absolute reflection of the mode of the Object. Thus Islām itself is like its Object in that it emulates its ontological nature as subsisting and unchanging—as being; and hence affirms itself to be complete and perfect as confirmed by God's words in the Holy

Qur'ān,[46] and it denies the possibility of ever being in need of completion or evolution towards perfection; and such concepts as *development* and *progress* and *perfection* when applied to man's life and history and destiny must indeed refer, in Islām, ultimately to the spiritual and real nature of man. If this were not so, then it can never really mean, for Islām, *true* development and progress and perfection, as it would mean only the development and progress and perfection of the animal in man; and that would not be his true evolution unless such evolution realizes in him his true nature as spirit.

Change, development and *progress,* according to the Islamic viewpoint, refer to the return to the genuine Islām enunciated and practised by the Holy Prophet, the members of his sanctified House and his noble Companions and their Followers, and the faith and practice of genuine Muslims after them, and they also refer to the self and mean its return to its original nature and religion (Islām). These concepts pertain to presupposed situations in which Muslims find themselves going astray and steeped in ignorance of Islām and are confused and unjust to their selves. In such situations, their endeavour to direct their selves back onto the Straight and True Path and to return to the condition of genuine Islām—such endeavour, which entails change, is development; and such return, which consists in development, is progress. Thus, for Islām, the process of movement towards genuine Islām by Muslims who have strayed away from it is development; and such development is the only one that can truly be termed as progress. Progress is neither 'becoming' or 'coming-into-being', nor movement towards that which is 'coming-into-being' and never becomes 'being', for the notion of 'something aimed at', or the 'goal' inherent in the concept 'progress' can only contain real

---

[46] *Al-Mā'idah* (5):4.

meaning when it refers to that which is already *clear* and permanently *established,* already *being.* Hence what is already clear and established, already in the state of being, cannot suffer change, nor is it subject to constant slipping from the grasp of achievement, nor constantly receding beyond attainment. The term 'progress' reflects a *definite direction* that is aligned to a *final purpose* that is meant to be achieved in life; if the direction sought is still vague, still coming-into-being, as it were, and the purpose aligned to it is not final, then how can involvement in it truly mean progress? Those who grope in the dark cannot be referred to as progressing, and they who say such people are progressing have merely uttered a lie against the true meaning and purpose of progress, and they have lied unto their selves!

Their similitude is that of a man
Who kindled a fire;
When it lighted all around him,
God took away their light
And left them in utter darkness.
So they could not see.
Deaf, dumb, and blind,
They will not return (to the path).
Or (another similitude)
Is that of a rain-laden cloud
From the sky: in it are zones
Of darkness, and thunder and lightning:
They press their fingers in their ears
To keep out the stunning thunder-clap,
The while they are in terror of death.
But God is ever round
The rejecters of Faith !
The lightning all but snatches away
Their sight; every time the light
(Helps) them, they walk therein,
And when the darkness grows on them,
They stand still.

And if God willed, He could take away
Their faculty of hearing and seeing;
For God hath power over all things.[47]

The Islamic worldview is not to be construed as a dualism, for although two elements are involved, yet the one is independent and self-subsistent while the other is dependent upon it; the one is absolute and the other relative; the one is real and the other a manifestation of that reality. So there is only One Reality and Truth, and all Islamic values pertain ultimately to It alone, so that to the Muslim, individually and collectively, all endeavour towards change and development and progress and perfection is invariably determined by the worldview that projects the vision of the One Reality and confirms the affirmation of the same Truth. In this way in practice Muslims have been able to live their lives in accordance with the belief without suffering any change to be wrought that would disrupt the harmony of Islām and of their own selves; without succumbing to the devastating touch of time, nor to the attendant challenges in the vicissitudes of worldly existence. The man of Islām has with him the Holy Qur'ān which is itself unchanged, unchanging and unchangeable; it is the Speech of God revealed in complete and final form to His Chosen Messenger and Last Prophet Muḥammad. It is the clear Guidance which he carries with him everywhere, not merely literally so, but more in his tongue and mind and heart, so that it becomes the very vital force that moves his human frame. I have said earlier, when referring to man's contemplation of his self, how every man is like an island set in isolation in a fathomless sea enveloped by darkness, saying that the loneliness his self knows is so utterly absolute because even *he* knows not his self completely. I must add that such utter loneliness basically springs from man's inability to

---

47 *Al-Baqarah* (2):17–20.

answer his own persistent ageless inner question to himself: "Who am I?" and "What is my ultimate destiny?" We say that such experience of utter loneliness, however, assails only the heart of the man who denies God, or doubts Him, or repudiates his soul's covenant with God; for it is, again, recognition and affirmation of that same covenant that established for man his identity in the order of Being and Existence. The man of Islām—he who confirms and affirms the covenant within his self—is never lonely for even when contemplating his self he knows intuitively, through acts of *'ibādah* that include constant recitation and reflection and contemplation of the words of God in the Holy Qur'ān, how close that self is with God, his Creator and Lord, Whom he ever contemplates in remembrance (*dhikr*) and with Whom he has intimate converse (*munājāt*). Such a man has identified his self to himself and knows his ultimate destiny, and he is secure within his self and free from the terrifying echoes of absolute loneliness and the breathless grip of silent fear. In affirmation of Being, the Holy Qur'ān, the source of Islām and projector of the Islamic worldview and the vision of the One Reality and Truth, is the expression of the finality and perfection of 'being' just as Islām is the phenomenological affirmation of 'being'; and he who conveyed the Holy Qur'ān to mankind himself represents the finality and perfection of 'being' in man. The Holy Prophet, upon whom be God's blessing and Peace !, is the Seal of the Prophets,[48] the universal and final Messenger of God to mankind,[49] whom he leads from darkness to light;[50] who is himself the Lamp spreading Light;[51] he is God's Mercy to all creatures,[52] and His favour to those who believe in him and

48 *Al-Aḥzāb* (33):40.

49 *Sabā* (34) 28.

50 *Al-Êalāq* (65) 11.

51 *Al-Aḥzāb* (33):46; *Al-Êalāq* (65) 11.

52 *Al-Anbiyā* ' (21) 107.

in what he brought[53] and he is God's favour even to the People of the Book,[54] who may yet come to believe in him. He is man whom God has created with a character exalted as the standard for mankind;[55] he is the Perfect Man and Exemplar *par excellence.* [56] He it is who even God and His Angels honour and bless as the greatest of men,[57] and all true believers, in compliance with God's Command, and in emulation of His Angels, do likewise, and have done and will do so in this world and the next for as long as God wills; and in the Hereafter to him will God vouchsafe the Lauded Station.[58] Muḥammad, the Messenger of God, is he whose very name is a miracle of fulfillment, for he alone among all mankind is constantly praised in every age and generation after him without end, so that even taking into account the ages and generations before him he still would be the only man to whom such praise is due. We praise him out of sincere love and respect and gratitude for having led us out of darkness into light, and he is loved above all other human beings including our selves. Our love and respect for him is such that neither time nor memory could dull, for he is in our selves in every age and generation—nay, he is closer than ourselves,[59] and we emulate his words (*qawl*) and model actions (*fi'l*) and silent confirmation (*taqrīr*) of usages known to him, so that next to the Holy Qur'ān he is our most excellent and perfect guide and exemplar in life. He is the perfect model for every Muslim male and female; adolescent, middle-aged and old, in such wise that Muslims do not suffer from the crises of identity. Because of him the

---

53 *Āli 'Imrān* (3) :164; *Al-Nisā* (4):170.
54 *Al-Mā-'idah* (5):21.
55 *Al-Qalam* (68):4.
56 *Al-Aḥzāb* (33) 21.
57 *Al-Aḥzāb* (33) :56.
58 *Banī Isrā'īl* (17) :79.
59 *Al-Aḥzāb* (3) 6.

external structure or pattern of Muslim society is not divided by the gap of generations such as we find prevalent in Western society.

Western civilization is constantly changing and 'becoming' without ever achieving 'being', except that its 'being' is and always has been a 'becoming'. This is and has been so by virtue of the fact that it acknowledges no single, established Ṛeality to fix its vision on; no single, valid Scripture to confirm and affirm in life; no single, human Guide whose words and deeds and actions and entire mode of life can serve as model to emulate in life, but that each and every individual must find for himself and herself each one's identity and meaning of life and destiny. Western civilization affirms the evanescent (*fanā'*) aspect of reality, and its values pertain to the secular, material and physical realities of existence. Western society is thus divided by gaps between the three generations: the youth, the middle-aged, and the old. Each separate generation moves within the confines of its own attempts at finding a meaning for its own self and life in an ageless search for the answers to the questions "Who am I?" and "What is my destiny?" The youth, who at that stage experience change in life, consider the values handed down by their fathers, the middle-aged, no longer useful nor relevant to their way of life. Consequently, they do not take the middle-aged as models to guide them in life, and hence demand of them their 'freedom' to choose their own destiny. The middle-aged, realizing that *their* values too, when they were in the prime of youth, did not succeed in guiding them in life, and now they know they are themselves unable to provide the necessary guidance for their sons, and so surrender 'freedom' which they seek to choose their destiny in the hope that youth may yet succeed where they had failed. Now the youth, in demanding 'freedom' to choose their own destiny, also know that they need guidance, which is unfortunately not available, for even from their very midst they are unable to bring forth a leader who can play the role of perfect model whose example can be emulated by others.

This disconcerting situation creates in youth uncertainty and much doubt about the future, and they desperately dare to hope that when *they* reach the middle-age they would then be able to remould the world nearer to their heart's desire. But the middle-aged, who play the central role in moulding and preserving their state, society, and world, know from experience in their youth that their former values now no longer serve a purpose and have lost their meaning in life; and since their former search for identity has failed, so their present lives do not reflect contentment of fulfillment and are void of happiness. Thus the values they now esteem, the values that now become for them the measure of their success in searching for meaning in their individual lives, are only those promoting secular and materialistic achievements pertaining to the state and society; and so they strive and relentlessly compete among themselves to gain high places in the social ladder, or wealth and power and world renown. In the midst of such struggle, they realize that their mental capacity and intelligence are beginning to weaken; physical power and vitality are beginning to deteriorate, and consternation and regret and sadness begin to take hold of their selves when there appear in successive series before their mental perception the vision of retirement from public life into the loneliness of old age. Consequently, they look to youth with nostalgia and set high hopes that the youth may yet bring forth the longed-for perfect model and exemplar in life for all society to emulate; and this attitude towards youth is the very core of the worship of Youth, which is one of the dominant features of Western civilization since ancient times. The crisis of identity experienced by the middle-aged is somewhat similar to that experienced by the youth, with the exception that, for the middle-aged, the 'freedom' to choose their destiny is increasingly limited, for time relentlessly moves on like a Greek tragedy to the very end. The old, in such a society, are mere creatures forgotten by society, because their very existence reminds the youth and middle-aged of what they would be like which they want to forget. The old remind them of dissolution and death; the old have lost physical power and vitality; they have lost success; they have lost memory and their use and function in society; they have lost friend and family—they have lost the future. When a society bases its philosophy of life upon secular foundations and espouses materialistic values to live by, it inevitably follows that the meaning and value and quality of life of the individual citizen therein is interpreted and measured in terms of his position as a citizen; his occupation and use and working and earning power in relation to the state. When in old age all this is gone, so likewise his identity—which is in fact moulded by the secular role he plays—is lost. The three generations that in such wise comprise Western society are forever engaged in the search for identity and meaning of life; are forever moving in the vicious circle of unattainment; each generation dissatisfied with its own self-evolved values of life; each generation finding itself a misfit. And this condition, we maintain, is what we mean by injustice (*ẓulm*). This condition is further aggravated by the fact that in Western society there exists also a crisis of identity between the sexes, in that women are engaged, as women, in the search for *their* own, separate identity.

Islamic society is not beset by such condition. The individuals within the generations that comprise it, whether male or female, have already established their identity and recognized their ultimate destiny; the former through recognition and confirmation of the covenant, and the latter through affirmation and realization of that covenant by means of sincere submission to God's will and obedience to His law such as enacted as Islām. The man who brought to us the Holy Qur'ān as it was revealed to him by God, who thus brought to us the Knowledge of our identity and destiny, whose own life is the most excellent and perfect interpretation of the Holy Qur'ān so that his life becomes for us the focus of emulation and true guiding spirit, is the Holy Prophet, may God bless and give him Peace ! By his teaching and example he has shown us the right and true practice of

Islām and of Islamic virtues; he is the perfect model for mankind not merely for one generation, but for all generations; not merely for a time, but for all time. Indeed, we say that the concept 'perfect model' can fulfill its true meaning only if he who is thus described, such as Muḥammad alone is, embodies within his self all the permanent human and spiritual values necessary for man's guidance in life, whose validity is such that they serve man not only for the span of his individual lifetime, but for as long as man lives in this world. So every generation of Muslims, emulating his example, passes on the way of life he patterned to the next in such wise that no gaps nor crises of identity occur between them, but that each preceding generation guides the next by confirming and affirming his example in their lives.

The problem of human identity and destiny is, to my mind, the root cause of all other problems that beset modern society. Many challenges have arisen in the midst of man's confusion throughout the ages, but none perhaps more serious and destructive to man than today's challenge posed by Western civilization. I venture to maintain that the greatest challenge that has surreptitiously arisen in our age is the challenge of knowledge, indeed, not as against ignorance; but knowledge as conceived and disseminated throughout the world by Western civilization; knowledge whose nature has become problematic because it has lost its true purpose due to being unjustly conceived, and has thus brought about chaos in man's life instead of, and rather than, peace and justice; knowledge which pretends to be real but which is productive of confusion and scepticism, which has elevated doubt and conjecture to the 'scientific' rank in methodology; knowledge which has, for the first time in history, brought chaos to the Three Kingdoms of Nature; the animal, vegetal and mineral. It seems to me important to emphasize that knowledge is not neutral, and can indeed be infused with a nature and content which masquerades as knowledge. Yet it is in fact, taken as a whole, not true knowledge, but its interpretation through the prism, as it were, the worldview, the intellectual vision and psychological perception of the civilization that now plays the key role in its formulation and dissemination. What is formulated and disseminated is knowledge infused with the character and personality of that civilization—knowledge presented and conveyed as knowledge in that guise so subtly fused together with the real so that others take it unawares *in toto* to be the real knowledge *per se.* What is the character and personality, the essence and spirit of Western civilization that has so transformed both itself and the world, bringing all who accept its interpretation of knowledge to a state of chaos leading to the brink of disaster? By 'Western civilization' I mean the civilization that has evolved out of the historical fusion of cultures, philosophies, values and aspirations of ancient Greece and Rome; their amalgamation with Judaism and Christianity, and their further development and formation by the Latin, Germanic, Celtic and Nordic peoples. From ancient Greece is derived the philosophical and epistemological elements and the foundations of education and of ethics and aesthetics; from Rome the elements of law and statecraft and government; from Judaism and Christianity the elements of religious faith; and from the Latin, Germanic, Celtic and Nordic peoples their independent and national spirit and traditional values, and the development and advancement of the natural and physical sciences and technology which they, together with the Slavic peoples, have pushed to such pinnacles of power. Islām too has made very significant contributions to Western civilization in the sphere of knowledge and in the inculcation of the rational and scientific spirit, but the knowledge and the rational and scientific spirit have been recast and remoulded to fit the crucible of Western culture so that they have become fused and amalgamated with all the other elements that form the character and personality of Western civilization. But the fusion and amalgamation thus evolved produced a characteristic dualism in the worldview and values of Western culture and civilization; a dualism that cannot be resolved into a harmonious unity, for it is formed of conflicting ideas, values, cultures, beliefs, philosophies, dogmas, doctrines and theologies altogether reflecting an all-pervasive dualistic vision of reality and truth locked in despairing combat. Dualism abides in all aspects of Western life and philosophy: the speculative, the social, the political, the cultural—just as it pervades with equal inexorableness the Western religion.

It formulates its vision of truth and reality not upon revealed knowledge and religious belief, but rather upon cultural tradition reinforced by strictly philosophical premises based upon speculations pertaining mainly to secular life centered upon man as physical entity and rational animal, setting great store upon man's intellectual capacity alone to unravel the mysteries of his total environment and involvement in existence, and to conceive out of the results of speculations based upon such premises his evolutionary ethical and moral values to guide and order his life accordingly. There can be no certainty in philosophical speculations in the sense of religious certainty based on revealed knowledge understood and experienced in Islām;[60] and because of this the knowledge and values that project the worldview and

---

60 See above, p. 75, reference to *yaqīn* (certainty). The Holy Qur'ān mentions three degrees or levels of certainty of knowledge: certainty derived by inference, whether deductive or inductive: *'ilm al-yaqīn*, (*Al-Takāthur* (102): 5); certainty derived by direct vision: *'ayn al-yaqīn* (*Al-Takāthur* (102): 7); and certainty derived by direct experience *ḥaqq al-yaqīn*(*Al-Ḥāqqah* (69): 51). These levels of certain knowledge pertain to truth, whether manifest or hidden, empirical or transcendental; and the certain knowledge of what is hidden has the same force of certainty as that of what is visible. These levels of certainty also pertain to that which is perceived by the spiritual organ of cognition, the heart (*al-qalb*), and refers to knowledge as belief and faith (*īmān*). See p. 65 above.

direct the life of such a civilization is subject to review and change.

The inquiring spirit of Western culture and civilization originated with disenchantment towards religion as that civilization understands it. Religion in the sense we mean as outlined here has never really taken root in Western civilization due to its excessive and misguided love of the world and secular life and of man and preoccupation with man's secular destiny. Its inquiring spirit is basically generated in a state of doubt and inner tension; the inner tension is the result of the clash of conflicting elements and opposing values in the sustained dualism, while the doubts maintain the state of inner tension. The state of inner tension in turn produces the insatiable desire to seek and to embark on a perpetual journey of discoveries. The quest insatiable and the journey perpetual because doubt ever prevails, so that what is sought is never really found, what is discovered never really satisfies its true purpose. It is like the thirsty traveller who at first sincerely sought the water of knowledge, but who later, having found it plain perhaps, proceeded to temper his cup with the salt of doubt so that his thirst now becomes insatiable though he drinks incessantly, and that in thus drinking the water that cannot slake his thirst, he has forgotten the original and true purpose for which the water was sought. The fundamental truths of religion are regarded, in such a scheme of things, as mere theories, or discarded altogether as futile illusions. Absolute values are denied and relative values affirmed; nothing can be certain, except the certainty that nothing can be certain. The logical consequence of such an attitude towards knowledge, which determines and is determined by the worldview, is to negate God and the Hereafter and affirm man and his world. Man is deified and Deity humanized, and the world becomes man's sole preoccupation so that even his own immortality consists in the continuation of his species and his culture in this world. What is called 'change' and 'development' and 'progress' in all their aspects as far as Western civilization is concerned is the result of the insatiable quest and perpetual journey spurred on by doubt and inner tension. The context in which the notions of change and development and progress is understood is always this-worldly, presenting a consistently materialistic worldview that can be termed as a kind of humanistic existentialism. The spirit of Western culture that describes itself as Promethean is like the Camusian Sisyphus who desperately hopes that all is well. I say *desperately hopes* that all is well because I suspect that the fact cannot be that all is well, for I believe that he can never really be truly happy in that state. The pursuit of knowledge, like the struggle to push the Stone from the plains up the Mountain where at the top it is destined to roll down again, becomes a kind of serious *game,* never ceasing, as if to distract the soul from the tragedy of unattainment. No wonder, then, that in Western culture *tragedy is* extolled as being among the noblest values in the *drama* of human existence !

Reliance upon the powers of the human intellect alone to guide man through life; adherance to the validity of the dualistic vision of reality and truth; affirmation of the reality of the evanescent-aspect of existence projecting a secular worldview; espousal of the doctrine of humanism; emulation of the allegedly universal reality of drama and tragedy in the spiritual, or transcendental, or inner life of man, making drama and tragedy real and dominant elements in human nature and existence—these elements altogether taken as a whole are, in my opinion, what constitute the substance, the spirit, the character and personality of Western culture and civilization. It is these elements that determine for that culture and civilization the moulding of its concept of knowledge and the direction of its purpose, the formulation of its contents and the systematization of its dissemination; so that the knowledge that is now systematically disseminated throughout the world is not necessarily *true* knowledge, but that which is imbued with the character and personality of Western culture and civilization, and charged with its spirit and geared to its purpose. And it is these elements, then, that must be identified and separated and isolated from the body of knowledge, so that knowledge may be distinguished from what is imbued with these elements, for these elements and what is imbued with them do not represent knowledge as such, but they only determine the characteristic form in which knowledge is conceived and evaluated and interpreted in accordance with the purpose aligned to the worldview of Western civilization. It follows too that apart from the identification and separation and isolation of these elements from the body of knowledge, which will no doubt also alter the conceptual form and values and interpretation of some of the contents of knowledge as it is now presented,[61] its very purpose and system of deployment and dissemination in institutions of learning and in the domain of education must needs be altered accordingly. It may be argued that what is suggested is but *another, alternative* interpretation of knowledge imbued with other conceptual forms and values aligned to another purpose which reflects another worldview; and that this being so, and by the same token, what is formulated and disseminated as knowledge might not necessarily reflect *true* knowledge. This, however, remains to be seen, for the test of true knowledge is in man himself, in that if, through an alternative interpretation of knowledge man knows himself and his ultimate destiny,[62] and in thus knowing he achieves happiness,[63] then that knowledge, in spite of its being imbued with certain elements that determine the characteristic form in which it is conceived and evaluated and interpreted in accordance with the purpose aligned to a particular worldview, is true knowledge; for such knowledge has fulfilled man's purpose for knowing.

---

61 'Some of the contents of knowledge' referred to here pertains mainly to the human sciences.

62 See above, pp. 65–74; 81–84.

63 See above, p. 65.

II

THE MEANING AND EXPERIENCE OF HAPPINESS IN ISLĀM

Happiness according to the perspective of Islām is expressed by the term *sa'ādah,* and it relates to two dimensions of existence: to the hereafter (*ukhrawiyyah*) and to the present world (*dunyawiyyah*). The contrary of *sa'ādah is shaqāwah,* which conveys the meaning of great misfortune and misery in general. With respect to the hereafter *sa'ādah* refers to ultimate happiness, which is everlasting felicity and bliss, the highest being the Vision of God, promised to those who in worldly life have lived in willing submission and conscious and knowing obedience of God's commands and prohibitions. This being so, we see that the relation of *sa'ādah* to the hereafter is very closely connected with its relation to the present world, with respect to which it relates to three things: (1) to the self (*nafsiyyah*) such as pertains to knowledge and good character; (2) to the body (*badaniyyah*) such as good health and security; and (3) to things external to the self and the body (*khārijiyyah*) such as wealth and other causes that promote the well being of the self, the body, and the external things and circumstances in relation to them.[64] Happiness in the present world pertains therefore not only to the secular life, it has also to do with life as interpreted

---

64 See al-Ghazālī, *Iḥyā' 'Ulūm al-Dīn,* Cairo, 1939, 4v., vol. 3, p.229. As for the terms *sa'ādah* and its contrary *shaqāwah,* these are ultimately derived from the Qur'ān, *Hūd,* (11): 105–108. With regard to the three things to which happiness relates in this world, see also Aristotle's *Nicomachean Ethics,* tr. Sir David Ross, O.U.P. London, 1963, Ethics I.8.1098b5.

and guided by religion whose source is Revelation.

As to the relation of happiness to the self, which we say pertains to knowledge and good character, Islām teaches that the seat of knowledge in man is a spiritual substance variously referred to in the Qur'ān as his heart (*qalb*), or his soul or self (*nafs*), or his intellect (*'aql*), or his spirit (*rūḥ*).

Since the self is intimately involved in a dual aspect of body and soul, it is described on the one hand as the animal soul (*al-nafs al-ḥayawāniyyah*) and on the other hand as the rational soul (*al-nafs al-nāṭiqah*); and its destiny in the attainment of happiness here, and of ultimate happiness in the hereafter, depends upon which aspect it chooses to align itself with in a preponderant way. Both aspects possess powers or faculties (*quwā*). The faculties of the animal soul are motive and perceptive; and those of the rational soul are active and cognitive. In so far as it functions as the active intellect it is the principle of movement of the human body. It is the practical reason, and directs individual actions in agreement with the theoretical faculty of the cognitive intellect. In relation to the motive power of the animal soul, which is responsible for the exertion of willing that desire or aversion shall issue in action, it produces human emotions. In relation to the perceptive power and its representative, estimative, and imaginative faculties it manages physical objects and produces human skills and arts; and in relation to its faculty of rational imagination it gives rise to premises and conclusions. In so far as it governs and manages the human body it induces ethical behaviour in man involving the recognition of vices and virtues.[65]

Virtue (*faḍīlah*) may be classified under a general heading of excellence of mind or discernment and good

---

65 See al-Ghazālī, *Ma'ārij al-Quds fi Madārij Ma'rifat al-Nafs*, Bayrūt, 1978, pp. 49–50; ibn Sīnā, *Kitāb al-Shifā'*, Cairo, 1975, p. 185; and *Kitāb al-Najāt*, Bayrūt, 1985, pp. 202–203. See further chapter IV, below.

character.[66] Character is a stable state of the soul. If this state causes actions commended by the intellect and by religion it is called good character. Good character may be achieved by learning and habituation, and in some cases it may come by nature as a divine gift. Character may change from bad to good, and conversely from good to bad.[67] The goal of good character is happiness, both in this world and in the hereafter. In order to produce virtue and good character the animal soul and its bodily faculties must be subordinated to the practical faculty of the rational soul, which directs individual action after deliberation in accord with what agrees with the theoretical faculty. In order to achieve good character the intellect must be trained in deliberate thinking and reflection. Only when this has been accomplished can it realize wisdom. The faculty of desire, when trained, will realize temperance, and that of anger courage. When desire and anger are subordinated to intellect justice is realized; and the mean (*al-wasaṭ*) *is* then to be achieved by these two bodily faculties after they have been trained and disciplined by the practical faculty of the rational soul leading to the attainment of good character. The training of the bodily faculties needs free choice.[68] Contrary to the invariable translation by most people of the word *ikhtiyār* by 'choice', we maintain that *ikhtiyār* does not simply mean 'choice'. The word *khayr,* meaning 'good', which is bound in meaning with *ikhtiyār* and being derived from the same root, determines that the choice meant is towards what is good. This point is most important when aligned to the philosophical question of freedom. A so-called 'choice' towards what is bad is therefore not a choice. Since we affirm that freedom is to act as our real and true nature demands, only the exercise of that

---

66 See al-Ghazālī's *Mīzān al-'Amal,* Bayrūt, 1986, p. 59.

67 *Mīzān,* p. 54, fol.

68 *Ibid,* pp. 55–56.

choice which is good can properly be called a 'free choice'. A choice for the better is an exercise of freedom. It presupposes knowledge of good and evil. A 'choice' for the worse is not a choice, as it is based upon ignorance and on the instigation of the soul that inclines towards the blameworthy aspects of the animal powers.

The philosophic virtues of temperance, courage, wisdom and justice are not in themselves sufficient to produce in the self the kind of happiness that is experienced to be abiding and not determined by external and temporal circumstances. We do agree that if happiness is understood to relate only to the temporal, secular dimension of life without any reference to the hereafter, it is a state that undergoes changes and variations in degrees from moment to moment; or it is something that cannot be consciously experienced from moment to moment here in this world, and can be judged as having been attained by one only when one's worldly life, if virtuously lived and attended by favourable circumstances, has come to an end. But we do not restrict our understanding of happiness only to the domain of temporal, secular life; for since we affirm that the relation of happiness to the hereafter has an intimate and considerable bearing upon its relation to worldly life, and since in the former case it is a spiritual and permanent condition, there is, even in its temporal and secular involvement, an element of happiness that we experience and are conscious of and that once attained is permanent. We do not agree, therefore with the Aristotelian position that virtue and happiness relate only to this world, and that consequently happiness as a permanent condition experienced consciously in the course of our worldly life is unattainable.

According to the tradition of Western thought there are two conceptions of happiness; the ancient, which goes back to Aristotle and which in the Middle Ages goes back also to Muslim philosophers and theologians such as chiefly Ibn Sīnā and al-Ghazālī; and the modern, which gradually emerged in Western history as a result of the process of secularization. This philosophic and scientific process with I call 'secularization' involves the diversting of spiritual meaning from the world of nature, the desacralization of politics from human affairs, and the deconsecration of values from the human mind and conduct, both the last two mentioned following logically from the first, which in my opinion found initial movement in the experience and consciousness of Western man in the philosophical foundations laid down chiefly by Aristotle himself.[69] It is the modern conception of happiness that is acknowledged to be prevalent in the West today, and this means that for that civilization the meaning of happiness, and necessarily of the virtues that lead to it, has undergone change, bringing with it not only moral decadence and crisis, but political dissension and conflict as well. Both the ancient and the modern conceptions agree that happiness is an end in itself, but whereas for the former the end is considered in terms of a standard for proper conduct, the latter considers it to be terminal psychological states having no relation with moral codes.[70] In reality, however, the so called modern conception of happiness, apart from the sophistication with which it is formulated and pursued, is not much different in essence from the ones known and practiced in ancient times by pagan societies.

Although philosophic virtues, which have been conceived apparently through human choice and by means of reason alone, are in themselves not sufficient for the realization of enduring happiness in the self, their acceptance is justified when they do not come into conflict with religion;

---

69 See my *Islām and Secularism*, Kuala Lumpur, 1978.

70 This is clearly reflected, for example, in the writings of two contemporary major thinkers in the West, namely Mortimer Adler in his *Reforming Education*, Macmillan, N.Y. 1988, *e.g.* pp. 81–89; 230–253; 254–274; and Alasdair MacIntyre in his *After Virtue*, University of Notre Dame Press, Indiana, 1984, *e.g.* pp. 1–5; 181–203; 226–243; 244–255; 256–263.

and their usefulness for the attainment of happiness is acknowledged when some reformulation of their meanings has been effected in agreement with religion. This reformulation is effected by drawing them into the conceptual ambit of other virtues of a higher order unknown to the Greek philosophical tradition, such as those virtues derived from the Qur'ān and from the life of the Prophet. Knowledge of God in accordance with Revelation is a religious virtue which is derived from wisdom; and wisdom itself, whether theoretical or practical, is a religious virtue because it is a gift of God and not an acquisition of unaided reason.

Religious virtues are classified into two kinds, the external (*ẓāhir*) and the internal (*bāṭin*) . The external pertains to fulfillment of the divine commandments such as acts of worship directed solely toward God; practices directed toward fellow men for the continued well-being of social and political order; the performance of the five essentials of the religion of Islām including ritual purity, recitation of the Qur'ān, remembrance of God, invocation; and fulfillment of the requirements of Islamic custom or habit such as religious etiquette regarding food, clothing, personal cleanliness, marriage, business transactions, things allowed and things forbidden, rules of neighbourliness, companionship, travel, observance of the model actions and sayings of the Prophet, and obligations of brotherhood in Islām.[71]

The internal virtues refer to the activities of the heart; activities that are grounded upon knowledge of God and of the self derived both from reason and from Revelation, and that require a positive disposition in the self inducing good intention (*niyyah*) to be followed by action (*'amal*) with sincerity of purpose (*ikhlāṣ*) and truthfulness to oneself (*ṣidq*).

---

71 A comprehensive and detailed account of the religious virtues sketched here in bare outline is to be found in the Quarters and Books of al-Ghazālī's *Iḥyā' (op. cit.)*, vols. 1–2.

Knowledge of the self leads to knowledge of its good and bad qualities, and to the assigning of duties to oneself to overcome the bad in order to purify the soul of impurities.[72] This action on the part of the self means that the rational soul must keep watch over the animal soul (*murāqabah*) to ensure that the duties assigned to oneself are carried out. It also entails self-examination to observe whether the carrying out of such duties has been executed in the proper way, and to correct any deviation from what is proper (*muḥāsabah*). *As* to the knowledge of God it means the knowledge of who He is, of His nature and oneness as He has described Himself in Revelation, and this knowledge leads to comprehension of the proper relationship between the self and God. In the Revelation also God speaks about His creation and about man's self as signs indicating His reality and truth;[73] and contemplation and reflection of His works and of the nature of man and the psychology of his soul are then prerequisites to the attainment of that knowledge. All this involves meditation (*tafakkur*) and brings about the gradual realization in the self of other virtues of a higher order, such as repentance (*tawbah*), patience (*ṣabr*), gratitude (*shukr*), hope (*rajā*), fear (*khawf*), divine unity (*tawḥīd*), trust (*tawakkul*), and finally the highest virtue for the attainment of happiness in worldy life, love of god (*maḥabbah*) .[74]

The external and internal virtues actually overlap one another, and the possibility of virtuous activities which

---

[72] The soul, according to the Qur'ān, is created in due proportion and order. It knows what is right for it and what is wrong for it. Its success is achieved when it is purified, and its failure is assured when it is corrupted (91: 70–10). The purification of the soul is to be achieved by means of virtue and good character as formulated and conceptualized in accordance with the tenets of Islām.

[73] *Fuṣṣilat* (41): 53.

[74] *Iḥyā',* vol. 4.

involve only the one without being in some way connected with the other is inconceivable. Their classification into external and internal is only to distinguish the inward activities of the heart, which characterize the latter, from the outward activities of the body; the emphasis on inner meaning evident in the latter, from the practice of what is apparent demonstrated in the former. Some may preponderate in the realization of the external virtues and some in that of the internal virtues; but it is not possible for some to realize only the external virtues without recourse to the internal virtues, nor for some to realize only the internal virtues without having accomplished the realization of virtues that are external. Thus both the external and internal virtues are necessary for the attainment of happiness in this life and ultimate happiness in the hereafter. Finally, since virtues classified as philosophic have been reformulated and assimilated into the religious framework wherein the interpretation of human destiny extends to horizons beyond temporal existence, and since this religious framework is established not only upon reason but upon reason as verified by Revelation, all virtue in Islām is religious.

In order to understand what *sa'ādah* means it seems to me necessary first to present a concise explanation of the meaning of its exact opposite *shaqāwah*. The Arabic lexicons from the earliest times and going back to Quranic usage describe *shaqāwah* as conveying the approximate equivalent in English of 'great misfortune', 'misery', 'straitness of circumstance', 'distress', 'disquietude', 'despair', 'adversity', 'suffering'. Every one of these conditions obviously involves serious internal and external activity. Indeed *shaqāwah* is a generic term as it encompasses all forms of misery, so that other terms expressing similar conditions but more specific in their contextual application are only constituent elements of *shaqāwah*. These include, among others for example, *khawf* (fear, of the unknown, of utter solitude and incommunicability, of death and what lies beyond, a foreboding of dread, *angst*); *ḥuzn* (grief, sorrow, sadness, roughness of soul); *ḍank* (narrowness, straitened, misery in the soul and in the intellect rendered incapable of fathoming something causing agitation of doubt in the heart); *ḥasrat* (profound grief and regret for something gone and never to be experienced again, such as—when referring to the hereafter—the exceedingly keen grief and regret of the man who turns away from God and spends his life in self-waste when he discovers after death how he has lost his soul and bitterly laments the impossibility of a return to worldly life to make amends). These terms are used specifically for those who turn away from God and reject His guidance, and are applied to conditions both in this world and in the hereafter. Other terms expressing misery of one kind or another and applicable to all in this life are, for example, *ḍīq* (straitened, of heart and mind, constrained); *hamm* (disquietude, anxiety, distress of heart and mind due to fear of impending calamity or harm); *ghamm* (same as *hamm,* only that the harm that is feared would come has come, so that it becomes anguish); *'usr* (hard, difficult and unpleasant of circumstance).

It seems to me that the above gist of the meaning of *shaqāwah* already clarifies that in its generic sense it refers to what is understood in the West as *tragedy* —tragedy not merely in its dramatic sense as a form of art, but more so in its philosophic sense as the drama of life enacted in the experience and consciousness of man when he rejects religion and turns away from God. This statement needs elaboration. According to Aristotle in the *Poetics* tragedy in its dramatic sense is an artistic imitation of an action that is serious, complete in itself, and of adequate magnitude, that is, for example, enacted in poetic language, having a moral purpose portraying character (*ethos*), and discursive understanding (*dianoia*) that enables the tragic character to exercise the power to say what is appropriate in a given situation. The protagonist in Greek drama must have stature, undergo physical as well as mental suffering, be brought low by an error of judgement due to lack of insight, a tragic flaw (*hamartia*), in the dramatic process that is brought about by some tempting opportunity (*kairos*). He must also have pride (*hubris*), a presumption against the gods which offends them. The casual factor is fate (*ananke*), which pursues the tragic character relentlessly with a fatefulness (*ate*), a curse, that runs inherited through generations. The framework of incidents upon which the drama is constructed forms a unity comprising a beginning, a middle, and an end; and within this unity of events there must occur a process of reversals (*peripeteia*) such as from happiness to sorrow, from good fortune to ill, and of discovery (*anagnorisis*) such as from ignorance to knowledge of something dreadful. The effect of tragedy is to arouse pity and fear in such a manner as to effect their purging from the soul and give it relief (*katharsis*).[75]

According to the Greek lexicons the purging that is meant by *katharsis* is of sin and of guilt from the soul or self.[76] This being so, and from what we have outlined above about the nature of tragedy in Greek drama, the purging of fear and of pity aroused by tragedy may be understood to mean fear in the self of impending misery brought about by a feeling of guilt due to sin committed in the past. Now tragedy is not merely a form of art, for the fact that it manifests itself so uniquely in the intellectual, religious and secular tradition of Western thought and spirituality in all ages and establishes itself in its mythology is succinct indication that tragedy—at least in the experience and consciousness of Western man—is a fact of life, and its dramatic form is only a reflection of what is happening in real life. It were as

---

75 *Poetics*, tr. with comm. by S. H. Butcher, 1911, The definition of tragedy is on 1449B.

76 *A Greek-English Lexicon*, comp. by H. G. Liddell and R. Scott, etc., Oxford, 1968, p. 851, col. 1; and F. E. Peters, *Greek Philosophical Lexicon*, New York, 1967, pp. 98–99.

though in that experience and consciousness there is made to dwell always that nagging guilt religion attributes to original sin committed by man's progenitor, who by a tragic flaw succumbed to tempting opportunity urged on by an adversary bent upon his fall from grace. In consequence of his fall a hereditary curse dogs his descendants causing them to sense the guilt that continues to plague their hearts and minds throughout the ages. Man's common ancestor was of high nobility brought low by the tragic flaw. In the beginning he dwelt in great honour and happiness in a different world. Then after his downfall he was banished to this world; and his descendants now find themselves in the middle part of the unity of events that are unfolding in a process of reversals and discoveries, and play their parts in conflict and violence. But the final discovery is yet to come in the dreaded end when every one must leave this world and return to come face to face with the truth. The obession with tragedy and with the art that depicts it is such that even religion had to be cast in the crucible of tragedy. The world has become a stage in which man contrives, enacts, and beholds his own drama of existence in order to effect the purging of fear and self-pity. Humanistic philosophy and the gradual process of secularization together with the rise of secular philosophy and science, made tragedy, instead of religion, the exaltation of man. Fear must be purged not by faith in God, but by the banishment of God from the realm of creation; self pity must be purged not by remembrance of God, but by pride in humanity and defiant acceptance of the human predicament. The causal factor in tragedy is no longer the old Greek Fate nor the God of religion, but social and individual conflicts, biological heredity, the psychology of the unconscious, defeat by frustration, man confronted by the mystery of the universe, the eternal quest of man, and the absurdity of life. Freedom of the will becomes a firm belief because it helps in the perpetual struggle against obstacles that prevent from reaching the goal. But the goal itself is evershifting. Can Sysiphus ever be happy in having eternally to push the stone up the hill where at the top it is destined to roll down again? Fitzgerald was not really translating the intended meaning of the Persian poet, even though that was what he claimed to do, when he wrote:

> O Thou, who Man of baser Earth didst make,
> And ev'n with Paradise devise the Snake;
> For all the Sin wherewith the Face of Man
> Is blacken'd—Man's forgiveness give—and take!

He was only expressing the prevalent spirit of defiance that rages in the experience and consciousness of man when he rejects God and turns away from His guidance.

The Qur'ān relates how Ādam was tempted by Satan, disobeyed God, and allowed himself to be seduced by Satan. Ādam and his consort, however, conscious of their error and unlike Satan, admitted their sin, were filled with remorse at their own injustice to themselves, and sought God's mercy and forgiveness. They both were forgiven, but were sent down together with Satan to this world to live a life of trial and tribulation. God assured Ādam and his progeny that guidance would come from Him and that whoever follows His guidance will not go astray nor fall into misery; but whoever turns away from remembrance of Him will surely live a miserable life assailed by doubt and inner tension heightened by blindness to the truth and to the reality of their predicament.[77]

The Quranic application of the meaning of *shaqāwah* in its various conjugated forms such as *shaqā,*[78] *yashqā,*[79] *tashqā,*[80] *ashqā,*[81] *al-ashqā,*[82] *shaqiyy,*[83] and *shiqwah*[84] relates,

---

77 *Al-A'rāf* (7):19–25; *Êā Hā* (20): 117–124; *Banī Isrā'īl* (7): 72.

78 *Hūd* (11): 106–107;

79 *Êā Hā* (20): 2;123.

80 *Êā Hā* (20):117.

81 *Al-Shams* (91):12.

82 *Al-A'lā* (87): 11; *Al-Layl* (92):15

83 *Hūd* (11):105; *Maryam* (19): 4; 32; 48.

84 *Al-Mu'minūn* (23): 107.

some to the hereafter, some to this world, and some to both. All of them refer to those who turn away from God and reject His guidance. *Shiqwah,* for example, refers to those who have lost their souls (*khasirū anfusahum*)[85] in this world by being overwhelmed by worldly pleasures leading them astray and making them fall into error. They may feel and think that they are happy in what they do in worldly life, but the underlying misery of their true condition that they may not now acknowledge because they have lost their souls but will be realized in the hereafter is unspeakable: a Day of Distress (*yawm al-ḥasrat*), of Sighs and Sobs, awaits them there.[86] Indeed according to the Qur'ān all mankind are in a condition of utter loss (*khusr*) except those who have true faith (*īmān*) and do righteous deeds, enjoin one another to the Truth and to patience.[87] The doing of good works is accomplished by means of virtues, *īmān* being the source of the principal ones, and good character. The meaning of happiness in this worldly life and ultimate happiness in the hereafter is then very closely bound up with *īmān,* whose general meaning as understood and experienced by those who have it is stated in the next chapter.[88] The root *amina* conveys the meaning of becoming secure, becoming free from fear. The infinitive noun of *amina: amnu,* means security, freedom from fear. The fear that is meant here is the fear of the unknown, of utter solitude and incommunicability, of death and what lies beyond, a foreboding of dread— in short it is the fear that refers to ultimate destiny. Those who have *īmān* and persevere in the doing of righteous deeds preserving themselves from disobedience of God are

---

85 *Al-An'ām* (6):12; 20; *Al-A'rāf (7):* 9; 53; *Hūd* (11): 21; *Al-Mu'minūn* (23): 103; *Al-Zumar* (39): 15; *Al-Shūrā* (42): 45.

86 *Maryam* (19): 39.

87 *Al-'Aṣr(* 103):2.

88 See below, p. 112.

then not affected by such fear (*khawf*), which is the contrary of security (*amnu*) .[89] The term 'fear' relates to two psychological conditions. When it refers to one who turns away from God and rejects His guidance it means fear as explained above; however, when it refers to one who submits to God and cleaves to His guidance, it means reverential fear or awe of His majesty, which also means to know Him. For such a one fear of God means fear of disobedience, of committing acts forbidden by God, of being evil, of being veiled from God and denied nearness to Him. Such fear, which arises from knowledge of God and His absolute freedom to do what He wills, and of human acts of transgression and their dreadful consequences, encourages the realization of virtues such as temperance (*'iffah*), abstinence (*wara'*), piety (*taqwā*), and truthfulness (*ṣidq*).[90] According to what has been and still is verified by "those who have faith (*āmanū*) and whose hearts are rendered tranquil (*taṭma'innu*) by remembrance (*dhikr*) of God, for surely in the remembrance of God are hearts made tranquil",[91] faith (*īmān*) and remembrance (*dhikr*) are necessary for the attainment of that stable and peaceful calmness of heart that is called *ṭuma'nīnah*. This condition refers to the state of the tranquil soul (*al-nafs al-muṭma' innah*) mentioned earlier.[92] *Êuma'nīnah* describes the calm, restful condition of the heart, which we said is an

89 *Al-Mā'idah* (5): 69; *Al-An'ām* (6): 48; *Al-A'rāf* (7): 35; *Yūnus* (10): 62; *Al-Aḥqāf* (46):13.

90 *Iḥyā',* vol. 4, p. 153. By 'piety' we mean cautiously guarding oneself from the commission of sins and the omission of duties. *Taqwā is* reverential awe of God's majesty; it is deliberate activity of guarding from disobedience by righteous conduct in accordance with virtue resulting in justice, *i.e.* being in the proper place of the self in relation to God such that peace is achieved in the soul.

91 *Al-Ra'd* (13): 28.

92 See above, p. 60.

aspect of the self.[93] It is freedom from worry resulting from doubt, freedom from disquietude; it is inward peace, satisfaction, joy, happiness, which comes about when the soul or self is submissive to God. Being submissive to God is what is known as freedom, for it is a return to one's true nature acknowledged by man's pre-existent soul when it sealed its covenant with God.[94] Being submissive to God involves remembrance in the heart of God's presence, and remembrance means recollection of God, recognition and acknowledgement of His Lordship. This being submissive to God is the soul's reconciliation with God, which causes to arise in the soul the consciousness of safety, security, freedom from corruption and failure, the consciousness of peace called *islām*. These activities of the soul or self imply a prior condition of consciousness in the soul of the truth that comes from guidance. This consciousness is that of certainty (*yaqīn*) of the truth. *Yaqīn* is the contrary of doubt (*shakk*) and conjecture (*ẓann*); it is the removal of doubt and conjecture from the heart and the verification of the truth in the past, present, and future. The Qur'ān mentions three degrees of certainty in knowledge: that which is derived by inference, whether deductive or inductive (*'ilm al-yaqīn*);[95] that which is derived by observation or direct vision (*'ayn al-yaqīn*);[96] and that which is derived by direct experience (*ḥaqq al-yaqīn*).[97] These degrees of certain knowledge pertain to truth, whether manifest or hidden, empirical or transcendental; and the certain knowledge of what is hidden has the same force of certainty as that of what is visible. These degrees of certainty also pertain to the heart and refer to

---

93 See below, pp. 145–146.

94 *Al-A'rāf* (7): 172.

95 *Al-Takāthur* (102): 5.

96 *Al-Takāthur* (102): 7.

97 *Al-Ḥāqqah* (69): 51.

faith (*īmān*).

We said that it is remembrance of God that brings about the state of tranquility in the soul; and that this and other virtuous activities imply a prior consciousness in the soul of the truth that comes from divine guidance. This consciousness arises as certainty (*yaqīn*). How then can one who forgets God find peace of heart and mind and calmness of soul when in reality forgetfulness of God involves also forgetfulness of the soul of itself? There can be no consciousness of certainty of the truth in the soul when that soul has forgotten itself, that is, when its rational aspect has been suppressed by its animal aspect such that it becomes conscious only of its involvement in its bodily faculties and the pleasures and amusements of worldly life, or the pursuit of secular philosophy and science and contemplation of facts derived from them, or even of both together. This is why the Qur'ān warns that those who forget God will be made to forget their souls or their selves.[98] The forgetting of the self here must mean, among other possible meanings, unconsciousness of the rational soul of itself, and consciousness only of the animal soul which inclines toward the satisfaction of bodily desires. One who forgets his self in this way is one who has lost his soul (*q.v. khusr*) and whose condition is "baser than the lowest of the low''.[99]

Feelings and emotions are involved in consciousness, and those who are conscious of God, verifying this consciousness by remembrance, experience in their feelings and emotions the consciousness of the happiness upon which their lives are established—I mean that their lives are secured upon a substratum of happiness. In their case the experience of suffering in the course of worldly life, which they must undergo from time to time just like the others, is

---

98 *Al-Ḥashr* (59): 19.

99 *Al-Ṫīn* (95): 4; p. 146 below; and for *khusr*, p. 103 above.

not consciously felt by them as misery in the tragic sense. Rather suffering is recognized by them to be probation, a testing of their faith in God and virtuousness of conduct in the face of hardship and calamity. Such suffering is not called *shaqāwah;* it is called *balā',* and the probation *ibtilā'* In spite of the suffering, then, they know and are conscious of the truth that the substratum upon which their lives is lived is ease and happiness, to which condition, they always return. The Qur'ān reveals this truth by declaring twice for emphasis the assurance that "with every hardship (*'usr*) there is relief (*yusr*)".[100] But as for those who turn away from God and are blind to His guidance, the substratum of life upon which they live is misery and tragedy, and no amount of feelings, or emotions, or activities they believe to be happiness is going to clear away that substratum. It is this condition that we believe to be the reason for their need of perpetual purging of the soul by means other than remembrance of God, such as by means of various forms of art and music contrived with magnitude and nobility of execution in a way that renders their predicament palatable to the aesthetic taste; by means of restless work and struggle against themselves, against others, against the world, against nature—to distract from the tragedy of unattainment, and to prevent a return to the substratum of life. That is why their philosophers speak of suicide as a philosophical problem. Unfortunately that is why also that from time to time there occur pessimistic outbursts of indignant anger in the form of violence somewhat like the sacrificial *sparagmos* of Old Greek tragedy. And that explains too the reason for the continual preoccupation with the quest of happiness regarded as an end in itself.

Happiness (*sa'ādah*) being the exact opposite of misery (*shaqāwah*) and as known in the experience and con-

---

[100] *Al-Inshirāḥ* (94): 5–6.

sciousness of those who are truly submissive to God and follow His guidance is not an end in itself because the highest good in this life is love of God. Enduring happiness in life refers not to the physical entity in man, not to the animal soul and body of man; nor is it a state of mind, or feeling that undergoes terminal states, nor pleasure nor amusement. It has to do with certainty (*yaqīn*) of the ultimate Truth and fulfillment of action in conformity with that certainty. And certainty is a permanent state of consciousness natural to what is permanent in man and perceived by his spiritual organ of cognition which is the heart (*qalb*). It is peace and security and tranquility of the heart (*ṭuma'nīnah*); it is knowledge (*ma'rifah*) and knowledge is true faith (*īmān*). It is knowledge of God as He has described Himself in genuine Revelation; it is also knowing one's rightful and hence proper place in the realm of creation and one's proper relationship with the Creator accompanied by requisite action (*'ibādah*) in conformity with that knowledge such that the condition which results is that of justice (*'adl*). It is only through such knowledge that love of God can be attained in earthly life.

From the foregoing brief but comprehensive exposition of the meaning and experience of happiness in Islām we derive conclusion that happiness in this life is not an end in itself; that the end of happiness is love of God; that in worldly life two levels of happiness can be discerned. The first level is psychological, temporal and terminal states which may be described as feelings or emotions, and which is attained when needs and wants are achieved by means of right conduct in accord with the virtues. The second level is spiritual, permanent, consciously experienced, becoming the substratum of worldly life which is affirmed to be probationary, the testing of conduct and virtuous activity being by good fortune or ill: *i.e.* not swayed to error by good fortune nor defeated in suffering by ill fortune. This second level, when attained, occurs concurrently with the first, except that wants are diminished and needs are satisfied. This second level of happiness is a preparation for a third level in the hereafter of which the highest stage is the Vision of God. There is no change in this meaning and experience of happiness in the consciousness of genuine believers throughout the ages.

We have discussed briefly but comprehensively and in a straighforward manner the meaning and experience of happiness as known in the consciousness of man when he is submissive to God and cleaves to His guidance. Happiness, we said, is related both to temporal, secular life as well as to the hereafter. Since religion is fundamental in its relation to man and to his well-being, the meaning of religion is first explained followed by a brief outline of the nature of man and the psychology of the human soul derived from reason and Revelation. As a perlude to an explanation of the nature of happiness which is here defined in terms of the opposite state, we maintained that the activity proper to man is virtuous activity of his body and his soul in accordance with reason aided by Revelation.

Virtuous activity is defined not merely in terms of philosophic virtues, but in terms of their reformulation within the conceptual ambit of religious virtues described as external and internal. In defining happiness in terms of its exact opposite, other related terms describing happiness and misery are brought into focus and explained. The explanation is made more meaningful by making comparative analysis of certain salient features of Aristotelian and modern Western conceptions of happiness with the Islamic conception of happiness in order to show significant divergences between the former and the latter. It is maintained that three levels of happiness are discerned in the Islamic conception, two of them in worldly life and one in the hereafter. In this summary exposition the Qur'ān is the direct source of our interpretation of happiness, which we maintain is verified in our experience and consciousness according to the various degrees of attainment, in belief and in practice, among the varying classes of people. It is also maintained that in our experience and consciousness there has been no change throughout the ages in the meaning of happiness in Islām. A general definition of happiness is set forth at the end. Finally, it may be noted that references to "those who turn to God and follow His guidance" are not necessarily meant to indicate only those who profess to adhere to the religion of Islām, just as those who profess to follow the religion of Islām are not all necessarily included among those who turn to God and follow His guidance.

III

ISLĀM AND THE PHILOSOPHY OF SCIENCE

The meaning of religion in Islām, as we have analysed in the first chapter, is expressed by the term *dīn*, which is not merely a concept, but is something which is translated into reality intimately and profoundly *lived* in human experience. Its ultimate source of meaning is derived from the Quranic revelation of the covenant (*al-mīthāq*) which man's pre-existent soul has sealed with God.[101] The very name of the religion: *Islām, is* in reality the definition of religion: *submission to God.* Already in the very idea of submission, feeling, belief, and action are implied; but the fundamental element in man's act of submission to God is his sense of *indebtedness* to God for His gift of existence, so that this sense of indebtedness—which involves recognition and acknowledgement of God as the giver of existence—is a prior condition to true submission (*islām*).[102] The ultimate aim of religion is for man to return to the state in which he was before he existed, and this involves the quest for his identity and transcendent destiny through right conduct. This 'returning' is what life is all about, and it involves the pursuit of true knowledge,[103]

---

101 See *Al-A'rāf* (7):172.

102 By 'true submission' (*islām,* the first letter in lower case) we mean conscious and willing submission for the whole of one's ethical life in the manner indicated and demonstrated by the Prophet and by the prophets sent before him.

103 By 'true knowledge' we understand it to mean knowledge that recognizes the limit of truth in its every object. See further below, pp. 134–135.

the understanding of God's signs and symbols in the pages of the book of nature by means of the guiding light of His words and interpreted in the sacred person of His messenger. It also involves the application of the sound senses to the experience of reality, and the application of the sound reason to the apprehension of truth.[104]

Religion (*islām*) and belief (*īmān*) are not identical, but they are mutually inseparable and indispensable. Belief in the sense we mean is to have faith, not quite in the sense faith is understood in English, but in the sense that it involves the becoming true to the trust by which God has confided in one, not by profession of belief with the tongue only, without the assent of the heart and the action of the body in conformity with it; and this is more than knowledge, which is prior to faith, so that it is also verification by deeds in accordance with what is known to be the truth.[105] It is recognition and acknowledgement of the truth necessitating its actualization in one's self. Recognition of the truth is in this case arrived at simply because it is clear in itself as apprehended by that intuitive faculty we call the heart, that is, by means of guidance (*hudā*) and not only by rational propositions and logical demonstrations. The truth is at once objective and subjective; and the objective and subjective, like religion and belief, are inseparable aspects of one reality. True religion is then not something that can succumb to the confusion arising from the objective-subjective dichotomy of the Greek philosophical tradition; nor is it that personal, individual, privatized and internalized 'religion of

---

104 On the meaning of religion or *dīn* in Islām, see chapter I above.

105 The 'truth' here means what has come down by way of revelation to the Prophet about the nature and reality of God, of His creation, of human destiny, of the relationship between man and God and man's individual responsibility and freedom.

humanity' that emerges out of the secularizing process which seeks to abolish the institutionalization of religious belief.

Religion in the sense we mean is not opposed to the desacralization of nature if it means the expulsion from our understanding of a magical or mythical conception of nature; for nature can still be regarded as a manifestation form of the sacred without myth or magic if we understand it to be the evolvement of ideal realities in the Divine consciousness whose effects have become manifest in the realms of sense and sensible experience. Nature in itself is not a divine entity, but a symbolic form which manifests the Divine. Indeed, in the sense we have conveyed, *all* nature, and not just a tree or a stone, proclaims the sacred to those who see the reality behind the appearance. Religion is only opposed to desacralization if it means the obliteration of all spiritual meaning in our understanding of nature, and the restriction of our way of knowing to the scientific method as advocated by secular philosophy and science.[106]

God is not a myth, an image, a symbol, that keeps changing with the times. He is Reality itself. Belief has cognitive content; and one of the main points of divergence between true religion and secular philosophy and science is the way in which the sources and methods of knowledge are understood.

Modern philosophy has become the interpreter of science, and organizes the results of the natural and social sciences into a world view. The interpretation in turn determines the direction which science is to take in its study of nature. It is this *interpretation* of the statements and general conclusions of science *and* the *direction* of science along the lines suggested by the interpretation that must be subjected to critical evaluation, as they pose for us today the most pro-

---

[106] See further my *Islām and Secularism,* (*op. cit.*) chapters I and II.

found problems that have confronted us generally in the course of our religious and intellectual history. Our evaluation must entail a critical examination of the methods of modern science; its concepts, presuppositions, and symbols; its empirical and rational aspects, and those impinging upon values and ethics; its interpretation of origins; its theory of knowledge; its presuppositions on the existence of an external world, of the uniformity of nature, and of the rationality of natural processes; its theory of the universe; its classification of the sciences; its limitations and inter-relations with one another of the sciences, and its social relations.

A gist of their basic assumptions is that science is the sole authentic knowledge; that this knowledge pertains only to phenomena; that this knowledge, including the basic statements and general conclusions of the science and philosophy derived from it, is peculiar to a particular age and may change in another age; that scientific statements must affirm only what is observed and confirmed by scientists; that what should be accepted are theories only that can be reduced to sensational elements, even though such theories might involve ideas pertaining to domains beyond the empirical spheres of experience; that universality should not be attributed to scientific formulas, nor should objects defined by universality be described as reality beyond what is observed; that the content of knowledge is a combination of realism, idealism, and pragmatism; that these three aspects of cognition together represent the foundation of the philosophy of science; that cognition is subjective, arbitrary, and conventional, and that in the relationship between the logical structure of knowledge and the empirical content of knowledge, the primacy of logic is affirmed; that mathematical theory is not a descriptive science making statements about the structure and processes of nature, and that it is in fact a logical theory; that since logic is indispensable to science, the role of language and logical systems in describing the structure and processes of nature is paramount; that truth and falsehood are properties of belief (*i.e.* belief in the sense of intellectual acceptance as true or existing of any statement or proposition) dependent upon the relations of belief to facts; that facts are neutral as far as truth and falsehood are concerned—they just *are.*

Contemporary science has evolved and developed out of a philosophy that since its earliest periods affirmed the coming into being of things out of each other. Everything existent is a progression, a development or evolution of what lies in latency in eternal matter. The world seen from this perspective is an independent, eternal universe; a selfsubsistent system evolving according to its own laws. The denial of the reality and existence of God is already implied in this philosophy. Its methods are chiefly philosophic rationalism, which tends to depend on reason alone without the aid of sense perception or experience; secular rationalism, which while accepting reason tends to rely more on sense experience, and denies authority and intuition and rejects Revelation and religion as sources of true knowledge; and philosophic empiricism or logical empiricism which bases all knowledge on observable facts, logical constructions and linguistic analysis. The vision of reality as seen according to the perspectives of both forms of rationalism and empiricism is based upon the restriction of reality to the natural world which is considered as the only level of reality. Such restriction follows from the reduction of the operational powers and capacities of the cognitive faculties and senses to the sphere of physical reality. In this system knowledge is valid only as it pertains to the natural order of events and their relationships; and the purpose of inquiry is to describe and to systematize what happens in nature, by which is meant the totality of objects and events in space and time. The world of nature is described in plain naturalistic and rational terms divested of spiritual significance or of symbolic interpretation, reducing its origin and reality solely to mere natural forces.

Rationalism, both the philosophic and the secular kind, and empiricism tend to deny authority and intuition as legitimate sources and methods of knowledge. Not that they deny the *existence* of authority and of intuition, but that they reduce authority and intuition to reason and experience. It is true that at the original instance in the case of both authority and intuition, there is always someone who experiences and who reasons; but it does not follow that because of this, authority and intuition should be reduced to reason and experience. If it is admitted that there are levels of reason and experience at the level of normal, human consciousness whose limitations are recognized, there is no reason to suppose that there are no higher levels of human experience and consciousness beyond the limits of normal reason and experience in which there are levels of intellectual and spiritual cognition and transcendental experience whose limits are known only to God.

As to intuition, most rationalist, secularist and empiricist thinkers and psychologists have reduced it to sensory observations and logical inferences that have long been brooded over by the mind, whose meaning becomes suddenly apprehended, or to latent sensory and emotional build-ups which are released all of a sudden in a burst of apprehension. But this is conjecture on their part, for there is no proof that the sudden flash of apprehension comes from sense experience; moreover, their denial of an intuitive faculty such as the heart, implied in their contention regarding intuition, is also conjectural.

Since it is man that perceives and conceives the world of objects and events external to him, the study of nature includes man himself. But the study of man, of mind, and of the self is also restricted to the methods of new sciences such as psychology, biology, and anthropology, which regard man only as a further development of the animal species, and which are none other than methodological extensions of the restriction of reason and experience to the level of physical reality. Moreover, in order to verify hypotheses and theories science, according to them, requires correspondence with observable fact, and yet since hypotheses and theories that contradict one another can correspond with observable fact, and since the preference for one as against the other of them is not dictated by any criterion of objective truth—because truth itself is made to conform with fact—such preference is then dictated simply by subjective and arbitrary considerations dependent upon convention. This dependence upon convention has created the tendency to regard society, rather than the individual man, as ultimate, real, and authoritative. Conventionalism reduces all institutional forms as creations of the so-called 'collective mind' of society. Knowledge itself, and even human language, are nothing but expressions and instruments of the collective mind of this unspeakable god called Society.

Finally, doubt is elevated as an epistemological method by means of which the rationalist and the secularist believe that truth is arrived at. But there is no proof that it is doubt and not something else other than doubt that enables one to arrive at truth. The arrival at truth is in reality the result of guidance, not of doubt. Doubt is a wavering between two opposites without preponderating over either one of them; it is a condition of being stationary in the midst of the two opposites without the heart inclining toward the one or the other. If the heart inclines more toward the one and not toward the other while yet not rejecting the other, it is conjecture; if the heart rejects the other, then it has entered the station of certainty. The heart's rejecting the other is a sign not of doubt as to its truth, but of positive recognition of its error or falsity. This is guidance. Doubt, whether it be definitive or provisional, leads either to conjecture or to another position of uncertainty, never to the truth—"and conjecture avails naught against truth." (Qur'ān 10:36)

Based upon the position established by our philosophical and scientific tradition as integrated into a coherent metaphysical system, we maintain that many important similarities are found between our position and that of modern, contemporary philosophy and science with regard to the sources and methods of knowledge; the unity of the rational and empirical ways of knowing; the combination of realism, idealism, and pragmatism as the cognitive foundation of a philosophy of science; the philosophy and science of process. But these similarities are apparent and pertain only to their external aspects, and they do not negate the profound differences that arise from our divergent worldviews and beliefs about the ultimate nature of Reality. Our affirmation of Revelation as *the* source of knowledge of ultimate reality and truth pertaining both to created things as well as to their Creator provides us with the foundation for a metaphysical framework in which to elaborate our philosophy of science as an integrated system descriptive of that reality and truth in a way which is not open to the methods of the secular philosophic rationalism and philosophic empiricism of modern philosophy and science.

In contrast to modern philosophy and science with regard to the sources and methods of knowledge, we maintain that knowledge comes from God and is acquired through the channels of the sound senses, true report based on authority, sound reason, and intuition. The meaning underlying the expression 'sound senses' points to perception and observation, and these comprise the five external senses of touch, smell, taste, sight and hearing which perform the function of perception of particulars in the external world. Corresponding to these are five internal senses which perceive internally the sensual images and their meanings, combine or separate them, conceive notions of them, preserve the conceptions thus conceived, and perform intellection of them. These are the common sense, the representation, the estimation, the retention and recollection, and the imagination. In the act of perception, the perceiver perceives the *form* of the external object, *i.e.* a representation of the external reality, and not the reality itself. What is perceived by the senses is then not the external reality as it is in itself, but its like as represented in the senses. The external reality is that from which the senses abstract its form. Similarly with regard to the *meaning*, the intelligibles are representations of realities that are imprinted upon the soul, because the intellect has already abstracted them from the accidental attachments that are foreign to their natures, such as quantity, quality, space and position. The difference between the form and the meaning of the sensual object is that the form is what is first perceived by the external sense, and then by the internal sense; the meaning is what the internal sense perceives of the sensual object without its having been previously perceived by the external sense.

As regards 'sound reason', we mean to understand reason not simply in the sense restricted to sensational elements; to that mental faculty that systematizes and interprets the facts of sensible experience in logical order, or that renders intelligible and manageable to the understanding the data of sensible experience, or that performs the abstraction of facts and sensible data and their relationships, and orders them in a law-giving operation that renders the world of nature understandable. Indeed, to be sure, reason is all this, but we maintain further that it is one of the aspects of the intellect and functions in conformity with it, not in opposition to it; and the intellect is a spiritual substance inherent in that spiritual organ of cognition we call the heart, which is the seat of intuition. In this way and through the mediacy of the intellect we have connected reason with intuition.

In the same way that we do not confine reason to sensational elements, we do not restrict intuition to the direct and immediate apprehension, by the knowing subject, of itself, of its conscious states, of other selves like itself, of an external world, of universals, of values or of rational truths. We understand by intuition also the direct and immediate apprehension of religious truths, of the reality and existence of God, of the reality of existences as opposed to essences—indeed, in its higher levels intuition is the intuition of existence itself. With reference to intuition at the higher levels of truth, intuition does not just come to anyone, but to one who has lived his life in the experience of religious truth by sincere, practical devotion to God, who has by means of intellectual attainment understood the nature of the oneness of God and what this oneness implies in an integrated metaphysical system, who has constantly meditated upon the nature of this reality, and who then, during deep contemplation and by God's will, is made to pass away from consciousness of his self and his subjective states and to enter into the state of higher selfhood, subsisting in God. When he returns to his human, subjective condition, he loses what he has found, but the knowledge of it remains with him. It is in the duration of subsistence in God, when he gains his higher selfhood, that the direct and immediate apprehension takes place. He has been given a glimpse of the nature of reality in that duration of coincidence with the Truth. In his case the cognitive content of his intuition of existence reveals to him the integrated system of reality as a whole.

With regard to intuition, and at the normal level of human consciousness, the higher levels to which great men of science and learning attain, in the moments of their decisive discoveries of laws and principles that govern the world of nature, are levels commensurate with the training, discipline, and development of their powers of reasoning and experiential capacities, and with the specific problems that confront them to which reason and experience are unable to give coherent meaning. The arrival at the meaning is through intuition, for it is intuition that synthesizes what reason and experience each sees separately without being able to combine into a coherent whole. Intuition comes to a man when he is prepared for it; when his reason and experience are trained and disciplined to receive and to interpret it. But whereas the levels of intuition to which rational and empirical methods might lead refer only to *specific* aspects of the nature of reality, and not to the whole of it, the levels of intuition at the higher levels of human consciousness to which prophets and saints attain give direct insight into the nature of reality *as a whole*. The prophet and the saint also require preparation to receive and to be able to interpret it; and their preparation does not consist only of the training, discipline, and development of their powers of reasoning and their capacities for sense experience, but also the training, discipline, and the development of their inner selves and the faculties of self concerned with the apprehension of truth-reality.

As to true report as a channel through which knowledge is acquired, it is of two kinds: that which is in sequence and continuity established by the tongues of people of whom reason cannot conceive that they would purpose together on a falsehood; and that which is brought by the Messenger of God. Authority, which is invested by general agreement in the first kind of true report, which includes that of scholars, scientists, and men of knowledge generally, may be questioned by the methods of reason and experience. But authority of the second kind of true report, which is also affirmed by general assent, is absolute. Authority is grounded ultimately upon intuitive experience, by which we mean both in the order of sense and sensible reality, and in the order of transcendental reality, such as intuition at the higher levels.

In contrast to the position of modern science and philosophy with regard to the sources and methods of knowledge, we maintain that just as there are levels of reason and experience, so are there levels of authority and intuition. Apart from the authority of men of science and learning generally, the highest level of authority in our view is the Holy Qur'ān and the Tradition including the sacred person of the Holy Prophet. They represent authority not only in the sense that they *communicate* the truth, but in the sense also that they *constitute* the truth. They represent authority that is established upon the higher levels of intellectual and spiritual cognition and transcendental experience that cannot simply be reduced to the normal level of reason and experience.

We define man as a 'rational animal' where the term 'rational' is signified by the term *nāṭiq*, which points to an innate faculty of knowing that apprehends the meaning of the universals and that formulates meaning. This formulation of meaning, which involves judgement, discrimination, and clarification, is what constitutes his rationality. The terms 'rational' (*nāṭiq*) and 'having the power to formulate meaning' (*dhū nuṭq*) are derived from the same root that conveys the basic meaning of 'speech', in the sense of human speech, so that they both signify a certain power and capacity innate in man to articulate words or symbolic forms in meaningful patterns. From the same root (*nuṭq*) is also derived the name for the science of discourse known as *al-manṭiq* (*i.e.* logic), developed for the construction of arguments, the formulation of methods of disputation, the discovery of fallacies, the theory of classification and definition, the basic notion of the syllogism, the conception of proof and demonstration, the general outlines of an intellectual method in the pursuit of truth. Man is, as it were, a 'language animal' or a 'speaking animal' (*al-ḥayawān al-nāṭiq*); and the articulation of linguistic symbols into meaningful patterns is no other than the outward, visible and audible expression of the inner, unseen reality which we call the intellect (*al-'aql*). The term *'aql* itself basically signifies a kind of 'binding' or 'withholding', so that in this respect it signifies an active, conscious entity that binds and withholds objects of knowledge by means of words or symbolic forms; and it indicates the same reality that is denoted by the terms 'heart' (*qalb*), 'spirit' (*rūḥ*), and 'self' (*nafs*). This conscious, active entity or reality has many names such as identified by the four terms above because of its many modes in its relations with the various levels of existence. The intellect is then a spiritual substance by which the rational soul recognizes truth and distinguishes truth from falsity. It is the reality that underlies the definition of man, and is indicated by everyone when he says "I".

In defining man as a 'rational animal', where we mean by rational the intelligential capacity for apprehending the meaning of the universals, the power of linguistic expression, the power responsible for the formulation of meaning —which involve acts of judgement, discrimination, distinction and clarification, and the articulation of symbolic forms in meaningful patterns—the meaning of 'meaning' (*ma'nā*) is the recognition of the place of anything in a system. Recognition occurs when the relation a thing has with others in the system becomes clarified and understood. The relation describes a certain order in terms of priority and posteriority as well as in terms of space and position. Meaning is an intelligible form with regard to which a word, an expression, or a symbol is applied to denote it. When that word, expression, or symbol becomes a notion in the mind (*'aql: nuṭq*) it is called the 'understood' (*mafhūm*). As an intelligible form that is formed in answer to the question "what is it?" it is called 'essence' (*māhiyyah*) . Considered as something that exists outside the mind, or objectively, it is called 'reality' (*ḥaqīqah*). Seen as a specific reality distinguished from the others, it is called 'individuality' or 'individual existence' (*huwiyyah*). Thus what constitutes meaning, or the definition of meaning, is recognition of the place of anything in a system, which occurs when the relation a thing has with others in the system becomes clarified and understood.[107]

We said that the relation describes a certain order. If everything in any system were in the same place, then there could be no recognition, there could be no meaning since there would be no relational criteria to judge, discriminate, distinguish and clarify. Indeed, there would be no system. For recognition to be possible there must be *specific difference* in things, there must be *essential relation* between things and, moreover, these *must remain as such;* for if the difference and the relation were not abiding but were in a state of constant change specifically and essentially, then recognition of

---

[107] See my *The Concept of Education. in Islām,* (*op. cit.*); p. 15.

things would be impossible and meaning would perish.

Thus in this we see that the intrinsic connection between meaning and knowledge has now become manifest, in that knowledge consists of units of meaning which are coherently related to other such units thereby forming notions, ideas, concepts, conceptions and judgements. Thought (*al-fikr*) is the soul's movement towards meaning, and this needs imagination (*al- khayāl*). Intuition, that is, either in the sense of sagacity (*al-ḥads*), or in the sense of illuminative experience (*al-wijdān*), is the arrival of the soul at meaning, or the arrival in the soul of meaning, either by acquisition through proof as in the former case, or it comes by itself as in the latter case.

The definition of man as a rational animal is a definition that sets a precise or concise limit (*ḥadd*) specifying the distinctive characteristic of what is being defined as man. The same kind of definition cannot obtain for knowledge because knowledge by nature defies the sort of limitation that defines categories within the divisions of genus and specific difference. Knowledge is limitless and its definition can only amount to a description of its nature (*rasm*) . We have already defined it thus as consisting of units of meaning coherently related to other such units thereby forming ideas, concepts, conceptions and judgements. Since we have defined meaning to be the recognition of the place of anything in a system, we now add that by 'place' we refer to 'proper place' in the various levels of human existence. Human existence may be considered as having different levels corresponding to the various spheres of operation of the external and internal senses. These are real (*ḥaqīqī*) existence, which is existence at the level of objective reality such as the external world; sensible (*ḥissī*) existence, which is confined to the faculties of sense and sensible experience including dreams, visions, illusions; imaginary (*khayālī*) existence, which is the existence of objects of sensible existence in the imagination when they are absent from human perception; intellectual (*'aqlī*) existence, which consists of abstract concepts in the human mind; analogous (*shibhī*) existence, which is constituted by things which do not exist in any of the levels above, but which do exist as something else resembling the things in a certain respect, or analogous to them. This level may also be considered as corresponding to that which is the sphere of operation of the discursive or cogitative (*fikrī*) faculty of the soul. At every one of these levels human perception of the objects of perception is not the same. In addition to these levels we affirm the existence of another level than rational truth; a suprarational or transcendental level of existence experienced by prophets and saints of God and men of discernment who are deeply rooted in knowledge. This last is the level of holy existence, in which things are apprehended as they really are. The concept of 'proper place', then, pertains to all these levels of human existence, which encompass the ontological, cosmological, and psychological domains, and which include man himself and the world of empirical things as well as the religious and ethical aspects of human existence. 'Proper' place means 'real' and 'true' place as denoted by the term *ḥaqq*. *Ḥaqq* signifies both reality and truth. As reality it denotes an ontological condition; as truth a logical condition; and it denotes a judgement or *ḥukm* conforming with the reality or the real situation.

One of the fundamental differences between our position and that of modern philosophy and science impinging upon the problem of formulating a philosophy of science revolves around the understanding of the meaning of *reality* and *truth* and their relation to *fact*. The understanding of what these terms designate has a profound bearing upon the understanding of the meaning of knowledge and the epistemological process and of values, and ultimately upon the understanding of the nature of man himself.

We use one word to mean generally both reality and truth, and this fact is in itself significant in conveying our understanding of the meaning of truth not merely as a property of statements, beliefs and judgements, but also as a property of the nature of reality. The word *ḥaqq* stands for both reality and truth. Its opposite is *bāṭil,* meaning non-reality or falsity. *Ḥaqq* means a suitableness to the requirements of wisdom, justice, rightness, truth, reality, propriety. It is a state, quality or property of being wise, just, right, true, real, proper; it is a state of being necessary, unavoidable, obligatory, due; it is a state of existence and encompasses everything. There is another word, *ṣidq,* meaning truth, whose opposite is *kidhb* meaning untruth or falsehood, that designates only truth pertaining to statements or uttered words; whereas the word *ḥaqq* not only refers to statements, but also to actions, feelings, beliefs, judgements, and the things and events in existence. The things and events in existence which *ḥaqq* designates pertain not only to their present condition, but also to their past as well as future condition. With regards to future condition *ḥaqq* means verification, realization, actualization. Indeed, that the meaning of *ḥaqq* is understood to encompass both reality and truth pertaining to the state of existence is due to the fact that it is one of the names of God describing Him as the absolute existence which is the *reality* and not the *concept* of existence.

To the generality of people, the nature of existence and its relation to separate, similar yet diverse realities which we call 'things' is that existence is a general, abstract concept common to all existences, that is, to everything and to anything without exception. The mind, when regarding external realities we call 'things', can first abstract them from existence and then predicate existence of them. The mind therefore attributes to the things what it considers to be their property of existence. Existence is then regarded as something superadded to, accidental to, and subsisting in things. In this mental process, the single, general, abstract concept becomes multiple and is rationally divided into portions corresponding to things. The existences of things are these portions, and these portions, along with the general, abstract concept of existence, are external to the 'essences' of things and are only mentally superadded to them.

According to this perspective, existence is something purely conceptual, whereas essences are real; essences are realities actualized extramentally. But we say further that in addition to the concept of existence there is another entity which is the reality of existence, by which existence as a pure concept comes to inhere in the mind as one of its effects. Existence as reality, unlike its conceptual counterpart, is not something static; it perpetually involves itself in a dynamic movement of ontological self-expression, articulating its infinite inner possibilities in gradations from the less determinate to the more determinate until it appears at the level of concrete forms, such that the particular existences which we regard as multiple and diverse 'things' having separate, individual 'essences' are nothing but the modes and aspects of the reality of existence. From this perspective, the *essence* of a thing is nothing more than an entity in concept only, whereas the *existence* of a thing is real. Indeed, the real and true essence of a thing is existence as individuated into a particular mode. It is this reality of existence that we have identified above as the all-encompassing Reality or Truth (*al-ḥaqq*), by which God as the absolute in all the forms of manifestation is called.

Since modern philosophy and science have come to realize that the fundamental nature of phenomena is process, the descriptive names that philosophers and scientists have applied to correspond with process must also reflect the dynamism involved in the very idea of process. They have applied such names as 'life' or 'vital impulse', or 'energy', implying the movement, the change, the becoming that are productive of the events in space-time. That they have chosen these names as descriptive of the reality manifested as process is itself an indication that they consider existence, unlike life, vital impulse, or energy, as a mere concept; and as a mere concept existence is indeed something static, clearly disqualifying it as corresponding with process. In this sense, their formulation of a philosophy of science, in contradiction with their position that the reality underlying phenomena is process, still revolves within the sphere of an essentialistic worldview, a worldview preoccupied with 'things' having independent and self subsistent 'essences', and of events, relations, and concepts pertaining to the things, making things point to themselves as the sole reality, and not to any other Reality beyond them that both *includes* as well as *excludes* them. Our position is that what is truly descriptive of the fundamental nature of phenomena as process is 'existence' because existence alone, both understood as a concept as well as a reality, is the most basic and universal entity known to us. It is true that existence understood as a concept is static and does not correspond with process. But we maintain that existence is not merely a concept, it is also a reality: it is not merely posited in the mind, but is also a real and actual entity independent of the mind. It is dynamic, active, creative and pregnant with infinite possibilities of ontological self-expression; it is an aspect of God that arises from the intrinsic nature of His names and attributes, and is therefore a 'conscious' entity acting in accordance with God's customary way of acting (*sunnat Allāh*). The so-called "laws of nature" are in reality God's customary way of acting, and understood as such, these "laws" are no longer seen as rigid because they are now open to infinite possibilities. Existence is then the primary, ultimate stuff of reality, whereas life, vital impulse, or energy and other such terms applied by philosophers and scientists to describe that fundamental entity, which is the reality underlying the nature of things, are all secondary to existence for they all are like properties or attributes of existence.

When we say that *ḥaqq* denotes both what is real as well as what is true, we are saying that *ḥaqq* has an aspect pertaining to the real and an aspect pertaining to the true in the sense that the real refers to the ontological and the true to the logical orders of existence. *Ḥaqq* as meaning the 'real' designates the reality of existence as well as its modes and aspects which we understand as 'events' and 'process'; as meaning the 'true' it designates a judgement conforming with the external realities that arise as 'things' out of the events or the process. This conformity involves a certain correspondence and coherence between the intellectual act of judgement and the external reality that is being perceived. As we said before in connection with perception, the realities that comprise the external world are not immediately or directly given in experience, but are abstractions of them in varying degrees performed by the external and internal senses, and transformed into knowledge of the external world by means of intellectual construction. Our conceptual knowledge then corresponds to the information conveyed to our consciousness or soul by the senses; and our conception of the external realities stand in a relation of coherence within a system of conceptual relations already imprinted upon the soul that convey to us our vision of the nature of Reality. Our position is that the correspondence and coherence that is of the nature of truth must satisfy the condition of coincidence with the requirements of wisdom and justice. Wisdom is the knowledge given by God that enables the recipient to know the right place, or to render correct judgement as to the right place of a thing or an object of knowledge. Justice is the condition whereby things or objects of knowledge are in their right places. Thus for it to be true, correspondence and coherence must coincide with right place. The notion of right or proper place involves necessity for every thing in the order of creation to be in that condition—that is, to be deployed in a certain order in terms of priority and posteriority as well as in terms of space and position and arranged according to various levels and degrees. Ontologically, created things are already so arranged, but man, out of ignorance of the just order pervading all creation, makes alterations and confuses the places of things such that injustice occurs. Injustice is the putting a thing not in its proper place; it is to fall short of or to exceed the limits of the proper place so that in the general order of things it is disharmony. Indeed, the very meaning of 'proper' is also included in that of *ḥaqq,* for it points to that which belongs to one, to one's own; it is the exact or the specific part that befits one's natural or essential constitution, to one's self; it is something inherent, a property, an essential attribute. The place of a person, a thing, an object of knowledge then does not merely refer to the location or the specific space occupied by the person, the thing, the object of knowledge; it is also the natural position, the position that conforms to the nature, both in the external world as well as in the imagination and in the mind, of the person, the thing, the object of knowledge. We do not agree, therefore, that knowledge pertains only to phenomena; that truth is only a property of statements or declarative sentences, or of beliefs and judgements from which statements are derived and which are dependent upon the relation of the belief or the judgement to some fact; that fact is neutral in its relation to truth and falsity. We maintain that truth is also a property of the nature of things in as much as they conform with a suitableness to the requirements of wisdom and justice, that is, to the requirements of the condition of being in their right or proper places. And this does not mean that truth is merely a correspondence of statement or judgement to fact, as that would make fact equivalent to truth. Even though a sentence may be true if it designates the fact, the mere existence of the fact does not necessarily make the fact into a truth. Truth is not simply conformity with fact because facts can be created by man and can therefore be not in their proper places, meaning that facts can be false. That facts can be created by man confirms the truth of our denial that facts are neutral in their relation to truth and falsity, for the very existence itself of such facts is dependent upon values belonging to the particular worldview of their creators. By truth involving a certain correspondence and coherence then we do not mean simply a correspondence of thought, idea, or belief with fact, unless the fact were in its proper place, that is, unless the fact coheres within an integrated system of interrelated truths as apprehended by the soul. The proper place of man, for example, is that he is to be considered as both spiritual and physical; that he is a living being possessing that inner faculty of knowing that apprehends the meaning of the universals; that has the power and capacity to articulate words or symbolic forms in meaningful patterns; he is spirit, soul, heart and intellect manifested in bodily form, and his spirit, soul, heart and intellect point to one and the same reality being named by many names because of its many modes in its relations with the various levels of existence encompassing the spiritual and physical domains. His reality and truth (*ḥaqq*) applies to both these domains. But if he were utterly secularized, if he were considered merely as something physical, an animal different from other animals only in degree and not in kind, then he would not in reality be considered to be in his proper place. And certain scientific propositions pertaining to him thus considered, such as those arising from the statements and general conclusions of genetic engineering, for example, even though supported by empirical evidence, are yet false because they serve premisses based upon a false interpretation of the nature of man, which in turn is dependent upon a false system purporting to describe the true order of reality.

As for the meaning of *ḥaqq* as reality, the proper term used to denote reality is *ḥaqīqah,* which is derived from *ḥaqq*. The distinction between *ḥaqq* and *ḥaqīqah* is that the former refers to ontological condition, order, or system as known by way of intuition; whereas the latter refers to ontological structure, to the very nature, being or self of a thing. *Ḥaqīqah* or reality is that by which a thing is what it is. Now *that* by which a thing is what it is has a twofold aspect; on the one hand since every thing that *is* partakes of reality, reality is then something that is common to everything. This something common to everything is existence. Thus one of the twofold aspect of that by which a thing is what it is is the 'being existent' of the thing. The other aspect of that by which a thing is what it is is its 'being-distinct' from any other. 'Being-existent' is common to all existents in the various levels of existence, and although existence is the stuff of reality, it is, strictly speaking, not the commonness that makes a thing to be *what* it is; it is rather the 'being-distinct' from any other that makes a thing to be what it is, for it is only by virtue of distinction that realities have come into existence. Therefore the fundamental nature of reality is *difference.*

Existence (*wujūd,* from *wujida* the passive form of *wajada*) denotes something found, discovered, perceived, known, sensed—by means of the external and internal senses, or of the intellect, or of the heart. Since existence as reality is the creative stuff of which things come to be, another form of the word (*ījād*) denotes something existentiated, created, originated. Since the reality that is existence pervades everything, it is self-sufficient in its eternal plenitude, and this meaning of not being in want, or need, is denoted by yet another form (*wājid*). When by means of higher intuition one comes to find the reality that exists, this 'finding' of existence is called *wijdān,* which we said earlier refers to the intuition of existence. So when we refer above to an aspect of that by which a thing is what it is as its 'being-existent', the 'being-existent' of a thing should not be interpreted as denoting something existing merely actually or currently in the external world; but as denoting also that category of existence in the interior condition of the reality of existence that is continually unfolding itself in gradations becoming the things that we see and behold. Existence means to have a place in the order of reality. Since existence particularized as the 'being existent' of a thing is one of the twofold aspect of reality, the referent of 'place', when we say that existence means to have a place in the order of reality, is then the 'being distinct' of a thing. The order of reality, according to us and in the aforementioned sense, cannot be restricted to the phenomenal world, or the world of empirical things in the realms of sense and sensible experience.

When we define knowledge as consisting of units of meaning that are coherently related to other such units thereby forming ideas, conceptions, and judgements; and we define meaning as the recognition of the place of anything in a system which occurs when the relation a thing has with others in the system becomes clarified and understood, we understand that it is such relation or network of relations that determines our recognition of the thing's proper place in the system. By 'the system' we are referring of course not only to the initial, partial system within a network of interrelated systems, but finally also to the ultimate, grandscale ontological system as a whole. We are in concerted agreement that all knowledge comes from God, and that the manner of its arrival and the senses and faculties that receive and interpret it are distinctly not the same. Since all knowledge comes from God, and is interpreted by the soul through its physical and spiritual or intelligential faculties, it follows that the epistemological definition would be that knowledge, with reference to God as being its source of origin, is the arrival of meaning in the soul; and with reference to the soul as being its active recipient and interpreter, knowledge is the arrival of the soul at meaning. The world of nature as depicted in the Holy Qur'ān is composed of symbolic forms (*āyāt*), like words in a book. Indeed, the world of nature is another form of the Divine Revelation analogous to the Holy Qur'ān itself, only that the great, open book of nature is something created; it presents itself in multiple and diverse forms that partake of symbolic existence by virtue of being continually articulated by the creative word of God. Now a word as it really is is a symbol, and to know it as it really is is to know what it stands for, what it symbolizes, what it means. If we were to regard a word as if it has an independent reality of its own, then it would no longer be a sign or a symbol as it is being made to point to itself, which is not what it really is. So in like manner the study of nature, of any thing, any object of knowledge in the world of created things, if the expression 'as it really is' is taken to mean its alleged independent reality, essentially and existentially, as if it were something ultimate and self-subsistent, then such study is devoid of real purpose and the pursuit of knowledge becomes a deviation from the truth, which necessarily puts into question the validity of such knowledge. For as it really is a thing is other than what it is, and that 'other' is what it *means*. Thus in the same manner that the study of words as *words* leads to deviation from the truth underlying them, the preoccupation in philosophy and physics with things as *things* leads to the erroneous, common sense belief in their existence outside the mind as aggregations of particles persisting through a certain period of time and moving in space, as if these particles were the ultimate material of the world. Whereas in reality the stuff of 'matter' consists of a series of events (*a'rāḍ*, sing. *'araḍ*), and physical phenomena are processes whose every detail is discontinuous. A thing like a word is then in reality ultimately a sign or a symbol, and a sign or a symbol is something that is apparent and is inseparable from something else not equally apparent, in such wise that when the former is perceived, the other, which cannot be perceived and which is of one predicament as the former, is known. That is why we have defined knowledge epistemologically as the arrival in the soul of the *meaning* of a thing, or the arrival of the soul at the *meaning* of a thing. The 'meaning of a thing' means the *right* meaning of it, and what we consider to be the 'right' meaning is in our view determined by the Islamic vision of reality and truth as projected by the Quranic conceptual system. Thus the phrases that we used previously, such as the 'true order of reality', the 'just order pervading all creation', the 'levels and degrees', and the 'general order of created things' in our reference to the 'system' of conceptual relations in which the 'proper places' of things are recognized, point to no other than the Quranic conceptual system. Correspondence and coherence as we understand them in connection with reality and truth refer to proper place in the former case and to the Quranic system in the latter case.

Knowledge is limitless because the objects of knowledge are without limit. But there is a limit of truth in every object of knowledge, so that the pursuit of true knowledge is not an endless search. Were its quest to be without end, then it would be impossible to attain to knowledge in the span of time to which there is a beginning and an end, and it would render knowledge itself to be meaningless. Knowledge of the truth about the world of empirical things can indeed be achieved and increased through inquiry made by generations of mankind. But true knowledge has an immediate bearing on the individual man as it pertains to his identity and destiny, and he cannot afford to suspend his judgement concerning its truth as it is not meant to be something that can be discovered eventually by future generations. That is why the crisis of truth occurring in every generation pertains to true knowledge, and the crisis of truth has perhaps never been so acute as in our age. Modern philosophy and science are unable to give a conclusive answer to the permanent question about truth. Their representatives attempt to clarify only the 'truth perspective' of the age in which the crisis of truth occurs, thus divesting truth of its objectivity. One can neither change, add to, nor embellish the truth so that it can become more true, nor can one fall short of it; in either of the cases it will not be the truth, but what is false. The truth is precisely itself, and nothing more or less. For every truth there is a limit that is true to that truth; the knowledge of that limit is wisdom. By it every truth is assigned its proper meaning which neither curtails nor transgresses it. There is a limit of truth in every object of knowledge, and every object of knowledge has a different limit of truth, some more recondite and difficult to discover than others, so that in our perpetual attempt to discover them there is no question of restricting inquiry, whose purpose, guided by wisdom, is to know such limits. True knowledge is therefore knowledge that recognizes the limit of truth in its every object.

The Holy Qur'ān itself speaks of its signs and symbols as consisting partly of those that are clear and established (*al-muḥkamāt*), and partly of those that are obscure and ambiguous (*al-mutashābihāt*). In correspondence with the signs and symbols of the Holy Qur'ān, the world of phenomena also consists of signs and symbols which we call 'things' that are clear and established in their meanings, and those that are obscure and ambiguous. The detecting, discovery and revealing of the concealed meanings of the ambiguous signs and symbols in the Holy Qur'ān is called allegorical interpretation (*ta'wīl*), and this is based upon the interpretation of those that are apparent (*tafsīr*). Thus, in the same manner that the interpretation of the obscure and ambiguous texts is to be based upon those that are clear and established, so the interpretation or the study and explanation of the obscure and ambiguous aspects of the things of the empirical world must be grounded upon what is already known and established. Although we said that some of the things that constitute the empirical world, the world of sense and sensible experience, are symbols whose meanings are clear and established, their being clear and established is understood by virtue of their being considered in their apparent meanings as arrived at by way of common sense. But since they are also physical in nature, they all are generally ambiguous because they appear to our consciousness to point to themselves, as if they each have independent, individual and self-subsistent reality. As symbols they are, to be sure, not something unreal, not merely appearance of the nature of illusion; but only provided they are understood to be something in profound and dependent connection with what they symbolize. Otherwise, considered as things in themselves, they *are* unreal, in the sense that they exist as such only in the mind, having no corresponding reality in the external world. What *are* existent in the external world and independent of the mind are realities in the process of actualization in particular and individual forms, which are modes and aspects of a single and dynamic all-encompassing Reality.

Supposing we are travelling in a car on a dark and stormy night heading for a place we have heard of but have never been to. Then we arrive at a main junction with many different roads leading to different places. At the centre of the junction there is a signpost with many arms of varying lengths pointing to the various directions signifying the way to the different places. The signpost and its arms are simply made and painted white, and along the pointed planks which serve as arms are engraved in bold, black letters the place names and their relative distances from that spot. As our car approaches and its headlights illumine the signpost and its many arms, we soon notice one of the arms bearing the name of the place of our destination. What we do next, if we are to pursue the object of our destination, would surely be to turn away from the signpost without much hesitation, and follow the road towards which the sign is pointing. We would be doing this because the sign is clear. But now supposing the signpost were made of marble finely wrought, and the pointing arms were sculptured into forms wondrous and beautiful, the place names and their relative distances from the spot chiselled into letters of pure gold and embellished with rare gems — would we then be able to seek out, without much hesitation and tarrying, the pointing arm that would show us the way to our destination; and would we then simply turn away from the signpost to follow the road directed? Indeed, what would most certainly happen in this case would be that we would stop the car and even get out into the rain with a torchlight to get a closer look at the marvelous sight before us. And we might even spend the night in the car to await the day for a more satisfying look. The sign in this case is not clear; it is ambiguous, and it points to itself more than it points to the object on which its very existence depends.

What we have said above should make it clear to us that science according to Islām is ultimately a kind of *ta'wīl* or allegorical interpretation of the empirical things that constitute the world of nature. As such science must base itself firmly upon the *tafsīr* or interpretation of the apparent or obvious meanings of the things in nature. Their apparent and obvious meanings have to do with their respective places within the system of relations; and their places become apparent to our understanding when the *limits* of their significance are recognized. *Ta'wīl* basically means getting to the ultimate, primordial meaning of something through a process of intellection. But even in this case, there are things whose ultimate meanings cannot be grasped by intellect; and those deeply rooted in knowledge accept them as they are through true belief which we call *īmān*. This is the position of truth: in that there are limits to the meaning of things, and their places are profoundly bound up with the limits of their significance.

Limitation is not a shortcoming. Our external and internal senses and faculties of imagination and cognition all have limited powers and potentials, each created to convey and conserve information concerning that for which it was appointed. There is pragmatic purpose in limitation, for by it we are able to perceive and conceive objects of knowledge and ideas about them and their relations so that we may put the knowledge of things to beneficial use. If we had senses whose powers are less limited, like the senses possessed by certain animals, our perception of things in everyday life would be different; for not only would the form, texture, colour and other characteristics of things be different from what they are as we normally perceive them, but also that some of them would not exist for us, and some of them would not exist at all, thereby affecting the very existence of human culture and civilization. Then again, if we had eyes whose powers are even more less limited than that of certain animals; eyes that could penetrate the veils of phenomena such that they could see the events and process underlying the phenomenal world, then the forms of things would vanish from our sight and we would not be able to derive from them the knowledge of particulars that lead to universals, and the very meaning of things would perish. The setting of limits to the channels and sources by which we obtain knowledge is therefore a blessing and a mercy from God in order that we may be able to understand the meanings of the objects of knowledge as well as to recognize their Creator.

Since the role of science is to be descriptive of facts, and facts undergo continual change by virtue of their underlying reality which is process, the secular aspect of modern philosophy and science considers change to be the ultimate nature of reality. That is why secularization as a philosophical program, in its attempt to correspond with the reality that is considered as absolute change, advocates change in all aspects of life, denies finality in worldview and propagates the belief in an open future. By 'change', which is movement involving space and time and presupposes diversity, philosophers and scientists usually mean either change of place or position, or qualitative and quantitative change which involves perpetual transformation or becoming. Some maintain that all motion is relative and there is no absolute motion; and some believe that change is merely due to psychological perception. The belief that knowledge pertains only to phenomena entails the belief that reality is change. We do not agree that change is merely psychological or 'subjective' since we affirm that movement is real. Our position that change is a reality should be understood without thereby implying that change is absolute; for we maintain that reality is at once both permanence *and* change, not in the sense that change is permanent, but in the sense that there is something permanent whereby change occurs. The implication underlying the concept of change is that the diverse things that constitute the world of phenomena somehow persist in existence and undergo movement or transformation. We maintain that phenomenal things do not persist in existence, but perish upon coming into existence, being continually replaced by new similars in a perpetual process. The perishing of things is called, after the Quranic expression, *hālik* or *fanā';* and the perpetual process of renewal, again after the Quranic expression, is called *khalq jadīd*—a new creation. The world is then ever new (*muḥdath*), it is novelty. Change, we say, occurs not at the level of phenomenal things, for they are ever-perishing, but at the level of their realities which contain within themselves all their future states. In this sense change is the actualization of potentialities inherent in the realities of things which, as they unfold their contents, preserve their complete identities through time. The world of phenomena, we said earlier, are processes whose every detail is discontinuous. The discontinuance of existence in its every detail is due to the ever-perishing nature of phenomena that are being replaced by new similars. Discontinuance in existence also involves the realities underlying all phenomena; but whereas the world of phenomena is ever-new, the realities change and yet remain the same. Their change is their unfolding of their potential states involving existential discontinuity at every state of actualization; their remaining the same is their regaining their identities. Thus the realities are ever-regaining continuance in existence, while their phenomenal modes and aspects perish upon actualization. This ever-regaining continuance in existence is called, to use another Quranic expression, *baqā'*. The dual aspect of the realities—permanence and change—presupposes a third metaphysical category between existence and non-existence, and this is the realm of the permanent entities (*al-a'yān al-thābitah*) which are aspects of the names and attributes of God. As to the Ultimate Reality that is God, even though He describes Himself in terms explicit of absolute dynamism, He is far too exalted to be conceived as being immersed in process descriptive of becoming or transformation.

In this chapter we have conveyed brief statements outlining our position on the meaning of religion and belief; on the nature of God; on secularization and the nature of modern, contemporary philosophy and science, and presented a gist of their basic assumptions and presuppositions. We pointed out that there are similarities between our position and that of modern philosophy and science regarding the nature of phenomena and of empirical reality as well as of the sources and methods of knowledge, while at the same time we maintained that there are profound differences in our respective understanding of them due ultimately to our affirmation of Revelation—and the Tradition deriving from it—as the source of true knowledge of ultimate reality. We have briefly outlined the contrast between our position and that of modern philosophy and science regarding perception, reason, intuition, and authority as sources and methods of knowledge. In this connection we maintained adherence to faculty psychology because it is aligned to the affirmation of existence of the soul, or intelligential spirit, as the ultimate reality of man and as the source of origin of human language. We stressed our concept of place beginning with our definition of meaning as the recognition of place within a system, showing also the conceptual connection between meaning and knowledge by defining the latter as coherent units of the former; we defined wisdom as knowledge of right place; justice as the condition of being in the right place; truth as conformity with right place; realities as permanent and separately placed entities; and existence as place in the order of reality. We explained the meanings of reality and truth, showing their relations of correspondence and coherence with fact. We distinguished the reality from the concept of existence, and maintained that the former is the truth underlying the nature of process. We defined true knowledge as recognition of the limit of truth in its every object. We referred to the Quranic system of conceptual interrelations and its methods of interpretation, saying that Islamic science must interpret the facts of existence in correspondence with that system, and not interpret that system in correspondence with the facts. We touched upon the problem of change or movement, and affirmed change and permanence together; and we maintained change and permanence only in the realities of things, and not in the things themselves as they are ever-perishing in their nature. We affirmed permanence also in God, neither implying by 'permanence' staticity, nor movement nor dynamicity that involves transformation or becoming; whereas in the realities change refers to actualization of their potentialities, while the real entities that establish their identities remain the same. What we have stated above in brief outline already implies, among other things, the primacy of the reality of existence; the dynamic nature of this reality that is continually unfolding itself in systematic gradation from the degrees of absoluteness to those of manifestation, determination, and individuation; the perpetual process of the new creation; the absence of a necessary relation between cause and effect, and its explanation in the Divine causality; the third metaphysical category between existence and nonexistence, which is the realm of the permanent entities; and the metaphysics of change and permanence pertaining to the realities. These constitute the fundamental bases of Islamic metaphysics, and it is within the framework of this metaphysics that our philosophy of science must be formulated.

IV

THE NATURE OF MAN AND THE PSYCHOLOGY OF THE HUMAN SOUL

Man has a dual nature, he is both body and soul, he is at once physical being and spirit.[108] God taught him the names (*al-asmā'*) of everything.[109] By the 'names' we infer that it means the knowledge (*al-'ilm*) of everything (*al-ashyā'*). This knowledge does not encompass knowledge of the specific nature of the essence (*al-dhāt*) or the inmost ground (*al-sirr*) of a thing (*shay'*) such as, for example, the spirit (*al-rūḥ*); it refers to knowledge of accidents (sing. *'araḍ*) and attributes (sing. *ṣifah*) pertaining to the essences of things sensible and intelligible (*maḥsūsāt* and *ma'qūlāt*) so as to make known the relations and distinctions existing between them, and to clarify their natures within these domains in order to discern and to understand their meanings, that is, their causes, uses, and specific individual purpose. Man is, however, also given limited knowledge of the spirit,[110] of his true and real self or soul,[111] and by means of this knowledge he is able to arrive at knowledge about God (*al-ma'rifah*) and His absolute oneness; that God is his true Lord (*al-rabb*) and object of worship (*al-ilāh*).[112] The seat of knowledge in man is a spiritual substance which is variously referred to in the Holy Qur'ān sometimes as his heart (*al-*

---

[108] *Al-Ḥijr* (15): 26–29; *Al-Mu'minūn*(23): 12

[109] *Al-Baqarah* (2): 31.

[110] *Banī Isrā'īl* (17): 85.

[111] *Ḥā Mīm* (41): 53.

[112] *Āli 'Imrān* (3): 81; *Al-A'rāf* (7): 172.

qalb), or his soul or self (*al-nafs*), or his spirit (*al-rūḥ*), or his intellect (*al-'aql*). In virtue of the truth that man knows God in His absolute unity as his Lord,[113] such knowledge, and the reality of the situation that necessarily follows from it, has bound man in a covenant (*al-mīthāq; al-'ahd*) determining his purpose and attitude and action with respect to his self in his relation to God.[114] This binding and determining of man to a covenant with God and to a precise nature in regard to his purpose, attitude, and action, is the binding and determining in religion (*al-dīn*) which entails true submission (*al-islām*).[115] Thus knowledge and religion are natural correlates in the nature of man, that is, the original nature in which God has created him (*al-fiṭrah*). Man's purpose is therefore to know and to serve God (*'ibādah*)[116] and his duty is obedience (*ṭā'ah*) to God, which conforms with his essential nature created for him by God.[117]

But man is also "composed of forgetfulness (*nisyān*)"— as a Prophetic tradition says[118], and he is called *insān* basically precisely because, having testified to himself the truth of the covenant he sealed with God, which entails obedience of His commands and prohibitions, he forgot (*nasiya*) to fulfill his duty and his purpose. Hence according to ibn 'Abbās with reference to a passage in the Holy Qur'ān,[119] the term *insān* is derived from *nasiya* when he said that man is called *insān* because, having covenanted with God, he forgot (*nasiya*).[120] Forgetfulness is the cause of man's disobedience, and this blameworthy nature inclines

---

113 *Al-A'raf* (7): 172.

114 *Ibid.*

115 See chapter I, above.

116 *Al-Dhāriyāt* (51): 66.

117 *Al-Rūm* (30): 30.

118 *Kashf al-Khafā'*, 2 vols. 4th pr, Bayrūt, 1985, vol. 2, p. 419, no. 2806. Al-Êabarānī, al-Tirmiẓī, ibn Abī Shaybah, from ibn 'Abbās.

119 *Êā Hā* (20): 115.

120 *LA*, vol. 6, p. 11, col. 1.

him towards injustice (*ẓulm*) and ignorance (*jahl*).[121] But God has equipped him with the powers and faculties of right vision and apprehension, of real savouring of truth, of right speech and communication; and He has indicated to him the right and the wrong with respect to the course of action he should take so that he might strive to attain his bright destiny.[122] The choice for the better (*ikhtiyār*) [123] is left to him. Moreover, God has equipped him with intelligence to know and distinguish reality from non-reality, truth from falsehood, and rectitude from error; and even though his intelligence—or rather his imaginative and estimative faculties—might confuse him,[124] and provided he is sincere and true to his noble nature, God, out of His bounty, mercy, and grace, will aid and guide him to attain to truth and right conduct. The supreme example of this is the case of the Prophet Ibrāhīm, upon whom be peace.[125] Man thus equipped and fortified is meant to be the vicegerent (*khalīfah*) of God on earth,[126] and as such the weighty burden of trust (*amānah*) *is* placed upon him—the trust and responsibility to rule according to God's will and purpose and His pleasure.[127] The trust implies responsibility to rule with justice, and the 'rule' means not simply ruling in the socio-political sense, nor in the controlling of nature in the scientific sense, but more fundamentally in its encompassing of the meaning of nature (*al-ṭabī'ah*), it means the ruling, governing, controlling and maintaining of man by his self or his rational soul.

The terms heart (*qalb*), soul or self (*nafs*), spirit (*rūḥ*),

---

121 *Al-Ahẓāb,* (33): 72.

122 *Al-Balad* (90): 8–10; *Al-Aḥqāf* (46): 26; *Al-Naḥl* (16): 78; *Al-Sajdah* (32): 9; *Al-Mulk* (67): 23; *Al-Mu'minūn* (23): 78.

123 See *Introduction* above, pp. 33–34

124 Al-Ghazālī, *Mishkāt al-Anwār,* Cairo, 1964, p.47.

125 *Al-An'ām* (6): 74–82.

126 *Al-Baqarah* (2): 30.

127 *Al-Aḥzāb* (33): 72.

and intellect (*'aql*) used in relation to the soul each conveys two meanings; the one referring to the material or physical aspect of man, or to the body; and the other to the non-material, imaginal and intelligential or spiritual aspect, or to the soul of man.[128] In general, and from the ethical point of view, the first meaning denotes that aspect from which originates the blameworthy qualities in man, and they are the animal powers which in spite of their being beneficial to man in some respects, are in conflict with the intellectual powers. The attachment of blameworthiness to the animal powers inherent in the physical aspect of man should not be confused with the idea of denigration of the human body, which is indeed against the teachings of Islām. The human being is created "in the best of moulds", but without true faith and good works he is worse than the lowly beasts.[129] It is against these non-beneficial aspects of the animal powers that the Holy Prophet urged us when he alluded to the greater struggle (*jihād*) of man, for they are the enemy within.[130] The second meaning refers to the reality of man and to his essence. To this meaning refers the well known Prophetic tradition: "Whosoever knows his self knows his Lord."

The real essence of man originated from the worlds of dominion (*al-malakūt*) and of command (*al-amr*).[131] When it inclines itself towards the right direction, the divine peace (*al-sakīnah*) will descend upon it,[132] and the effusion of divine liberality will successively be diffused in it until it achieves tranquility in the remembrance of God and abides in the knowledge of His divinity, and soars towards the high-

---

128 *Iḥyā',* vol. 3, p. 3; *Ma'ārij,* p. 15 fol.

129 *Al-Êīn* (95): 4–5.

130 Bayhaqī, *Zuhd,* from Jābir. Ibn Hajar says this *ḥadīth is* well known. *Kashf al-Khafā',* vol. 1, p. 511, no. 1362.

131 *Yā Sīn* (36): 83; *Al-Mu'minūn* (23): 88.

132 *Al-Baqarah* (2): 248; *Al-Tawbah* (9): 26;40; *Al-Fatḥ* (48): 4.

est levels of the angelic horizons. The Holy Qur'ān calls this state of the soul and tranquil soul (*al-nafs al-muṭma'innah*).[133] The faculties or powers of the soul are like armies engaged in constant battles of alternate success. Sometimes the soul is drawn towards its intellectual powers and encounters the intelligibles whereby their eternal truths cause it to affirm its loyalty to God; and sometimes its animal powers drag it down to the lowest foothills of the bestial nature. This vacillation in the state of the soul is the state of the soul that censures itself (*al-nafs al-lawwāmah*);[134] it is in earnest struggle with its animal powers. By means of knowledge, moral excellence, and good works it is possible for man to attain to the angelic nature, and when he does, he no longer has in common with his fellow man the animal nature in him except in outward form and fashion. But if he falls into the degrading depths of the bestial nature and remains captive in that condition, then he is severed from the nature common to humanity and appears as man only in shape and construction. This is the state of the soul that incites to evil (*al-nafs al-ammārah bi 'l-sū'*).[135]

In its specific sense, and when referring to the heart, the first meaning indicates the pine-shaped lump of muscular flesh situated to the left side in the breast. It is the circulator of blood to every part of the body and the fountain-head of the subtile vapour that is the vehicle of the physical animal spirit. Through this vehicle the animal spirit rises from its fountain-head in the heart to the brain through the veins to all parts of the body. This spirit is the conveyor of animal life and is common to all animals. When it passes away it causes the death of the external senses involving that of the body as a whole. As for the intellect, it performs

---

133 *Al-Fajr* (89): 27.

134 *Al-Qiyāmah* (75): 2.

135 *Yūsuf* (12): 53.

abstractions of objects of the external world and contemplates the realities of things, and its functions are localized in various regions of the brain. The soul or self sometimes denotes the individual, concrete existence of a thing or person.[136]

With reference to the meanings of the four terms used in relation to the soul when they pertain to the soul of man, they all indicate an indivisible, identical entity, a spiritual substance which is the reality or very essence of man. In this sense they point to a unifying principle referred to as the *kamāl* or perfection of a being, to the mode of existence of that which transforms something potential to something actual.[137] This entity, which is a spiritual subtlety (*al-laṭīfah al rūḥāniyyah*), is a thing created, but it is immortal; it is not measured in terms of extent in space and time, or of quantity; it is conscious of itself and is the locus of intelligibles; and the way to know it is only through intellect and by means of observing the activities that originate in it. It has many names because of its accidental modes or states (*aḥwāl*). Thus when it is involved in intellection and apprehension it is called 'intellect'; when it governs the body it is called 'soul'; when it is engaged in receiving intuitive illumination it is called 'heart'; and when it reverts to its own world of abstract entities it is called 'spirit'. Indeed, it is in reality always engaged in manifesting itself in all its states.

The soul possesses faculties or powers (*quwā*) which become manifest in its relation to bodies. In plants they are the powers of nutrition (*al-ghādhiyyah*), growth (*al-nāmiyyah*), and generation or reproduction (*al-muwallidah*). These powers, in their general and not their specific senses, exist also in animals; and in man, whose body belongs to the animal species, there are powers of volition or action at will

---

136 *Ma'ārij*, pp. 15–18.

137 *Ma'ārij*, pp. 21–22; *Shifā'*, pp. 9–10; *Najāt*, p. 197.

(*al-muḥarrikah*), and perception (*al-mudrikah*) in addition to those of nutrition, growth, and reproduction. All these powers belong to the soul, and in view of their common inherence generally in the different bodies as well as their separate inherence specifically in accordance with the natures of the different species, the soul is somewhat like a genus divided into three different souls respectively: the vegetative (*al-nabātiyyah*), the animal (*al-ḥayawāniyyah*), and the human (*al-insāniyyah*) or the rational (*al-nāṭiqah*).

The powers peculiar to the animal soul are motive and perceptive, each of which is of two kinds. The motive power operates as the arouser of action (*al-bā'ithah 'alā 'l-fi'l*) on the one hand, and as itself active (*fā'ilah*) or actuator on the other. As the arouser of action it directs movement attracted by what it considers beneficial or harmful. When attracted by what it imagines to be something beneficial to it, its desire for it arouses its active power to attain it. When attracted by what it considers to be harmful to it, its aversion for it arouses its active power to avoid or overcome it. It is appetitive (*nuzū'iyyah*), and its activity is directed by two sub-faculties: the faculty of desire (*al-shahwāniyyah*), and the faculty of anger (*al-ghaḍabiyyah*). *As* actuator it initiates and communicates movement starting the operation of the nerves, muscles, tendons, and ligaments towards fulfilling its purpose in accordance with what it desires or opposes.[138]

As for the perceptive power, this comprises the five external senses (*al-ḥawāss*) in the developmental order of touch, smell, taste, sight, and hearing respectively. These perform the function of perception of particulars in the external world. In addition to these there are five internal senses which perceive internally the sensual images and their meanings, combine or separate them, conceive notions of them, preserve the conceptions thus conceived, and per-

---

[138] *Ma'ārij*, p. 37 fol.; *Shifā'*, p. 33; *Najāt*, pp. 197–198.

form intellection of them.[139]

The perceptive powers of the internal senses may be classified into three kinds: some perceive but do not retain their objects; some retain objects but do not act upon them; some perceive their objects and act upon them. Perception is either of the form or the meaning (i.e. the intention or denotation) of the sensible objects; and the senses that retain their objects either retain their forms or their meanings; and those that act upon their objects act upon their forms or their meanings. The perceiver sometimes perceives directly and sometimes indirectly through another perceptive power. The difference between the form and the meaning is that the form is what is first perceived by the external sense, and then by the internal sense; the meaning is what the internal sense perceives of the sensed object without its having been previously perceived by the external sense. In the act of perception, the perceiver perceives the *form* of the external object, that is, an *image* or *representation* of the external reality, and not the reality itself. What is perceived by the senses is then not the external reality, but its like as represented in the senses. The external reality is that from which the senses abstract its form. Similarly, with regard to the meaning, the intelligible forms are representations of realities that are imprinted upon the soul, because the intellect has already abstracted them from the accidental attachments that are foreign to their natures, such as quantity, quality, space, and position.[140]

The existence of the internal senses is established by way of intuition (*al-wijdān*) .[141] The first of these internal

139 *Ma'ārij, p.* 41; *Shifā',* pp. 33–34; *Najāt,* p. 198.

140 *Ma'ārij,* pp. 44–45; *Najāt,* pp. 200–201.

141 The term *wijdān* is used by al-Ghazālī in the *Ma'ārij* (p. 45). Here it is understood in its general sense as intuition based on introspection.

senses receives the information brought in by the external senses and combines and separates internal images or representations of the external sensible objects. It is the common sense (*al-ḥiss al-mushtarak*),[142] also called the phantasy (*fanṭāsiā*). The common sense directly receives the data of the five external senses. It is necessary that the external sensible objects be first present to the external senses before they can be perceived by the common sense. It perceives only their individual sensible particulars, and not their intelligible universals, and it is able to sense pleasure and pain, both as perceived in the imagination as well as in the external sensible objects. It gathers together the sensed forms, combining and separating similar and dissimilar forms so as to make perception possible. This perception of forms, which are internal images or representations of the sensed objects, is called phantasy, and its recorder is the sensitive imagination (*al-khayāl*) or the representative faculty (*al-khayāliyyah*). The common sense, it may be further noted, only receives the data provided by the external senses, gathering together similar as well as dissimilar ones, but does not retain what it receives.

The function of recording and retaining the images or forms of the external objects received by the common sense belongs to the second internal sense called the representative faculty which we just mentioned. This faculty retains the images representing the external objects when the objects are no longer present to the external senses, and thus records the information received by the common sense

---

[142] *I.e.* an internal sense common to all the five external senses. It unites the sensations of all the senses in a general sensation or perception. On *al-ḥiss al-mushtarak*, see *Al-Shifā'*, pp. 145 fol. The Latin translation is *communis sensus*, from which the term 'common sense' is derived. Here, then, common sense is used as a technical term, and not in its general everyday usage as something quite evident or obvious.

from the external senses and preserves their images, their individual and collective meanings, and representations already existing therein for presentation to the third internal sense, which is the estimative faculty (*al-wahmiyyah*).

This faculty perceives of the individual, sensible particulars, their particular, nonsensible meanings, like enmity and love, and performs the function of judgement concerning right and wrong and good and bad pertaining to its objects as if they were sensible objects of the external world. The estimation is where judgements and opinions are formed, and unless governed by the intellect it and the imaginative powers related to it are the sources of errors of judgement.[143] By means of this faculty, for example, the soul denies the intellectual substances that are not bounded nor located; by it the soul affirms the existence of a void encompassing the universe; and by it also the soul is made to accept the validity of syllogisms based on sophistical premises and to differ in the arrival at the conclusion. The estimative faculty presides over judgements not in the analytical way that characterizes intellectual judgements, but in the imaginative way determined by memory images through a process of association from past experience, or not by memory images, but by an instinctive interpretation of the image perceived by the soul without going through any process of association from past experience.[144]

Just as the representative faculty conserves forms which it receives from the common sense, the fourth internal sense, called the retentive and recollective faculty (*al-ḥāfiẓah* and *al-dhākirah*), retains meanings and conserves them for the estimative faculty which perceives these meanings. The retentive faculty retains particular meanings and memorizes them for close inspection and appraisal by the

---

143 *Mishkāt*, p. 47.
144 *Ma'ārij*, p. 46.

perceiver for so long as they remain in it. When they become absent from retention and the perceiver wishes to recall them, then it is called the recollective faculty. The relation of the retentive faculty to meanings is like the relation of the representative faculty to sensible things whose images are formed in the common sense.

The fifth internal sense is the imaginative faculty (*al-mutakhayyilah*). It perceives forms, then combines and separates them in an act of classification; adds to them and takes away from them so that the soul may perceive their meanings and connect them with the forms or images. It is the natural disposition of this faculty to perform the function of appraisal in orderly or non-orderly fashion, so that in that way the soul may use it to formulate any order it pleases. The soul uses this faculty for the purpose of classification by means of combining and separating its objects, sometimes through the practical reason and sometimes through the theoretical reason. Its essential nature is to perform the function of combining and separating, and not of perception. When the soul uses it as an intellectual instrument it is cogitative; and when it is used according to its natural disposition it is imaginative. The soul perceives what this faculty combines and separates of the forms through the mediacy of the common sense as well as through the mediacy of the estimative faculty. In its developed form this faculty apprehends ideas beyond the spheres of sense and sensual images. It is a specifically human faculty not found in the lower animals. By means of this faculty are established principles of necessary and universal application.

The fifth internal sense, then, has a dual function which is related to the animal and the human souls respectively. In this sense, this faculty has two aspects: an aspect to the senses, and an aspect to the intellect. In the former case it receives sensual forms as the sense perceives it, that is either as a reality or as something metaphorical. As a reality it presents the form as it is in itself; as a metaphor it presents the form not as it is in itself, but as the form is seen by it to be as it is in itself, for example, a mirage. In the latter case it receives the intelligible forms as the cogitative faculty apprehends it, that is, as true or false. As something true it is the form as it really is; as something false it is the form not as it really is, but as the form is perceived by it to be as it really is, for example, magic or heresy, or any other erroneous judgement of facts.[145] In relation to the animal soul it is the faculty of sensitive imagination (*al-mutakhayyal*) which is productive of technical and artistic skills; in relation to the human soul it is the faculty of rational imagination (*al-mufakkirah*). In relation to the human, rational soul this faculty is cogitative. It functions as the manager of the data of theoretical reason, combining and arranging them as premises from which it deduces informing knowledge.

Then from this knowledge it derives conclusions, and from two such conclusions it derives another and combines them yet again acquiring new conclusions and so on.[146]

These then are the five internal senses explained in a brief and general way. With reference to their classification into three kinds we may now identify them: the perceiver of forms is the common sense, and its conserver is the imagination or representative faculty. The perceiver of meanings is the estimation, and its conserver is the retentive and recollective faculty. That which perceives and acts upon its objects is the imaginative faculty, while that which only perceives and does not act upon its objects is the estimation and the common sense. These internal senses do not have specific sense organs as intermediary instruments performing specific functions like those of the external senses, but they are of an imaginal and intellectual nature and have connections with physical intermediaries, and their various functions are localized in the anterior, posterior, and middle

---

145 *Ma'ārij*, p. 77.

146 *Ibid*, pp. 45–47.

regions of the brain.[147]

The faculties of the soul are not separate entities each acting differently apart from the soul itself. They appear to be so and perform different functions some of them prior in time to others not because they are essentially different from each other, but because of the localization of functions through different organs, and whose functions become actualized at different times, and due to the different states in which the soul is involved. In this respect, the faculties of the soul are in reality the soul itself as it manifests itself in accordance with its various modes.

The human, rational soul also possesses two powers which are both aspects of the same intellect. One of these is active (*'āmilah*), and the other cognitive (*'ālimah*). In so far as it functions as the active intellect it is the principle of movement of the human body. It is the practical reason, and directs individual actions in agreement with the theoretical faculty of the cognitive intellect. In relation to the motive power of the animal soul, which is responsible for the exertion of willing that desire or aversion shall issue in action, it produces human emotions. In relation to the perceptive power and its representative, estimative, and imaginative faculties it manages physical objects and produces human skills and arts; and in relation to its faculty of rational imagination it gives rise to premises and conclusions. In so far as it governs and manages the human body it induces ethical behaviour in man involving the recognition of vices and virtues.[148]

The soul may be considered as having two aspects in relation to receiving and giving-effects: an aspect towards what is lower in degree than itself, such as the body; and an aspect towards what is higher in degree than itself, such as the world of spirit whence it originated. In connection with

---

147 *Ma'ārij*, pp. 47–48; *Shifā'*, pp. 145–150.

148 *Ma'ārij*, pp. 49–50; *Shifā'*, p. 185; *Najāt*, pp. 202–203.

what it receives from what is above it for its benefit and its action, it is a recipient of effects; and in connection with what is below it, the soul cannot be a recipient, but a giver of effects.[149] From this aspect of the soul that inclines towards what is lower issues ethical principles and the notion of vices and virtues for the guidance of the body; and from the aspect that looks to what is higher it receives knowledge. As a recipient of the creative power of knowledge through intellection and intuition it is the cognitive intellect. The power of the cognitive intellect is speculative (*naẓariyyah*). It is predisposed to the management of universal forms absolutely separated from matter; its purpose is the abstraction of intelligibles from matter, space, and position; it acts upon concepts of concepts such as the secondary intelligibles (*al-ma'qulat al-thāniyah*).[150] If the universal forms are not completely separated from matter, but are separated only in various degrees of separation which still have material connections, such as concepts of objects of the external world or the primary intelligibles (*al-ma'qūlāt al-ūlā*),[151] then it will effect their absolute separation by means of abstraction. If the universal forms are in themselves abstract, then it takes them as they are.

The process of abstraction of sensibles to intelligibles, which is in reality an epistemological process towards the arrival at meaning, undergoes various grades of completion leading to perfection. It begins already in the initial act of perception by sense; then it attains to a slightly higher degree of completion by means of the imagination, and a more refined one by the estimation even before attaining to

---

149 *I.e.* effects that are good or those that are bad. See the three degrees of the soul mentioned in pp. 146–147 above.

150 *I.e.* like the concept 'rational animal' as derived from another concept 'man'.

151 *I.e.* like the concept 'man' as corresponding to a particular, existent human being.

complete and perfect abstraction by the intellect.[152]

The sensible, particular forms that have already been imprinted in the estimation, imagination, and sensation before the arrival of intelligible, universal forms in the intellect, reside in physical entities representing perceptive powers and faculties whose functions are localized in the body. When these forms are present in these faculties and are retained by their conservers, they serve as intellectual forms, or forms whose complete abstraction requires the exercise of the intellect. As to the relation of the intellect to the rational imagination, the contents of the imagination serve the intellect as potential intelligibles, becoming actual intelligibles when the intellect appraises them; not in the sense of being transformed into another form from their state of potentiality in the imagination, or of being transferred therefrom, for they remain as they are in the imagination and maintain their character as images. Only that when the intellect appraises the images, they produce an effect like the effect that comes about when light falls upon sensible things enveloped in darkness making them visible. Thus the actual intelligibles are something else other than the forms of the imagination, which only serve to generate other forms in the intellect when the intellect appraises them, that is, considers, compares and analyses them, and then abstracts them from their material attachments and arrives at their universal meanings. The intellect first distinguishes their essential natures from their accidental attachments, their similar and dissimilar characteristics, then from the many meanings in the similars it is able to arrive at their single universal meaning; and from the similar meaning in each of the dissimilars it is able to arrive at their multiple meanings. The intellect then has the power of deriving many meanings

---

152 See *Ma'ārij,* pp. 61–62; *Shifā',* pp. 50–51 fol; *Najāt,* pp. 207–210.

from the single, and a single meaning from the many. This intellective activity becomes manifest in our formulation of the logical divisions of genus, species, and differentia; the formulation of our syllogisms that enable us to arrive at conclusions; the formulation of definitions.[153]

In respect of its being a recipient of effects from what is above it, the speculative power of the cognitive intellect has many relations and operations. It is not a merely passive recipient, for that which is a recipient of something else is a recipient in terms of power and act.[154]

Power is meant in three ways in terms of priority and posteriority: as absolute potency (*al-isti'dād al-muṭlaq*); as possible (*mumkinah*) or possessive (*malakah*); and as perfection (*kamāl*) . Absolute potency is the state of being mere potentiality capable of receiving effects; it is pure power without the act, like the power in the child to write. As the child grows and develops into a youth, the power in the potentiality of receiving effects becomes gradually actualized by means of the instrument of actualization to that extent which is possible for him to receive at this stage without need of the mediacy of any physical instrument.[155] He now knows how to use the ink, and the pen; and understands the simple letters thus possessing the capacity to write them. Then when he becomes an adult, the power becomes actualized completely by means of the instrument of actualization, such that he can act whenever he pleases without need of acquisition, but that it is sufficient for him merely to intend the act and he acts, like the power in the writer who has reached consummation in his skill and knowledge when he is not writing. Indeed, it is the intellect that is the agent or

---

153 *Shifā'*, pp. 208–211; *Ma'ārij*, p. 126.

154 *Ma'ārij*, p. 51; *Shifā'*, p. 39; *Najāt*, p. 204.

155 Without need of the mediacy of any physical instrument, because the real instrument of actualization is the intellect, as we state presently.

instrument of actualization of the power that lies in potentiality in the various stages of human development from infancy to maturity.[156]

The relations and operations of the speculative power of the cognitive intellect involve four aspects of the intellect governing the stages of human intellectual development from mere potency to perfect actualization. The first aspect is called the material intellect (*al-'aql al-hayūlānī*). It is so called by way of analogy with the Greek concept of primary matter (*al-hayūlā:* Greek *hylê*), which is pure matter without form, but capable of receiving all forms. There is, however, a difference between the Greek concept of primary matter and the material intellect we speak of here; and that is that while primary matter is capable of receiving *all* forms, the material intellect is capable of receiving only forms that its particular potentiality or power is capable of receiving and this latent capacity is not the same for every individual.[157] The second aspect is the possible intellect (*al-'aql al-mumkin*) or the possessive intellect (*al-'aql bi'l-malakah*), which is able, by means of the power that has become activated in it, to receive from the primary intelligibles the first principles established by premises upon which rest self-evident truths, that is, those obtained not by means of deduction nor by verification, but necessarily—such as apprehension of the truth in the statement that the whole of something is greater than the parts, or that things equal to one and the same thing are equal to one another. Related to the material intellect, this intellect is active, for while the former has only the power without the act such that nothing can issue forth from it, nor has the instrument of actualization ever been achieved by it, it is the latter intellect that is the agent for bringing forth what is potential in the former in accordance with the power

---

[156] *Ma'ārij,* p. 91; *Shifā',* pp. 39–40; *Najāt,* p. 204.

[157] See below p. 163 and note 160.

to produce that is possible in itself at this stage. Related to the possessive intellect, this intellect that is in action makes possible for the former the reception of speculative forms from the primary intelligibles, by means of which it becomes possible for the former to arrive at the secondary intelligibles. The possessive intellect does not appraise these forms or give insights into their true natures, but merely acts as their repository. In this respect the intellect is possessive because it is able to possess and conserve the forms for further action by what comes after it. At this level, it is again the intellect-in-action that appraises the speculative forms by its act; it performs intellection of them, and perceives that it performs the intellection. It is called the intellect-in-action (*al-'aql bi'l-fi'l*) because it is the agent for bringing forth by act, and it performs intellection whenever it pleases without need of the effort of acquisition. In relation to what comes after it, the intellect-in-action may be called the potential intellect(*al-'aql bi'l-quwwah*); for the active nature of the intellect, in relation to its capacity to act absolutely, appraises further the forms present in it by means of act, and by the same means it performs intellection of them and further performs intellection of its intellection. At this stage of its actualization it is called the acquired intellect (*al-'aql al-mustafād*). It is called acquired because it perceives clearly that when the potential intellect passes over into absolute actuality, it does so by virtue of an intellect that is always in act, and that when this intellect that is always in act makes a specific contact with the potential intellect, it imprints into the latter a specific form, so that the intellect acquires these forms from outside itself.[158]

From the foregoing it becomes clear that there are three stages through which the human intellect passes in its intellectual development from pure potentiality to actuality.

---

[158] *Ma'ārij*, p. 52; *Shifā'*, pp. 39–40; *Najāt*, p. 205

The first stage is that of the material intellect, which is nothing but a pure potency of receiving intelligible forms. When its dormant state is activated by intelligible impressions coming from the intellect-in-action, it becomes possible for it to possess the intelligible forms without actually thinking upon them. At this stage the material intellect has imprinted upon it the intelligible forms and becomes their conserver. It is no longer in a state of absolute potentiality; it is now a possible intellect possessing principles of knowledge. This is the second stage. Then when at this stage of the possible intellect, it is again activated by the intellect-in-action, it appraises the intelligible forms imprinted upon it. When it has all the speculative forms and acquisition ceases, the possible intellect passes into a state of settled tendency to think upon them. Its former state of relative potentiality has now become perfected potentiality. At this stage the possible intellect as intellect-in-action becomes capable of performing the act of thinking by itself, and the tendency to do so has become habitual to it. This is the third stage wherein the possible intellect becomes the possessive intellect. These developmental stages are common in all mankind, but in some cases there is indeed a fourth stage. When the possessive intellect actually reflects upon its own contents, that is, when it thinks, and thinks the thought it is thinking, it has reached the stage of absolute actuality and becomes the acquired intellect.

Since the potential intellect cannot by itself become actual, the actualization of the human intellect from absolute potentiality to absolute actuality presupposes the existence of an external intelligence which is always in act and which transforms the human intellect from the state of pure latency to that of perfect actuality. This external intelligence is the Active Intelligence (*al-'aql al-fa'āl*) identified as the Holy Spirit (*al-rūḥ al-qudus*),[159] and ultimately as God. In

---

159 *Ma'ārij*, p.124. Al-Ghazālī adduces as proof of the identity of

relation to the human intellect, the Active Intelligence is the intellect-in-action which rouses the potential material intellect from its state of dormancy by activating in it the thought of universal forms and eternal truths thereby transforming it into the possible intellect. Then, becoming more and more actualized (*i.e.* as the possessive intellect) by means of the illumination which it receives from the intellect-in-action, the human intellect becomes capable of self-intellection (*i.e.* the stage of the acquired intellect) and resembles the Active Intelligence. In relation to the Active Intelligence, the acquired intellect is like the potential material intellect, becoming transformed into a higher form when it receives illumination from the former. Thus the human intellect may be classified as follows:

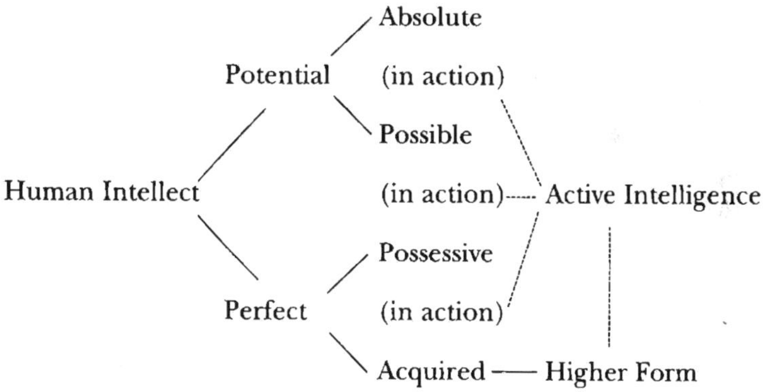

These, then, are the various degrees of power in the relations and operations of the speculative nature of the cognitive intellect. In this we see that the consummation of the animal genus and the human species is accomplished in the acquired intellect. Now this acquired intellect attains to

---

the Active Intelligence the Sacred Texts: *Al-Najm* (53): 5–6; *Al-Shūrā* (42): 51; and *Al-Takwīr* (81): 19–20; *Ma'ārij*, p.123.

higher forms of intellect graded in various degrees of excellence. In relation to the higher planes of existence, the acquired intellect is none other than the holy intellect (*al-'aql al-qudsī*), which characterizes the intellects of the prophets, the saints, and the learned who are established in knowledge, each according to their various degrees of excellence. Although the human soul is common in mankind it differs in potency,[160] and it differs in individuals due to differences in the accidents that make up every personality; and the potential power in the material intellect is therefore not equal in capacity for everyone. The potency in the intellect is ordered according to nobility of soul, the highest being that of the Holy Prophet.[161]

The intellect is essentially a spiritual substance; it is non-material and separate from matter and only its act is connected with matter. A material or physical entity such as a body can neither receive nor contain intelligibles; nor can intelligibles reside in a body because a physical entity is divisible, and whatever resides in it is also divisible. Since the intelligible is a single, universal form it is indivisible, and it is impossible for it to reside in bodily entities.[162] Intelligible forms, and even forms of the cognitive imagination, have no physical repository. The internal senses in the body receive only sensible, particular forms whose images and meanings are conserved in the representative and the retentive or recollective faculties which serve the imaginative powers. If the soul, which does not retain such forms, wishes to review rational concepts pertaining to them necessitating a reconsideration of the forms through the medium of these faculties, it merely has to recall them as they exist in their repositories. If, however, they no longer exist in their repositories

---

160 *Al-Baqarah* (2): 286; *Al-A'rāf* (7): 42; *Al-Mu'minūn* (23): 62.

161 *Ma'ārij*, p. 53; *Shifā'*, pp. 212–220.

162 *Ma'ārij*, p. 123. *Najāt*, pp. 213–216.

then their reappraisal by the rational soul necessitates a process of reacquisition. As for the intelligible forms, the intellect utilizes their meanings after they have been imprinted in it. It does not possess the actual intelligible realities themselves, as they are contained neither in the body nor in any physical entity as we have already stated, nor in the soul because if they were the soul would have been aware of them; and its being aware of them simply means the act of intellection by the rational soul or intellect, and this refers to their forms or meanings as imprinted in it, not to the intelligible realities themselves. Since these intelligible realities are neither in the body nor in the soul, they must be external to them. Their separate existence external to them means either their being self-subsistent entities, or entities inhering in a substance whence they originate and whose predisposition is to imprint intelligible forms in the human soul. It is not possible for them to be self-subsistent, for intelligible realities inhere in a substance; and thus it follows that their repository and source of origin is that substance we call the Active Intelligence.[163]

The relation of the Active Intelligence to the soul is like that of the sun to the eye.[164] Without light coming from the sun, the eyes in darkness remain as potential organs of vision; and the objects of sight remain potentially visible. Only when the sun sheds its light do the eyes become actually seeing, and their objects become actual visibles. So in like manner does the potential intellect become actual intellect, and the potential intelligibles become actual intelligibles by means of the light that is shed by the Active Intelligence upon the soul. When the intellective power of the soul - that is, the potential intellect - appraises the par-

---

163 *Ma'ārij,* p.124.

164 *Ma'ārij,* p.125; *Shifā',* p. 208; *Najāt,* p. 231. See also above, pp. 157–158.

ticulars in the imagination, this act of appraisal puts it in a state of readiness to receive the universal intelligible from the Active Intelligence by way of illumination. The arrival at the meanings of the particular images whose material attachments have all been abstracted by the illumination of the Active Intelligence is due to an immediate apprehension in the soul or intellect caused by the illumination that comes directly from the Active Intelligence. The elements of meanings that are in the images are then not the cause of the production of their like in the intellect. The action of the Active Intelligence upon the potential intellect, causing the latter's immediate apprehension which transforms it into an actual intellect, is very much like the immediate apprehension arrived at by the intellect of the necessary connection between the premises and the conclusion in a syllogism. The activity of the soul in the appraisal of the particulars is then simply to bring itself to a state of readiness to receive the intelligibles from the Active Intelligence.[165]

In relation to the soul, the intellect is a faculty or power of the soul that becomes manifest in man as the rational soul. This intellective power is something different from the rational soul, since the active agent is the soul, and the intellect is in this respect its instrument, like the knife and the cutting. But in reality intellect, soul, and mind, point to the same entity, being called intellect because the entity is perceptive; being called soul because the entity governs the body; being called mind because the entity is predisposed to the apprehension of realities.

The human soul, though independent of the body, yet requires the body in this physical world in order to acquire principles of ideas and beliefs. By means of its relationship with the body, the rational soul makes use of the animal powers to gain, among the data supplied to it by the senses,

---

[165] *Ma'ārij*, p. 125; *Shifā'*, p. 208.

the particulars. Through the particulars it acquires, among other things, four informing matters:

(1) The isolation of single universals from particulars by way of abstraction of their meanings from matter and from material connections and connective relations; and consideration of the common and differentiating factors in their essential and accidental existence. Through this process the soul acquires the principles of ideas by utilizing the imagination and the estimation, such as the genus and the differentia, the general and the particular accident.[166]

(2) The establishment of comparative relations and ratios between the single universals in the manner of negation and affirmation.

(3) The acquisition of empirical premises, which are obtained by means of the senses through sensible experience, and by means of the process of reasoning from parallel cases, or analogy, through repeated observation.

(4) Reports that are successively transmitted on which rest true beliefs.[167]

We have thus far been explaining in a brief and general way the soul's intellective activity in the course of its

---

166 A genus is a class of objects of knowledge more extensive than the species; for example, 'animal'. A differentia is a property distinguishing a species from other species of the same genus; for example, 'rational' from the genus 'animal'. An accident is an occurrence, a happening, an event, an essential property of substance that is continually being replaced by similars. A particular accident is an inseparable accident of a class of objects, such as the 'blackness' of crows. A general accident is a separable accident which allows some members of a class to differ from other members of the same class, such as the 'white' or 'fat' horses from the 'black' or 'lean' horses; it equally allows a thing to differ from itself at different times, as it happens in all cases of things that grow and decay.

167 *Ma'ārij*, pp. 101–102; *Shifā'*, p. 197; *Najāt*, pp. 220–221.

cognitive involvement in the material and intelligible domains of existence, the world of gross matter and the world of pure ideas. We pointed out that this activity consists in the abstraction of matter and its attendant attachments by means of its external and internal senses and of the intellect. Since we said that the soul is a spiritual substance independent of the body, and since this explanation of the soul's intellective activity and cognitive involvement pertains to the worlds of matter and intellect, of body and mind, it may be erroneously construed that when the body no longer lives the soul simply reverts to a purely intellectual world of utter abstraction.[168] But the soul's consciousness of itself is not only something intellectual in nature, it is something imaginal as well; and this means that not only the intellective power of the soul, but the imaginative power also survive

---

168 The psychology of the human soul sketched in the foregoing pages, which we have paraphrased from the *Ma'ārij* of al-Ghazālī, has largely been derived by al-Ghazālī from the *Shifā'* and the *Najāt* of ibn Sīnā as indicated in the reference notes. However, al-Ghazālī has added important modifications of his own. He has in fact also given a résumé of the theory of the philosophers on the animal and rational powers of the soul in his *Tahāfut* (Cairo, 1321H., pp. 70–71), saying that what they affirmed does not contradict religion - on the contrary, religion lends its support to their theory in this matter. Only their claim with regard to the primacy of the intellect as the sole guide to knowledge of the ultimate nature of reality is disputed (*Tahāfut,* p. 71). Religion, apart from stressing the cognitive role of the intellect (*'aql*) emphasizes no less the role of the heart (*qalb*) as a spiritual organ of cognition. The heart, also called *fu'ād,* is the organ of spiritual perception (see for example in the Holy Qur'ān, *Al-Najm* (53): 11). This spiritual perception, which is of the nature of perceptive experience and tasting, is connected with the imaginative faculty of the soul. See the schema of the soul on p. 176 below.

physical death. Imagination is a cognitive power of the soul. We are not here referring to that aspect of the imagination that is called phantasy, but to a spiritual or intelligential 'creative' imagination reflective of a real world of images (*'ālam al-mithāl*) ontologically existing independently between the world of gross matter and the world of pure ideas. This intermediary world reflects realities in the world of pure intelligibles which are in turn projected by it in the form of imperfect reflections in the world of sense and sensible experience.[169] The things in the world of images, which are reflections of realities in the intelligible world, exist in reality, their nature as images being neither purely intelligible nor grossly material. Images, like those in the dream state, have form and extension and quantity, and yet they are not material; they partake of both aspects of reality, the material and the intelligible, but are in nature neither the one nor the other. They are thus unlike the Platonic Ideas which are pure abstractions of the intellect.[170] Thus when we speak of the intellect's abstraction of matter and its accidental attach-

---

169 The world of images or *'ālam al-mithāl* corresponds in theological terms to the *barzakh,* that is, an intermediary world into which he who dies enters and remains for a period from the time of death to resurrection.

170 The idea of a real world of images (*'ālam al-mithāl*) and the science of symbolism pertaining to the interpretation of the reflections of that world in our world of sense and sensible experience, have their roots in al-Ghazālī and perhaps also in ibn Sīnā. In the *Ma'ārij,* al-Ghazālī has given an elaborate though concise explanation of the powers of the imagination (pp. 135–145; see also pp. 125–134). This was developed in Muslim metaphysical thinking especially by ibn 'Arabī, who derived many of his interpretations on the nature of reality from the writings of al-Ghazālī. See further the *Mishkāt* of al-Ghazālī, which is a profound commentary on the Verse of Light in the Sacred Text, and the conclusion to 'Afīfī's general introduction to the *Mishkāt,* pp. 34–35. See also ibn 'Arabī,

ments, it should not be understood thereby to mean that the soul effects a complete denudation of forms in the intelligibles; it is the *materiality* in matter that is abstracted by the intellect, and not the *imaginality* as well, for images are not matter and materiality does not pertain to them. The imagination that we mean, which is a cognitive faculty or power of the soul, like intellect, is immaterial, and therefore does not 'contain' the images. When we speak of intelligible forms being 'in' the mind, or images being 'in' the cognitive imagination, we do not mean that these forms or images are 'contained' in them; it is rather that they are *constructions* of the intellect or mind during the course of its intellection of them such that they are 'present' to the intellect, and hence referred to as being 'in' the mind; and *productions* of the cognitive imagination as it involves itself in projecting the sensible world.

In our present state, the intellect's inability to conceive or perceive abstract entities is not due to its essential nature, nor is it due to the nature of the abstract entities, but rather it is due to its own preoccupation with the body which is needed by it as we have mentioned. This being engrossed with the affairs of the body prevents it from perceiving the abstract realities in their original nature because the body acts as an obstruction. When, however, consciousness of the body and of the subjective self or ego is subdued, the intellect will be able to make contact with the Active Intelligence and will then be capable of perceiving the abstract realities as they are.[171]

Unlike the intellect, which undergoes a transformation from a state of potentiality to that of actuality, the imagination is from the beginning active. That aspect of the imagination whose powers are directed towards the world of

---

Fuṣūṣ, Cairo, 1946, pp. 99–104; and 'Afifi's *ta'līqāt* to the *Fuṣūṣ,* pp. 74–76; 105–118.

171 *Ma'arij,* p.127; see also *Najāt,* pp. 219–220.

sense and sensible experience is the sensitive imagination or phantasy. It serves the practical intellect by providing it with the forms or images and meanings of particular objects of knowledge. It is also the source of fictitious productions. In contrast to the sensitive imagination, that aspect of the imagination whose powers are directed towards the realms of the intellect and the spiritual realities is the cognitive imagination, which is capable of reflecting the forms of the real world of images. However, because of the intermediary position of the world of images, and due to the dual function of the imagination that is aligned to it, being involved in the operation of its powers both with the sensible and intelligible realms, the imagination cannot preoccupy itself with its own world of real images without distraction. [172]

We said in a note that the heart (*qalb*) *is* a subtile organ of cognition connected with the imaginative faculty of the soul. It is like a mirror that is ever-turning in different directions. When forms appear in front of it their images are reflected therein. The forms themselves remain always in their places outside the mirror, so that they are not transferred therein to the extent that the mirror may contain them. Only their images are reflected in the mirror. In like manner also, only when the mirror of the heart is turned towards the right direction without being distracted towards any other, and provided that it is not deficient in its reflective power and has achieved pellucid quality will the human soul be able to perceive clearly the real and true forms of the intelligential and spiritual realm.[173] Imagine yourself to be inside an opaque sphere. This sphere is within another such sphere, and that other within yet another one, all having each a single aperture. Now all these spheres are turning, rotating in different directions. Only when you have the

---

[172] *Ma'arij*, p.137.
[173] *Ma'ārij*, p. 93.

power to make the spheres turn and rotate in such a way that their apertures would come in a line of conjunction with each other will the light from outside shine through, enabling you to see both what is within and without.

The power of imagination is not equal in men and differs according to their degrees of intellectual excellence and nobility of soul. In some it is stronger than in others, so that some may be able to see true visions of that intermediary world and others may not. We who affirm prophecy cannot deny the possibility that the forms of the world of images that are reflected in the cognitive imagination may get imprinted in the sensitive imagination or phantasy to the extent that the perceiver of these forms may actually see them in their sensible guise. Indeed, in the case of the Holy Prophet, for example, his cognitive imagination was so powerful that he was able to perceive intelligible realities in their sensible forms (*e.g.* the Angel in the form of a man); and sensible realities in their intelligible forms (*e.g.* the dead as alive in the other world).[174]

The function of the imagination is then to create sensible things, or rather it is the soul itself that creates sensible things and perceptible forms from within itself as well as images of unperceived objects. The thinking and feeling entity to which perception, whether sensitive, imaginative and intellective, is attributed is then in reality not the external and internal senses, but the soul itself exercising its cognitive powers of intelligence and imagination. The soul is therefore not something passive; it is creative, and through perception, imagination and intelligence it participates in the 'creation' and interpretation of the worlds of sense and sensible experience, of images, and of intelligible forms or ideas.

The soul, according to a tradition of the Holy Prophet,

---

[174] *Ma'ārij,* p.78.

is created before the body,[175] meaning it existed long before the body. Some commentators think that the word for 'body' (sing. *jasad*) applied in the tradition, does not refer to organic bodies such as the human body, but rather to celestial or physical bodies. As for the word for 'spirit' (sing. *rūḥ*) occurring in the same tradition and understood as referring to the soul, they say that it refers to angelic entities. Their view in this matter reflects their position which amounts to a denial of the pre-existence of the soul, and seems to have originated from the position taken by ibn Sīnā, who argued according to the principles of physics, that it is impossible for the soul to exist before the body. Its pre-existence according to those principles entails either its being a simple unity or a plurality, both of which are impossible. Moreover, ibn Sīnā's argument against the pre-existence of the soul is directed against the doctrine of metempsychosis (*al-tanāsukh*).[176] Some Muslim thinkers and writers seem to have taken such arguments as conclusive and deny the pre-existence of the soul. As for the passage in the Holy Qur'ān referring to the creation of man where God says that after having fashioned him (*i.e.* formed him as body), He breathed into him of His spirit,[177] this does not demonstrate conclusively that the existence of the body is prior to that of the soul. It can also be interpreted that the spirit that was breathed into the body already implied the soul's pre-exis-

---

175 This is a well known *hādīth* also reported in *Ma'ārij*, p.111. Al-Ghazālī, however, has given an interpretation of it aligned with the position of the philosophers who, following Aristotle, maintained that every soul is created to suit a particular body, thereby denying the pre-existence of the soul. But this position, as we will state presently, appears to have no real cogency and if so must be regarded as untenable.

176 *Shifā'*, pp. 198–201; 202 fol; *Najāt*, pp. 222–230. See also *Ma'ārij*, pp. 105–115.

177 *Al-Ḥijr*, (15): 29 .

tence. Moreover, in another passage in the Holy Qur'ān God says: 'It is We Who created you (*i.e.* the spirits or souls) and then We formed you (i.e. the bodies).[178] With regard to the interpretation of the term *jasad* being meant, in the tradition referred to above, to denote not the organic or human body, but the physical or celestial body, the testimony of linguistic usage demonstrates that *jasad is* synonymous with *badan,* which invariably refers to the organic and the human body; whereas a physical or celestial body is usually denoted by the term *jisim,* even though *jisim* too may be employed synonymously with *jasad.* The usual distinction between *jisim* and *jasad is,* however, that the former refers to body in the genus of quantity, whereas the latter refers to body in the genus of animal.[179]

But we do not agree with their position on the soul. Their adherence to the principles of physics in denying the pre-existence of the soul reflects the position of the essentialists or those who affirm the primacy of quiddity over existence. We maintain that their position on the soul is confused, and indeed ibn Sīnā himself seems to have contradicted his own position on the preexistence of the soul in his psychology and his oriental philosophy, where the soul's prior existence is implied.[180] We do not admit that the principles of physics must necessarily be brought to bear insofar as the nature of the soul is concerned. Moreover, we do not concede that our affirmation of pre-existence of the soul has

---

178 *Al-A'rāf,* (7): 11. More specific, *Al-A'lā* (87): 2

179 See my *Commentary on the Ḥujjat al-Ṣiddīq,* Ministry of Culture Malaysia, Kuala Lumpur, 1986, p. 330, note 463. Cp. *Lisān al 'Arab,* vol. 3, p.l20, cols. 1 & 2; vol. 12, p. 99, col. 1.

180 *E.g. al-Najāt,* p. 223; and Fazlur Rahman's commentary in *Avicenna's Psychology,* London, 1952, p. 107, with reference to Ch.XII, p. 57. See also ibn Sīnā's poem on the soul called *Al-Qaṣīdatu 'l-'Ayniyyah,* tr. by A.J. Arberry in *Avicenna's Theology,* London, 1951 pp. 77–78.

anything to do with the doctrine of metempsychosis, which - insofar as it pertains to the world - we likewise reject.[181] Nor do we admit, in affirming the soul's pre-existence in relation to the body, that we believe the soul to be necessarily eternal, for we affirm that it is created. Furthermore, in line with those who affirm the primacy of existence over quiddity, our position on the pre-existence of the soul may not simply be equated with Platonism or Neoplatonism. We say, with al-Junayd and others,[182] that the soul's pre-existence refers to a state of being unlike that of existence that is known to us, but to an existence in the interior condition of Being, in the consciousness of God. To this state of existence refer God's words in the Holy Qur'ān when He called to the souls: "Am I not your Lord?", and they answered: "Yes indeed!" [183] By virtue of the power that God gave them to respond to His call, we infer that the soul knows God as its Lord; it knows itself as His creature; it knows other souls as distinct from itself; and it possesses power to apprehend what knowledge communicates. For this reason - that is, the soul's possession of a cognitive power enabling it to identify its Lord and Creator, itself, and others like itself, and to make distinctions as well as to formulate and communicate meaningful signs by means of an innate power of speech (*i.e. nuṭq* with reference to the term *qawl*) - the soul is called the 'rational' soul.[184] This also means that the soul already has some form

---

[181] See *Tahāfut,* pp. 86–87.

[182] Junayd, *Kitāb al-Mīthāq,* pp.40–43; al-Kalābādhī, *Kitāb al-Ta'arruf;* Bayrūt, 1400/1980, p.68.

[183] *Al-A'rāf* (7): 172.

[184] *I.e. al-nafs al-nāṭiqah. Nāṭiq* signifies the reasoning powers, the rational faculty, and corresponds to the Greek *logos* and the Latin *ratio.* It points to an inner faculty that apprehends realities and formulates meaning involving judgement, discrimination and clarification. It is derived from the same Arabic root that conveys the basic meaning of 'speech', signifying a certain

of knowledge of the realms spiritual before its attachment to the body. The human body and the world of sense and sensible experience provide the soul with a school for its training to know God also, this time through the veils of His Creation.

---

power and capacity to articulate words or symbolic forms in meaningful pattern. *Manṭiq,* the Arabic word for logic, is derived from the same root and includes within its semantic structure what is conveyed by *ma'qūl,* which is the intelligible character of a thing as grasped by the mind. In this sense, *ratio* can be understood as being synonymous with *ma'qūl,* which in Latin is *intentio.* According to al-Ghazālī, this entity that we call the 'rational soul' and which we identify with that which is referred to in the Quranic passage mentioned above, signifies the second aspect of the heart (*qalb*) referred to in page 5 above. This entity is also identified by him as the spirit of man (*rūḥ*) that carries the trust (*amānah*) granted by God, and that is by nature created with the power and capacity to be the abiding center of knowledge. It is, by its saying "Yes indeed!" (*balā*), that which affirms the Divine unity. It is also the original root (*aṣl*) of mankind, to which ultimate state of existence it will return in the world to come. See *Ma'arij,* p. 17.

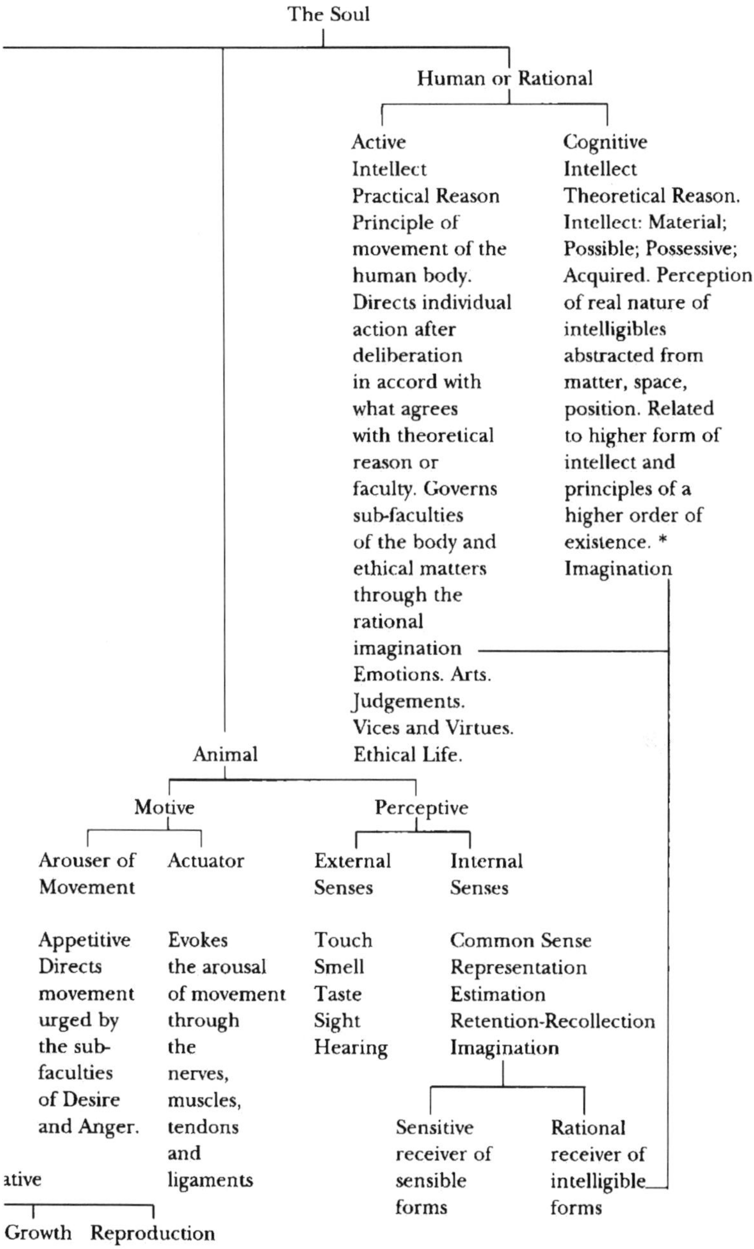
The Soul
Human or Rational
Active
Intellect
Practical Reason
Principle of movement of the human body. Directs individual action after deliberation in accord with what agrees with theoretical reason or faculty. Governs sub-faculties of the body and ethical matters through the rational imagination
Emotions. Arts. Judgements. Vices and Virtues. Ethical Life.
Cognitive
Intellect
Theoretical Reason.
Intellect: Material; Possible; Possessive; Acquired. Perception of real nature of intelligibles abstracted from matter, space, position. Related to higher form of intellect and principles of a higher order of existence. *
Imagination
Animal
Motive
Perceptive
Arouser of Movement
Actuator
External Senses
Internal Senses
Appetitive Directs movement urged by the sub-faculties of Desire and Anger.
Evokes the arousal of movement through the nerves, muscles, tendons and ligaments
Touch
Smell
Taste
Sight
Hearing
Common Sense
Representation
Estimation
Retention-Recollection
Imagination
Sensitive receiver of sensible forms
Rational receiver of intelligible forms
ative
Growth
Reproduction

V

THE INTUITION OF EXISTENCE

The metaphysical vision of the world and of the ultimate reality envisaged in Islām is quite different from that projected by the statements and general conclusions of modern philosophy and science.[185] We maintain that all knowledge of reality and of truth, and the projection of a true vision of the ultimate nature of things is originally derived through the medium of intuition.[186] The intuition that we mean cannot simply be reduced to that which operates solely at the physical level of discursive reason based upon sense-experience, for since we affirm in man the possession of physical as well as intelligential or spiritual powers and faculties which refer back to the spiritual entity, sometimes called intellect, or heart, or soul, or self, it follows that man's rational, imaginal and empirical existence must involve both the physical and spiritual levels.[187]

In the view of man at the physical level, or at the everyday, ordinary level of reason and sense experience, the world appears to him as composed of so many diverse and variegated forms, each separated from the other by its own, individual shape, size, colour and character, its own delimitation and determination as such, so that each appears to him as an independent, self-subsistent object, or entity possessed of individual reality or essence. In this view of reality

---

185 See above, chapter III.

186 Even knowledge of intelligible truths is ultimately derived from intuitive principles. See ibn Sīnā, *Kitāb al-Najāt,* (*op. cit.*), p. 206.

187 See above, chapter IV.

at this level of experience, the phenomenal world, in which man himself is included, presents itself as a world of variety and multiplicity, wherein all cognitive and volitive processes occur within the necessary framework of the subject-object dichotomy. Experience which operates at this level must involve separateness everywhere and in all things; and for this reason the men of spiritual experience and discernment call this condition that of 'separation' (*farq*) - to be sure, that of the 'first separation' (*al-farq al-awwal*) .

Calling this condition of separateness at this level of experience as that of the 'first separation' means that there is a possibility for man—depending upon his intellectual development, his religious and spiritual state of affairs, and upon God's grace— to *transcend* it and then to *return* to it, so that for him his experience of the phenomenal world *after* his return to it would then become a condition of the *'second* separation' (*al-farq al-thānī*). Indeed, for such a man, and although the same world of multiplicity in separateness confronts him again, that world is no longer seen as the same as that which he knew before, at the stage of the 'first separation' which is common to all; for during his transcending of it he experiences a verification of its true nature, he has attained to certain knowledge of its real nature in such wise that he *now,* at the stage of the 'second separation', sees it in an altogether different light. This state of transcending the 'first separation' involves a transformation in the man, without which he would continue to be bound to the ordinary level of reason and experience in his existence.

The 'separation' that we are discussing conveys in fact two connotations. The first connotation refers to the 'separation' of God or the Absolute from the world of creation in the manner as conceived by man. We say 'in the manner as conceived by man' because in reality there is no such 'separation'. Thus the condition of 'separation' is a condition made necessary by human reason and experience at the ordinary level, in which his faculties of cognition and volition perform their normal functions. The fact that this condition is called that of the '*first* separation'—apart from implying the possibility of a further condition known as that of the '*second* separation' as we have pointed out—implies also a condition *prior* to it, in which there was no such 'separation'. The terms 'first' and 'second' prefixed to 'separation' refer to the human condition at different levels of experience. In the same way, the term 'prior' prefixed to 'separation' also refers to man though not, to be sure, to the human condition. It refers to man in the spiritual condition, that is, to his pre-existent soul *before* he became man as human being. This condition of 'pre-separation' is alluded to in the Holy Qur'ān:

> 'When thy Lord drew forth from the Children of Ādam - from their loins - their descendents, and made them witness unto their selves (declaring): "Am I not your Lord?" - they said: "Yes indeed! we do witness"[188]

Al-Junayd, in explanation of this passage, says:

> In this verse God tells you that He spoke to them at a time when they did not exist, except insofar as they existed for Him. This existence is not the same type of existence as is usually attributed to God's creatures, it is a type of existence which only God knows and only He is aware of. God knows their existence, embracing them, sees them in the beginning when they are non-existent and oblivious of their future existence in this world...[189] In their timeless existence

---

[188] *Al-A'rāf* (7): 172.

[189] *Kitāb al-Fanā'*, in Ali Hassan Abdel-Kader's *The Life, Personality and Writings of al-Junayd*, London, 1976, p. 32 of the Arabic text of the *Rasā'il*. The English translation is on p. 153.

> before Him and in their state of unity with Him it is He who has granted them their being. When He called them and they answered quickly, their answer was a gracious and generous gift from Him... He gave them knowledge of Him when they were only concepts which He had conceived ....[190]

Here the souls of mankind were made to 'witness' (*ashhada*) unto their selves the actuality of God's Lordship in the sense that they *actually know by direct experience and vision* (*shuhūd*) the Reality and Truth that is revealed to them. In this way and by their own admission they had sealed a Covenant with God recognizing and acknowledging Him as their Lord (*rabb*), that is, their Absolute Possessor, Owner, Creator, Ruler, Governor, Master, Cherisher, Sustainer. Such recognition and acknowledgement, which is the fundamental basis of religion in Islām,[191] entails consciousness of the distinction between their Lord and their selves. This consciousness of distinction between Lord and servant (*'abd*), however, occurred within the spiritual context of 'union', and not the human context of 'separation'. We will have recourse to elaborate upon this subject again in due course. The second connotation refers to 'separation' in the consciousness and experience of separateness everywhere and in all things that make up the world of phenomena, as we have explained.

The view of man at the physical, or everyday, ordinary level of reason and sense experience, in which things that make up the world of multiplicity take their concrete, separate forms and identities, is the view of the generality of the people (*'awāmm*).They see only the reality of the multiplicity before them, and nothing beyond that. However, among

---

190 *Ibid, Kitāb al-Mīthāq,* pp. 40–41/160–161.

191 See above, chapter I.

people adhering to this common view of reality are those who attained to a higher degree of perception of truth. They recognize that what appears before them is not the sole reality, and that there is another, entirely different reality beyond, which they conceive theologically as God, Who is separate from the world and Whose relationship to it is that of Creator without any 'inner connection' between Him and His creation. A further extension of this dualistic view of reality is the view among philosophers, theologians and scientists that the external things of the world that comprise the world together with all its parts possess cores of self-subsistent, substantial realities or quiddities which become subjects or our knowledge because of their being qualified by their inherent property of existence. The existence of an object is seen as a quality or property of its quiddity, as if its quiddity could subsist by itself prior to its existence. In this view, a *real* distinction was made between quiddity, which they refer to as 'essence', and existence; the former conceived ontologically as real substance, the latter as a mere accident of real substance. The philosophical controversy pertaining to the problem of essence and existence, which has been brought to the fore in the West in contemporary times by the upholders of essentialism and existentialism respectively, derives its origin from this basically common view of the nature reality.

The view of reality based on the ordinary level of reason and sense experience, and the philosophical and scientific developments that evolve from it, has undoubtedly led philosophical and scientific speculations to the preoccupation with *things* and their 'essences' at the expense of *existence* itself. Seen from the perspective of Islamic metaphysics and philosophy as based on Quranic wisdom or *ḥikmah,* our position is that we do not make a real distinction between essence and existence, that is to say, we posit such distinction only in the mind, and not in the extra-mental reality itself. In the extra-mental reality itself, what is seen as the qualification of so many diverse and variegated 'essenses' by existence is in our view the multiple determinations and delimitations into particular forms of the all-embracing and pervasive Existence Itself, so that *that* by which things are what they really are, or the selves and realities of things which are their very existences, is no other than the all-encompassing reality of Existence actualizing Its multiple and diverse modes in a perpetual act of expansion and contraction in gradations from the levels of Its absoluteness to those of Its manifold determinations till It reaches the realms of sense and sensible things. A 'thing' in itself—that is, considered independently of the Reality by which it is it—is not something in a state of 'be-ing', as it is a perishing thing; what has come to 'be' is an actualization of one of the modes of the Reality in the guise of that thing, such that what we behold and consider to be the thing is that mode being actualized. Thus according to our perspective it is Existence (*wujūd*) that is the real 'essences' of things; and what is mentally or conceptually posited as 'essences' or quiddities (*māhiyyat*) are in reality accidents (*a'rāḍ*) of existence.[192]

As demonstrated by the Holy Prophet's supreme experience and by what he brought, all knowledge comes from God, and is interpreted by the soul through its physical and spiritual faculties. We have already said elsewhere that epistemologically knowledge, with reference to God as being its source of origin, is the arrival *in* the soul of the meaning of a thing or an object of knowledge; and with reference to the soul as being its interpreter, knowledge is the arrival of the soul *at* the meaning of a thing or an object of knowledge. Thus, at the rational and empirical level of ordinary experience, in which the subject-object dichotomy prevails and imposes its condition upon cognition and volition; in which the ego-consciousness of the subject necessarily confronts

---

192 A more elaborate exposition of this subject is given in chapter VI below.

the multiplicity of external objects of reason and sense experience, knowledge refers to the soul's intussusception of the *meanings* of such objects and not of the *objects themselves,* seeing that these objects are accidental in their nature and, therefore, *do not endure two durations.* There is, as we have said, another level of experience; and even at this higher, spiritual level, reason and experience remain as valid channels by which knowledge is attained, only that they are of a transcendental order. At this level the rational has merged with the intellectual, and the empirical with what pertains to authentic spiritual experiences such as 'inner witnessing' (*shuhūd*), ' tasting' (*dhawq*), 'presence' (*ḥuḍūr*) and other interrelated states of trans-empirical awareness (*aḥwāl*) . At this level knowledge means 'unification' (*tawḥīd*) of the soul with the very Truth that underlies all meaning. Here the soul not only understands, but knows reality and truth by real and direct experience. Real and direct experience consists in 'union' of the knower and the known.[193]

---

[193] At the level of ordinary reason and experience, the 'known' refers to the meaning of things, and not to the things themselves; and 'union' - if we apply such a term at that level does not mean union with the material objects of sense perception, but with their intelligible forms that have been abstracted by the intellect from all their characteristics of materiality. The elements of meaning derived by the intellect from the objects of sense perception are not found in the objects themselves, but are constructions of the intellect or soul as it receives illumination from the Active Intelligence. The material objects in the world of sense and sensible experience are in themselves particulars which the intellect transforms into universals; in themselves they merely provide the ground for the special occurrence that gives rise to the soul's projection of perceptible forms from within itself. At the higher level, 'union' of the knower and the known means the identity of thought and being or existence. Existence has different degrees, and the Absolute Existence or the Truth has a degree unique to

We have pointed out in the case of one who transcends the stage of the 'first separation', that such a one must first undergo a transformation. The transformation pertains to the subject's ego-consciousness. Knowledge as 'union' of the knower and the known can only happen when the knower's ego-consciousness, or subjective consciousness, has 'passed away' (*fanā'*). It must be noted that even at the phenomenal, empirical level of existence one comes to know that when one is engaging oneself in deep meditation or contemplation on some affair which demands one's complete attention, one is not at the same time aware of one's bodily parts. In a limited sense one's subjective consciousness, during the loss of awareness of one's bodily parts which are the main constitutents of the subjective self, is subdued because the soul is directing its concentration elsewhere. Thus when even at this level of existence in the world of sense and sensible experience we can admit of such experience as reveals some insight into the nature of the soul's power and activity in its arrival at meaning, there is no reason to suppose that that power and activity ends here and cannot transcend this level to operate at other higher and congener levels of existence about which we are now discussing.

Since the myriad and variegated forms, clearly defined as so many independent objects comprising the world of multiplicity, are seen as such by the knowing subject, the 'passing away', of the subjective consciousness necessarily involves the 'passing away' also of the forms that define the multiplicity of phenomena into separate objects of cognition and volition. But at the same time, the passing away of the forms is not altogether a subjective affairs; for the multiplic-

---

Himself, and a degree in relation to other than Himself. 'Union' refers to the latter aspect of the Truth. 'Union' with the Truth therefore means union not with the Truth as He is in Himself, but as He manifests Himself in the form of one of His Names and Attributes.

ity of existents represented by the myriad forms are themselves discontinous in their existing, so that the forms are continually perishing. Thus *fanā',* when it occurs, occurs both subjectively and objectively; it involves both the psychological and the ontological conditions of existence; it is a coincidence between the losing of the subjective consciousness which entails the losing also of the objects of that consciousness, and the actual disappearance of the objects themselves. The 'passing away' of the subjective consciousness does not necessarily entail—at least at the initial stage—the annulment of awareness in the subject of the distinction between his self as the seer and the object as the seen; the subject here is still aware of his self in being able to distinguish the seeing subject and the object seen.[194] So the subject-object relation still holds at this initial stage of *fanā',* although the transformation that he experiences, both in himself and in the multiplicity of objects, of necessity renders it to be not quite the same condition of dichotomy as the subject-object relation in the stage of the 'first-separation', wherein all things are involved in the sway of conditions at the normal, everyday level of experience. Were it not for the subject's continued awareness of his self at this initial stage of *fanā',* then such experience would not result in the attainment of certain knowledge (*ma'rifah*) of the true nature of things as he reflects and contemplates upon it later, when he returns to the sobriety of his normal, phenomenal consciousness.

At the initial stage of the 'passing away' of his subjective consciousness, then, the knower is able to 'witness' the 'passing away' of the forms that define the multiplicity of phenomena into separate objects. What the knower as seer sees is the 'gathering together' (*jam'*) of the myriad forms of the phenomenal world into a single, unified Reality. This

---

[194] Cf. ibn 'Arabī, *Fuṣūṣ al-Ḥikam,* (*op. cit.*), p. 91.

'inner witnessing' is the seeing and experiencing of Multiplicity (*kathrah*) gathered together into Unity (*waḥdah*). The tremendous inner turmoil that accompanies this overpowering vision is at the same time heightened by God's revelation of an aspect of Himself (*tajallī*) in the knower by means of one of His Names (*asmā'*) or Attributes (*ṣifāt*). God in His aspect as the Absolute Being in all the forms of manifestation is 'the Truth' (*al-ḥaqq*). It is in fact God's self-revelation in the man in that particular aspect that brings about the state of *fanā'*, that makes him naught and deprives him of consciousness of his individual existence. Ultimately, when the human light is extinguished and the creaturely spirit passes away, there would not even be a trace of consciousness left in the ego of its passing away. The man has at this stage 'passed away from the passing away' (*fanā' al-fanā'*). In exchange for what God has deprived him of, God puts in the man, without incarnation (*ḥulūl*), a spiritual substance (*laṭīfah*) which is of His Essence (*dhāt*) and is neither separate from Him nor joined to man. God's revelation of an aspect of Himself is made to that spiritual substance, named the Holy Spirit (*al-rūḥ al-qudus*),[195] for He is never revealed except to Himself. We call that substance 'a man' because it is an exchange for what God has deprived of the man, taking the man's place instead of the man. At this stage the subject-object dichotomy no longer exists.[196]

If the experience of *fanā'* ceases at this stage because the man's spiritual capacity and preparedness cannot withstand it, and when later the man, regaining his phenomenal

---

195 The Holy Spirit is in philosophical terms identified as the Active Intelligence which illumines the human soul with knowledge of the realities when the soul has attained to higher forms of the acquired intellect (see further chapter IV above).

196 Cf. 'Abd al-Kārim al-Jīlī, *Al-Insān al-Kāmil,* 2v., Cairo, 1956, vol. 1. p. 62.

consciousness, returns to the level of the human condition in which the world of multiplicity again confronts him in its myriad forms, his reflection and contemplation of the experience he has undergone, in the absence of God's guidance and succour, might convey to him the erroneous conviction that the world together with all its parts is nothing but sheer illusion. Due to his own imperfect spiritual state, and to his incomplete experience of the 'unveiling' (*kashf*), he might then believe that the separate and multiple things are mere figments of the imagination; that these particulars in existence are really what the mind conjures up, and that in reality there is no particularization in existence. He will believe that everything is in reality God in the pantheistic or even monistic sense. He thinks that God is the world and the world is God, and his self is God and God is his self. Swayed by his own, subjective vision, he has become one of those who, like him, have slipped from the Right Path and fallen into the abyss of error and heresy. Among such people also are those who are not people of genuine experience, but who derive a semblance of such knowledge from discursive reason, and then misconstrue the matter in their own imagination, without any real experience of *fanā'* or *kashf*.

But not all those who genuinely experienced incomplete 'unveiling' become involved in error and heresy. Those whom God guides and aids in persevering on the right course (i.e. the recipients of *tawfiq*) are aware of the incompleteness of their vision of Reality and Truth which they witnessed during this state of 'unveiling'; and they are aware also that the 'unveiling' itself is only an initial one, an incomplete one. While they are prone to the urge to affirm the oneness aspect of reality only, in harmony with the reality of their experience of Unity, they nevertheless confirm the truth of religion as brought by the Holy Prophet, and accept the experience of the Veracious as a truer and higher degree of spiritual attainment and discernment then theirs. They also confirm in their acts the *sunnah* of the Holy Prophet, and they acknowledge in their selves the religious distinction between 'Lord' (*rabb*) and 'servant' (*'abd*), between Creator and creature, and act in accordance with its necessary requirements. In our classification of human perception of truth and reality, theirs is to be distinguished from the generality, whose characteristic condition we have already described, as belonging to a higher degree. In the spiritual hierarchy of man, they are known as the 'elect' (*al-khawāṣṣ*) amongst God's servants and are among those constant obeyers whom God has drawn close to Himself, the genuine saints (*awliyā'*) or 'friends' of God.

In their spiritual condition, they have realized in their selves the true experience of what is called 'proverty' (*faqr*), or that 'anxious need' or condition of being in 'utter want' that stirs intense agitation and anxiety of vital magnitude, that is born out of the experience of *fanā'* followed by *fanā' al-fanā'*. In their 'passing away' they 'witnessed' the complete annullment of all phenomena in such wise that only the Aspect of God remains;[197] and in their 'passing away from the passing away' they experienced their own complete annullment; so that when they regain their individual existence and phenomenal consciousness, the realization of the truth that *only the Aspect of God remains* conveys to them such a tremendously awesome awareness of utter dependence for their existence and consciousness upon God alone. They know, by what has been realized for them, the nothingness of all things *conceived as things-in-themselves,* and they know also, by what has been realized in them, the nothingness of their subjective selves *as their own independent selves,* and so what they now know is that all 'other' (*ghayr*) than God, all 'that-which-is-other-than-God' (*mā siwā Allāh*), only appears to subsist by 'borrowed' existence. Just as the debtor, borrowing an indefinitely extended loan lives by it, and for that

---

[197] A verification of the passage in the Holy Qur'ān, *Al-Raḥmān* (55): 26–27.

living depends solely on his creditor, realizes his dire need and anxiety for the creditor's continued maintenance of the loan; even more so—nay, immeasurably more crucial in its awesome totality—when in this case the debt is that of *existence* itself; existence not only in this phenomenal world, but in that spiritual world also, to which all must in the end return. Existence is indeed God's gift, but it is in reality a gift that belongs only to God Who, as it were, 'lends' it as a 'personal' favour. Hence the recipient who is rightly guided is aware that he is in a state of being in debt to God for his existence, for he knows that it is entirely dependent upon God's existence, and realizes that it is like a 'borrowing' from Him. They who know this condition of being reduced to the state of dire need of God and anxiety speak of such 'poverty' as "a blackened face in both worlds" (*i.e. "al-faqr sawād al-wajh fī al-dārayn"*). So the self-devastating consciousness in true 'proverty' is realized when one knows by direct experience that only the Aspect of God remains, as the saying puts it: *"Idhā tamma al-faqr fa huwa Allāh"* - "When poverty is complete it is indeed God."

The highest level in the hierarchy of mankind according to spiritual degrees of perception of truth consists of the 'super elect' (*al-khawāṣṣ al-khawāṣṣ*). The experience of *fanā'*, in their case, does not cease at the stage of *fanā' al-fanā'*, as is the case with the 'elect' (*al-khawāṣṣ*). The man whose spiritual condition is perfect and mature, and who is under God's guidance, being a recipient of His aid (*tawfīq*), will be resuscitated, *while still in that state,* even before he regains his normal condition of phenomenal consciousness, from the utter oblivion of *fanā' al-fanā'*. What he has actually experienced in that state is the reality and truth that underlies the meaning of the words of the Holy Prophet: *"Kāna Allāhu wa lā shay' a ma'ahu"*—"God was, and there was nothing with Him."[198] This saying does not only refer to the

---

[198] A well known *ḥadīth* mentioned in the *Ṣaḥīḥ* of al-Bukhārī in

period of pre-creation when God alone 'existed'; it also means that God has been, is, and will continue to *be* alone, as He was (*Huwa al-āna kamā kāna*). All phenomena are *in themselves* as construed by the imagination really nothing; they are in a constant state of perishing (*fān*),[199] in which no two instants of time measure a process in their perishing, as their perishing is not a 'process' happening to the *same* phenomena. As one series of phenomena is made naught, another resembling them take their turn, and so on, so that in reality 'only the Aspect of God remains'. This is the eternal order of Being, and hence He always is as He was, with nothing subsisting besides Him. The manner of God's Aspect 'remaining' is not static; He is forever in some 'operation' (*shā'n*):[200] producing, bringing to naught the production, and reproducing. So He is, in His Aspect as the Absolute Existence, as it were, the 'Substratum' which makes possible the appearance and disappearance and reappearance of all phenomena in continuous series.

Having been resuscitated from the state of 'passing away from the passing away' without regaining his phenomenal consciousness, what he 'witnesses' next is the final 'unveiling'. We have said that in the initial 'unveiling' he 'witnesses' the 'assembling together' (*jam'*) of all forms of the phenomenal world into a single, unified Reality. He sees with a spiritual vision as if it were by ocular vision all Multiplicity gathered together into Unity. In other words, he sees the 'perishing' of all phenomena and the 'remaining' of the Reality underlying them. Now in the final 'unveiling', he 'witnesses' the single, unified Reality again taking the myriad forms of the phenomenal world without Itself

---

the chapter on the Divine Unity (*al-tawḥīd*) and the beginning of creation. Also in the *Musnad* of ibn Ḥanbal, vol.2, p. 134.

199 *Al-Raḥmān* (55): 26.

200 *Al-Raḥmān* (55): 29.

becoming multiple. He sees with a spiritual vision the Unity individuating Itself into Multiplicity without impairing Its original Unity, and yet 'connecting' or 'relating' the Multiplicity with Itself in such wise that, although the Unity takes on the forms of Multiplicity, It still distinguishes Itself from the latter and remains always in Its original nature. In other words, he sees the inner articulations of the Unity, in which the Unity is neither joined to nor separate from the Multiplicity, and which goes on in continuous operation. This continuous operation of Unity articulating Itself into Multiplicity and back again into Unity as witnessed by the spiritual adept is called the 'gathering of gathering' (*jam' al-jam'*).[201] In this state, which is no longer the same state as the previously experienced *fanā'* but the *final stage* of it, the man realizes his true selfhood and 'subsists' in God (*baqā'*).[202] His experience of *fanā' al-fanā'* is what the masters of spiritual experience and discernment call 'absorption' (*istighrāq*). In his experience of the 'gathering' and then, after utter oblivion (*istighrāq*), the 'gathering of gathering', God, out of His favour and bounty has revealed to him, as it were, a fragmentary vision of the continuous operation of His self-manifestations and determinations and particularizations that appear as the forms of the sensible world. We say that his vision of Multiplicity in Unity and Unity in Multiplicity is 'fragmentary' because when God gives him back his subjective consciousness and he regains his individual existence and consciousness of phenomena, he knows that what he

---

[201] The inner articulations of the Unity correspond to the dynamic creative activity of the reality of existence, or the Absolute Existence, in terms of expansion (*i.e.* existentiating) and contraction (*i.e.* annihilating) in continuous series.

[202] *I.e.* he has returned to the state he was before being qualified by external existence, which corresponds to the ontological plane of the third metaphysical category between existence and non-existence.

has 'witnessed' was a 'fragment', so to speak, of the continuous series of self-determinations and particularizations of the absolute Unity. His remembrance, reflection and contemplation of that vision at this stage constitute that Knowledge in him whose reality and truth is established by the certainty of direct experience (*ḥaqq al-yaqīn*). His experience of *baqā'* or 'subsistence' in God necessarily does not cease, for it would not be a 'subsistence' if it were temporary. We speak of the *vision* as 'fragmentary', so that it is the 'witnessing' of it (*i.e.* of the 'gathering of gathering') that is temporary; but the subsequent *knowledge* of it is permanent. His return to individual existence and phenomenal consciousness is accompanied by a condition of recovery as if from a state of intoxication (*sukr*), or insensibility; a condition of alertness, wakefulness and clarity. "All men are asleep", said the Holy Prophet, "only when they die do they wake up" (*Al-nāsu niyāmun fa idhā mātū intabahū*).[203] We must interpret the words 'when they die', *in this case* as having a double meaning: one to physical death and the other meaning when they 'die' to self, to subjective consciousness of the self, and not to physical death; for the Holy Prophet also said, with reference to dying to self as we mean here: "Die before ye die" (*Mūtū qabla an tamūtū*), that is 'die to self before ye actually die physically'.[204] So, in this case, the

---

203 This *ḥadīth* is also well known. Some maintain that it was a saying of 'Alī ibn Abī Êālib. But it cannot be denied that 'Alī, if the saying were indeed his, could have gotten the idea from the Holy Prophet. Cf. *Fuṣūṣ al-Ḥikam,* p. 159. see also *Futūḥāt.* IV, p. 457–637. III, p. 285 (250); p. 285 (251); p. 286 (251).

204 Shabistarī says that death occurs to man in three sorts: the one occuring to him every moment; the death of the conscious ego; the death compulsory on him. Lāhijī, commenting on this, says that the first is the new creation (which we will explain in due course); the second is death to the world, as in accordance with the tradition: "Die before ye die"; the third is

man's condition of alertness and clarity, of wakefulness, on returning from the experience of the 'gathering of gathering' (previous to which he has in fact 'died' to self), is called *ṣaḥw:* 'sobriety'. Although from the point of view of his individual existence he is the same man, yet he is no longer in fact the same man. That former self was 'dead', he has 'died' before he actually died, and he has regained, in that dying, his higher selfhood and subsists in God. He has returned, in recollection, to that state of wakefulness when his true self, his soul, had seen God in clarity, and had declared "Yea!" to God's "Am I not your Lord?"[205] So now he 'lives in God', confirming and affirming what he as his true self had witnessed unto itself on the Day of *Alastu.* Although he now sees the sensible world of multiplicity confronting him again, although 'separation' again comes into force, yet it is no longer for him the same world as the one he knew before; for he now *knows* that the myriad forms that constitute the Multiplicity are in reality so many different aspects of 'the Truth' (*al-ḥaqq*) Who 'clothes' Himself in their guises; are so many manifestations and determinations and particularizations of the Absolute Being Who, as the Reality underlying the sensible world, is called 'the Truth'. He also knows that the separate things considered independently are nothing in themselves, and the certainty of this truth is borne out in his experiences of the 'gathering' and of 'utter oblivion'. But considered as so many particular determinations and self-relevations of the 'Truth', the separate things of the sensible world are no mere illusion; they do exist and possess ontological status. They are 'theatres of manifestation' (sing. *maẓhar*), the manifestation-forms that determine the particular forms of self revelations of the Truth. Thus

---

the separation of the soul and body. See *Gulshan-i Rāz,* Lahore, 1978, p. 65, couplets 664–665.

205 *Al-A'rāf* (7):172.

this stage of returning to the condition of 'separation' is called the 'second separation' (*al-farq al-thānī*), and it is sometimes also called the 'separation after gathering' or the 'separation after union' (*al-farq ba'd al-jam'*) .

This was perhaps the profounder meaning of the vision of the Prophet Mūsā on the Mount (*Al-A'rāf* (7):143). He had asked his Lord to show Himself to him that he might look upon his Lord. His Lord had addressed him saying that he can by no means see Him with the naked eye in his present condition, but told him to look at the mountain to see that if it remains standing firm then perhaps he might see Him. When his Lord manifested Himself (*tajallā*) upon the Mount, it disintegrated as if pressed down or pulverized to ground level (*dakkan*). The Prophet, witnessing this overwhelming occurence, fell to the ground gasping for breath and became unconscious (*kharra ṣa'iqan*). Then when his consciousness was restored to him as if recovering from a swoon or intoxication (*afāqa*), he realized the meaning of his experience and turned to God in repentance, glorifying Him and confessing his belief with great intensity. It is possible that the reference to looking at the mountain to see whether it *remains standing firm* alludes to its *reappearance* after its disappearance to the vision of one involved in the *fanā' - baqā'* experience. Seeing the mountain remain standing firm would be the vision of the man of the 'second separation', who sees both the mountain vanishing in the Reality, and the Reality *renewing the mountain* in a perpetual act of creation.

Speaking of the same experience as we have outlined here, al-Ghazālī, alluding to the people of the 'second separation', that is the elect and the super-elect, says:

> ... the Knowers (*al-'ārifūn*) rise from the plain of metaphor (*majāz: i.e.* from the level of the phenomenal things, whose ontological status is merely that of a 'metaphorical existence', that is, to which existence is not literally applicable, or

of which existence cannot really be predicated) to the pinnacle of reality (*ḥaqīqah*); and they complete their ascent and perceive through direct ocular vision (*al-mushāhadah al-'iyāniyyah*) that there is nothing in existence but God Most Exalted, and that every thing perishes save His Aspect (*wajh:* lit. Face),[206] not because it perishes at one particular moment, but rather because it is perishing eternally and everlastingly, since it cannot be conceived otherwise. For everything other that He, when considered *in itself,* is pure non-existence (*'adam maḥḍ*); and when considered from the standpoint of the existence which it receives from the First Truth (*al-awwal al-ḥaqq*), is seen as existent—not in itself, but solely from the standpoint of the Originator of its existence—so that the sole existent is the Aspect of God Most Exalted. Everything thus has a double aspect: an aspect unto itself, and an aspect unto its Lord; in respect of itself it is non-existent (*'adam*), in respect of its Lord it is existent (*mawjūd*). Therefore, there is no existent save God Most Exalted and His Aspect, and hence 'every thing is perishing save His Aspect', eternally and everlastingly. These Knowers have no need to await the rising on the Day of Resurrection to hear the Creator's call: "To whom is the sovereignty this Day?—to God, the One, the Irresistible!", because this call peals endlessly in their ears. Nor do they understand by their saying 'God is Greater' (*Allāhu akbar*) that He is 'greater' than others. God forbid! For there is 'with' Him no other in existence for

---

206 Al-Qur'ān: *Al-Qaṣaṣ* (28):88: *Kullu shay'in hālikun illā wajhahu.*

Him to be greater than it. None has the rank of 'withness' (*al-ma'iyyah*) with Him, but only that of 'consequentialness' (*al-taba'iyyah*); indeed, none has existence at all save through the aspect that follows from Him, so that what exists is only His Aspect. Now it is absurd that He should be 'greater' than His own Aspect. The meaning is rather that He is much Greater than to be called 'greater' by way of relation and comparison—too Great indeed for anyone, be he prophet or angel, to comprehend the real nature of His Greatness. None knows God with real knowledge of Him but God, for every known comes within the circumsective sway of the knower, and this is the very negation of Majesty and Greatness...[207] The Knowers (on their return) after their ascent to the empyrean of reality confess in concerted agreement that they saw naught in existence save the One Truth. Among them, however, are those who attain to this state through illuminative knowledge (*'irfān 'ilmi*), and others through direct experience or immediate tasting (*dhawq*). The (forms of) Multiplicity pass away from them (*i.e.* their vision) in its totality. They were drowned in the absolute Unity, and their intelligences were effaced in it, and they became therein as those utterly bewildered. No capacity remained in them; neither to recall aught other than God, nor to recall even their own selves, so that nothing was with them save God. They became intoxicated with an intoxication in which the sway of their intelligences vanished... Then when their

[207] *Mishkāt al-Anwār,* (*op. cit.*), pp. 55-56. My translation.

> intoxication abated, and they returned to the sway of the intelligence, which is God's balance-scale upon earth, they knew that that (experience of absorption in the absolute Unity) had not been *actual* union (*ittiḥād*), but only something *resembling* union ... Now this state, when it prevails, is called in relation to him who experiences it, 'annihilation' (*fanā'*), nay 'annihilation of annihilation' (*fanā' al-fanā'*), for he has become extinct to his own self and extinct to his own extinction; for he becomes unconscious of his self in this state and unconscious of his own unconsciousness, since were he conscious of his own unconsciousness he would be conscious of his self. In relation to the one immersed in it, the state is called in the language of metaphor 'union' (*ittiḥād*), or in the language of reality 'unification' (*tawḥīd*) .[208]

We said earlier that the condition of a 'first separation' not only involves the possibility of a condition of a 'second separation', but also a condition prior to it of a 'pre-separation'. We said further that this condition of 'pre-separation' occurred in the spiritual context of 'union', when the souls of mankind confirmed and affirmed their individual and collective Covenant (*mīthāq*) with God, recognizing and acknowledging Him as their Lord. Their recognition and acknowledgement of the supreme truth indeed involve some sort of 'separation' - that is, some consciousness of distinction between Lord and servant, between Creator and creature. This means that even in the spiritual context some form of subject-object relation still holds, setting a limitation to man's cognition. God cannot be known to man in His Essence because, as such, He is beyond all determinations

---

208 *Ibid.*, p. 57. My translation.

into particular entities (*i.e. lā ta'ayyun*) . He can thus be known only in a limited way when He manifests Himself to the perfect man through some definite Name or Attribute. And when He manifests Himself in this way, He always reveals Himself as the Lord (*al-rabb*); and knowing Him as 'Lord' is the ultimate kind of knowing God possible for man. It is true that the perfect man knows *about* God in a way that seeks to encompass the profounder mysteries of His Being and Existence, such as that which he can infer intuitively from his reflection and contemplation of what has been given to him in his spiritual experiences, from which the metaphysical vision of Reality is formulated and established in Islām. But all that knowledge ultimately has its source and basis on the knowledge of the self and of the Lord. The Holy Prophet said: "He who knows his self knows his Lord', and he means by 'self' the true self, so that what he said means: "he who knows his true self (by realization in the final stage of *fanā'*, that is, the stage of *baqā'*) knows his Lord (through being that self, who *already* knows God as Lord when that self sealed the Covenant with God recognizing and acknowledging His Lordship)."

Thus the term 'separation', in its three senses meant in this exposition, always involves a subject-object relation. But the degrees of separateness in the relation is by no means the same in 'pre-separation', 'first separation' and 'second separation'. When we speak of 'pre-separation', we do not mean that there was absolutely no 'separation' in that spiritual condition, for since the capacity of the souls to *recognize* and *acknowledge* their Lord necessarily involves discernment of *distinction* on the part of the souls between their Lord and their selves, and between their selves among themselves, the distinction discerned implies the persistence of a 'separation' in their condition . However, the 'separation' involved here is discerned in the context of 'union', which is no other than that of 'subsistence' in God (*baqā'*). From the point of view of the stage of the 'first separation', the 'separation' that we have just described between the self and the

Lord is not a 'separation'; it is a 'union', and hence in that sense it describes a condition or stage of 'pre-separation'. In the case of the 'second separation' the 'separation' involved is not the same as that in force in the 'first separation'. The condition of the 'second separation', when looked at from the point of view of the 'first separation', involves *both* 'union' and 'separation'. It is 'union' in one sense and 'separation' in another, since on the one hand it involves the spiritual condition of the man who has transcended himself in self realization, and on the other hand it also involves the physical condition of that man who has returned to phenomenal consciousness. The man sees on the one hand the Multiplicity in the Unity and on the other hand the Unity in the Multiplicity. This is why the masters of spiritual experience and discernment call such a man the 'possessor of two eyes' (*dhū al-'aynayn*).[209] It were as though the man, having transcended his phenomenal self by being transported into another condition in the state of self realization, there saw what he as that self had always seen; and now upon his return to normal consciousness, seeing things as they were before, he yet continues to see them *as they really are*,[210] that

---

[209] The triple division of human perception of truth as we have explained in the foregoing pages is upheld by all genuine Ṣūfīs. See, for example Jāmī in his *Naqd al-Nuṣūṣ fī sharḥ Naqsh al-Fuṣūṣ*, edited with notes and introductions in Persian and English by W.C. Chittick, Persian foreword by Sayyid Jalāl al-Dīn Āshtiyānī, Tehran, 1977; p. 142, note 147. See also Sayyid Ḥaydar Āmulī. *Jāmi' al-Asrār wa Manba' al-Anwār* bound together with his *Risālah Naqd al-Nuqūd fī Ma'rifah al-Wujūd*, eds. H. Corbin and Osman Yahia, Tehran. 1969/1347, pp. 112–112; p. 220.

[210] I allude here to the Holy Prophet's prayer: *Allāhumma arinā' l-ashyā'a kamā hiya.*" "O God! Show us things as they really are". Perhaps it is on account of this *ḥadīth* that, in my estimation, the early Muslim philosophers coined the term *māhiyyah*

is, as they exist in reality seen by his true self. Thus, although both the stages of 'pre-separation' and 'first separation' are common to all mankind, even if the former refers to the spiritual condition and the latter to the physical, the stage of the 'second separation', which only the relatively few among mankind attain to, is in fact more akin to that of 'pre-separation'.

In the same way that, in the condition of 'pre-separation', the man as his true self subsists in God, so even in his physical condition, the man at the stage of the 'second separation' has realized his true self and spiritually subsists in God as he was before he acquired external existence. And in his phenomenal existence, he constantly confirms and affirms the reality and truth of his Lord, as in his original Covenant, in true submission as enacted in Islām.[211] His *taṣdīq,* or verification of Truth or 'truthing', is of that higher degree of *īmān* that characterizes the level of 'excellence' (*iḥsān*) whose nature is indicated by the Holy Prophet in a *ḥadīth* related by 'Umar ibn al-Khaṭṭāb and transmitted by Muslim and Abū Hurayrah, when he said of *iḥsān:* "that you should worship God as if you saw Him. . . " (*an ta'buda Allaha ka annaka tarāhu...*). Indeed, the man at the stage of the 'second separation', which is that of *baqā',* sees God everywhere in his spiritual vision, so that for him is realized the full meaning of the text: 'Wheresoever you turn *there* is the Aspect of God' (*fa aynamā tuwallū fa thamma wajh Allāh*).[212]

The intuition of existence, then, comes about through the mediacy of the ' spiritual witnessing' (*shuhūd*), which can take the form of cognition whose seat is the pure intel-

---

(from *mā, i.e.* 'what'; and *hiya, i.e.* 'is it'). The *ḥadīth* is quoted by Fakhr al-Dīn al Rāzī in his *Tafsīr al-Kabīr,* vol. 21 p.37.

211 Cf. chapter I, pp. 7; 11–12; 18–20.

212 *Al-Baqarah* (2): 115. See also *Rasā'il al-Junayd,* (*op. cit*) *Risālah* no. 10.

lect;[213] or through the mediacy of the 'savouring' or 'tasting' (*dhawq*) in direct illuminative experience by which the heart comes to know directly and to verify what it knows; or through the mediacy of both forms of cognition (as al-Ghazālī says in the quotation on p. 195 above). Both *shuhūd* and *dhawq* occur when the veil of separate objects and phenomenal forms is removed from the cognitive vision of one who is involved in the *fanā'-baqā'* experience. The removal of this veil is called *kashf*. *Al-kashf* is akin to the ocular vision.[214] It is the laying bare of something covered. 'Covered' here pertains to what is covered to one's state of being or feeling (*ḥāl*), or to one's cognition (*'ilm* or *'irfān*), or to one's sight or vision (*'ayn*). It is the removal, by God's grace, of the covering from one's state of being, or cognition, or vision that enables one to feel, or to know, or to see the reality- truth.[215] It is certain knowledge based on true verification, direct apprehension, and clear vision, uninterrupted by any distraction. The covering that is meant and that is caused, by God's grace, to be lifted in the experience of *kashf*, is the

---

213 We identify the pure intellect, which is intellect abstracted from all physical attachments and bodily relations, with the higher forms of the acquired intellect. See chapter IV, p. 162.

214 Al-Sarrāj, *Kitāb al-Luma'*, ed. R.A. Nicholson, London, 1963, p. 346.

215 We have formulated this definition of *kashf* based upon Quranic usage. See for example, with reference to the removal of what is covered to one's state of being or feeling, *Al-An'ām* (6): 41;17, which refers to the removal of distress and affliction; likewise *Al-Naḥl* (16):54; *Al-Anbiyā'* (21):84; *Al-Zumar* (39) :38; *Banī Isrā'īl* (17) :56; *Yūnus* (10) :12;107; *Al-Naml* (27:62; the removal of penalty, *Al-A'rāf* (7):134-135; *Yūnus* (10):98; *Al-Dukhān* (44):12;15, *Al-Zukhruf* (43):50; with reference to knowledge, the laying bare of some deep secret or mystery, *Al-Najm* (53): 58; *Nūn al-Qalam* (68): 42; with reference to vision, *Al-Naml* (27): 44; *Qāf* (50): 22.

covering of the heart, which is as the eye to the pure intellect, and which is the spiritual organ of cognition at the higher levels of knowledge.[216] The lifting of the covering of the eye of the pure intellect, such that the one from whom that covering is lifted sees as in the ocular vision the Truth or the Reality, pertains to one who we have described as the man of the 'second separation'. Such a one not only 'sees' by direct vision, but 'verifies' by direct experience the Reality of Existence expanding over all and every existing thing, articulating Its multiple and diverse individuations while yet retaining Its unity.[217] The intuition of existence is none other than the man's 'coincidence' in the very act of Existence itself, and hence it is also called *wujūd.* The state of existential intuition is preceded by a state of inner agitation or ecstasis called *wajd.* What follows is the passing away of the individual self or subjective consciousness (*fanā'*), and if the man is steadfast in his spiritual condition he attains the state of his true selfhood and subsists (*baqā'*) in God. It is

---

216 It is to the vision of the heart that the Holy Prophet alluded when he, upon whom be peace, said: 'Worship God as if you saw Him..." On another occasion he also spoke of seeing God with our hearts (see *Kashf al-Maḥjūb,* London, 1911, p. 329). That the heart is the spiritual organ of sight is derived from the Holy Qur'ān. There God speaks of His covering and sealing of hearts, and says that those who are blind (*a'mā*) in this world would be blind in the hereafter, and further astray from the path (*Banī Isrā'īl* (17):72. Not that their *eyes* would be blind, since their sight (*baṣar*) would then be sharp (*Qāf* (50):22), but that in spite of that their *hearts* would be blind. See further *Al Ḥajj* (22):46, and Qāshānī, *Sharḥ Fuṣūṣ,* p. 155.

217 The viewing with the eyes (*al-mu'āyanah*) involves confronting what is viewed and not doubting what the eyes see. Thus it points to the presence (*ḥuḍūr*) to God of the heart of the man in the state of uninterrupted contemplation, such that the man becomes absent to himself and experiences the intuition of existence.

only in this latter state of subsistence that he 'finds' (*wajada*) God. This 'finding' is *wijdān*. In this sense *wujūd is* the finding of the Truth in existence, and this is possible only after the extinction of the human condition - that is the loss of consciousness of the subjective self or ego.[218]

As regards *al-dhawq*, the basic meaning is 'taste' in the sense applicable to both pleasure and pain alike.[219] It refers, in the epistemological context here described, to a kind of intuitive knowledge brought about by a spiritual perception that accompanies the direct experience of verification. The transcendental vision that it entails refers to that of the pure intellect (*'aql mujarrad*); and the spiritual degree of the person in that condition of intellect is that of the archetypal realities, in which degree the knower's verification and cognition of the transcendent Reality and Truth is called genuine *dhawq*. We see here the close relationship between *dhawq* and *kashf*; and indeed also between these and *wajd*. *Dhawq* comes before *wajd*, and the latter state is arrived at by means of pure devotion to God and intimate converse with Him until He addresses the heart of the person who is so engrossed in contemplation of Him to the exclusion of all else so that it then 'sees' from what it was freed, and there occurs the agitation called *wajd*, for it has found what was lost. This finding, we said earlier, is called *wujūd*, or *wijdān*, which we have described as the intuition of existence. When the person recovers from the vision he loses what he found, but the knowledge of it remains with him.

With reference to the intuition of existence, the transempirical vision is called *shuhūd* or 'witnessing'. The vision of the Reality or Truth that is here seen ultimately refers to that of the soul of man in its primordial state when

---

[218] See al-Qushayrī, *al-Risālah*, Beirut, 1957, p. 34.

[219] This is evident from the Holy Qur'ān, *e.g. Hūd* (11) :9, 10; *Al-Sajdah* (41): 50; *Al-Dukhān* (44): 49; *Al-Qamar* (54): 48.

God made it to witness unto itself the reality and truth of God's Lordship in His calling to the souls: "Am I not Lord?" Man's response in recognition of that reality and truth is his unconditional acknowledgement, confirmed within his self in his saying "Yes indeed!"; and this acknowledgement is confirmed by means of verification by direct experience of what is 'seen' (*q.v. shahida*). This refers to the original witnessing (*shuhūd*), to which state the man of the 'second separation' returns.

There can be no unveiling of the real nature of the phenomenal forms in their variety and multiplicity and separate existences unless man transcends himself, that is, his human condition, by which he is bound at the stage of the 'first separation'; and this necessarily involves a transformation in him, without which he would be forever bound to the ordinary level of cognition and volition. His transformation is brought about as he attains to successively higher intellectual and spiritual stations, raising him to that stage whereby he is able, by God's grace, to transcend himself and gain his higher selfhood. The transformation entails—as al-Ghazālī says alluding to a passage in the Holy Qur'ān—that "this earth to him be changed into that which is not earth, and likewise the heavens".[220]

They who have experienced the 'second separation', when they contemplate the Truth, return (in recollection of what they have experienced of the passing away of their faculties of rational perception and of their individual egos which entails the passing away also of the phenomenal forms) to the state they were in before, when God made them absent to themselves and to the world and present with Him; and then afterwards when God granted them their individual consciousness and made them separate from Him and present to the world again, they know by personal veri-

---

220 *Mishkāt al-Anwār,* p. 50; *Ibrāhīm* (14): 48.

fication that everything—their phenomenal selves psychologically and all created things ontologically —is perishing save His modes and aspects, in guises that are never repeated for two consecutive durations. They have seen the Unity of Absolute Existence that has become Multiplicity, and the Multiplicity reverting to its original Unity without that Unity being impaired by any change in its oneness and its perfection. To this condition refers al-Junayd's words: "... they are dazzled by the sight of the effulgences from Him..."[221] They realize that all existents are in their nature His modes and aspects, whereas the phenomenal forms in whose guises they appear momentarily are in themselves pure nonexistence. As they are in themselves they are that which is other than God (*mā siwā Allāh*); they are, when 'linked' to Him, or when considered in association with Him, "left without a trace"; when the splendour of His sun appears the lights of the stars vanish, they cannot 'exist-with' the Absolute, as ibn 'Aṭā' Allāh al-Iskandarī says:

> According to the People of Unity and Illuminative Knowledge (*ahl al-tawḥīd wa al-ma'rifah*) neither 'existence' nor 'loss-of-existence' (*faqd*) may be predicated of that which is other than God Most Exalted, for that which is other than God cannot 'exist-with' God because God is Unique; nor may 'loss-of-existence' be predicated of that which is other than God because only that which has existed is capable of qualification by loss of existence...*etc.*[222]

A passage in the *Kitāb al-Lumā'* of al-Sarrāj clarifies the meaning of 'loss-of-existence' (*faqd*) about which we are now considering:

---

[221] *Kitāb al-Mīthāq, op. cit.*, p. 41/161–2.

[222] Quoted in Nūr al-Dīn al-Rānīrī's *Ḥujjat al-Ṣiddīq*, p. 20. See my *Commentary* on the *Ḥujjat*, p. 98.

> The 'existent' (*al-mawjūd*) and the 'lost-to-existence' (*al-mafqūd*) are two terms signifying opposites. The 'existent' is that which has issued forth from the domain of 'non-existence' (*al-'adam*) to the domain of 'existence' (*al-wujūd*); whereas the 'lost-to-existence' is that which has departed from the domain of 'existence' to the domain of 'non-existence'. Dhū al-Nūn—God's mercy be upon him!—said: "Grieve not for the 'lost-to-existence', for it is a recollection (of 'existence') to an existent slave." The 'non-existent' (*al-ma'dūm*) is that which 'is not', and which 'its being found' is not possible, but if one 'finds not' a thing while yet 'its being found' is possible, then that thing is called the 'lost-to-existence', and it is not called the 'non-existent'.[223]

Now *al-faqd* signifies, according to al-Bayḍāwī, 'the thing's being absent from the range of perception by sense so that its place is not known'. Al-Bayḍāwī is here referring to a passage in the Holy Qur'ān: *Qālū wa aqbalū 'alayhim mā dhā tafqidūna* (12:71),[224] that is: 'They said, turning towards them: "What is it that ye miss?" What is being missed here is 'the great beaker of the king' (*suwā'a al-maliki*) which the Prophet Yūsuf has concealed in his brother's (Benjamin's) saddle-bag.[225] Because the drinking cup is concealed in the saddlebag they (the Egyptians) miss (*nafqidu*) it—that is, they *do not see* it anywhere and they *do not know* its hiding place. In this case 'absent from the range of perception by sense' means 'lost to sight'. But it also means, however, that

---

223 *Op. cit.*; p. 339 of the Arabic text. My translation. It is clear from this that the 'non-existent' is what cannot *essentially* exist as external existence, but it is nevertheless what can exist in the interior condition of Being.

224 See his *Anwār al-Tanzīl wa Asrār al-Ta'wīl*, 2 vols. Cairo, 1939.

225 *Yūsuf* (1 2): 71–72

the beaker is not *lost* to the *memory*—it still exists in the memory of the Egyptians, for otherwise they would not have been able to *miss* it. So in spite of its loss the fact that it is remembered means that it is still something existent only that its place is not known. The apparent meaning of Dhū al-Nūn's words, quoted by al-Sarrāj, can be interpreted in the same way. When referring to the individual self in the stage of spiritual experience which follows *wajd,* the word *wujūd,* as we have already indicated, does not mean 'existence' in the usual sense. In *wajd* the spiritual state is the initial state of *fanā' or* 'self-extinction', in which the one who experiences *wajd* (the *wājid*) loses individual consciousness of the self. Following this state, and if he remains steadfast in his condition, he then 'finds' (*wajada*) God.[226] In this explanation *faqada is* the opposite of *wajada,* and *fāqid* the opposite of *wājid,* and *faqd* that of *wajd. Faqd* is a description of the last stages of *fanā',* when the man returns to self-consciousness without attaining to the state of *baqā'.*

In the quotation from al-Sarrāj, *al-mafqūd* means the 'lost-to-existence' and it is defined as something that has departed from the domain of existence to that of non-existence. *Faqd is* defined as *loss* of existence, not as *existence* that is lost—it is the *loss* that is the dominant connotation in *faqd,* not the *existence.* Thus it is, as al-Iskandarī says, that it can only be said of "that which has existed". Since it has become apparent from what has been explicated that that which is other than God is neither in the state of existence (*wujūd*) nor in that of loss of existence (*faqd*), this means that it is also not in the state of being-existent (*mawjūd*), nor of being lost to existence (*mafqūd*). To say that that which is other than God, or the world, is absolute non-existence (*'adam muṭlaq*) is equally erroneous, as the world, somehow, does

---

[226] See 'Affifi's commentary on the *Fuṣūṣ, op. cit.,* p. 310. See also al-Qushayrī's *Risālah,* p. 34 where this meaning of *wujūd* is given.

'exist'. If the world is neither in the state of existence nor in that of absolute non-existence, what then is its state? 'The world together with all its parts is nothing but a series of accidents (*a'rāḍ*), and that of which they are accidents (*al-ma'rūḍ i.e.* the subtratum) is God.'[227] "The world is nothing but His self-manifestation (*i.e. tajallī*)."[228] To say that the world 'exists', means only that it is 'coming-into-existence' between two durations, and even then it is subject to annihilation since the accident does not endure two durations—and others like them are continually being created to replace them. The world's 'existence' is bounded on either side by non-existence. The world *qua* world cannot be described as something that has lost its existence, as that would imply that it has existed, and this is denied because it never 'is' a real thing at each moment of itself; it cannot be described as having lost its existence for it never in fact comes into existence to the extent that its annihilation can be described as a 'loss'. Existence in its absolute and not in its relative sense is the prerogative of God alone.

We said that the world *qua* world never 'is' a real thing at each moment of itself because it is in reality ever perishing. But the world *qua* the self-manifestation of God in His Aspect as the Absolute Existence is ever regaining subsistence. That which is other than God, or the world of creation as a whole, has then a double aspect: as something apparently separate and self subsistent outside the Reality which is Absolute Existence; and as something which manifests the individuations of the Absolute Existence appearing in Its various grades and in accordance with the limitations of Its modes and aspects which are continually being replaced by similars in a new creation. The world in its first aspect is the 'creation' of the sensitive imagination

---

[227] *Fuṣūṣ,* pp. 125–126.

[228] *Ibid.*, p. 81.

(*mutawahham*), something which the estimative faculty of the soul considers to have ontological independence which it does not possess in reality. But the world in its second aspect, in its multiplicity and variety, is like so many different mirrors each reflecting something real. Its reflection of something real makes the reflection deceive the beholder who takes it to be the real object. What is other than God pertains to the world in both its aspects: in the first aspect it is neither existent nor subject to loss of existence; in its second aspect, however, the world is something that *was* existent and *is* lost to existence. In its first aspect the world is conceived as something having continuance in existence, subsisting independently, and composed of quiddities to which existence is conceptually superadded as seen from the essentialistic viewpoint of the metaphysics of substance and accident. This aspect of the world emerges as a result of the normal operation of the ordinary level of perception and conception, and the philosophical as well as scientific development of it into an interpretation of the nature of reality is nothing but a sophisticated elaboration of the ordinary level of reason and experience. The world in this aspect is essentially nothing; not only because the quiddities that are made to comprise it are merely mental in nature, but also because it is ever-perishing, and only the perpetual renewal of its similars creates in the mind the notion of its continuance in existence as if it were a self-subsistent, independent entity possessed of being. In its second aspect the world is something that comes into existence at each moment of itself independent of the mind. Each moment of itself is discontinuous, a moment which is its 'being-existent': it only is in that atomic duration, it being replaced by another similar to it, and that other by yet another perpetually. Everything involved in this series of the renewal of its creation retains its unity and identity as that particular thing owing to its reality or archetype, over which and in which form Existence expands from the level of Its absoluteness to the levels of Its determinations and individuations in evermore concrete forms. The archetype itself—though it too undergoes the renewal process—retains its original identity and remains always in the interior condition of Being. This second aspect of the world is real, and has itself two aspects: (1) as Existence Itself, in which case it is the Absolute Existence as it involves itself in dynamic movement; (2) as modes of Existence, in which case it is the individuations of Absolute Existence that have descended to the level of sense and sensible experience.

God in His Aspect as the Truth or the Reality, that is, the Absolute Existence, is then not identical with the things that we see and behold—just as He is not identical with His Names and Attributes when they represent His qualification of Himself in their forms; for qualified as such He is not as He is in Himself. God as He is in Himself is above being qualified even by absoluteness, as He is in that degree unconditioned by any condition, and therefore unknown and unknowable except to Himself.

From the foregoing explanation it is already clear to those possessed of understanding that God cannot be likened to created things; that He is neither substance, nor body, nor accident; that He is neither in a place nor in time; that He is not a recipient for accidents, nor is He a locus for originated things—even though He sometimes appears *as if He were* a unique 'substance' or 'substratum' in which inhere all accidents, and at other times *as if He were* the 'accidents' inhering in that 'substratum'.

We have been speaking, with reference to the *fanā'-baqā'* structure in the intuition of existence, about what is verified by the men of discernment as the objective, metaphysical and ontological aspect of the world of created things in relation to God. In everything that we have said, the double aspect of realities from the highest to the lowest levels of existence has been repeatedly indicated. Now, correspondingly, in the subjective, psychological aspect of the matter relating to man, the same double aspect is unified in the experience of the coincidence of opposites. The terminology defining the duration in which *fanā'* occurs is *waqt* or 'time', by which they mean the cutting off of serial time from one's individual consciousness such that one comes to be in a time without past or future; a time which is something of the nature of eternity and in which one is immersed in the coincidence of opposites (*coincidentia oppositorum*). There are two such 'times' (*awqāt*) during which *fanā'* occurs; one refers to the state of *wajd*—the spiritual agitation that precedes the 'finding' of the Truth (*wijdān*), which is none other than the intuition of existence (*wujūd*); the other refers to the state of *faqd*—the 'losing' (*fiqdān*) of what was found that precedes the return to individual consciousness. What was lost is the true self that had witnessed and verified the Truth, or the Aspect of God as the Absolute Existence; what was lost is the state in which he was before he existed as external existence.[229] In this sense also, what was lost is his vision of the Truth, for he was in a state of 'union' and 'presence', and is now in a state of 'separation' and 'absence'. It is possible that the one who is immersed in 'time' in the sense described above may, without the state (*ḥāl*) of actual vision (*i.e. al-mushāhadah al-'iyāniyyah*) which God causes to descend upon him, become distressed by the separation, for he has *felt* but has not fully *seen*, and feeling turns to genuine grief at what is lost and begets other feelings which only emphasize the condition of individual consciousness of phenomenal existence. To such a one also surely refer Dhū al-Nūn's words quoted earlier from al-Sarrāj. But the possessor of *waqt* coupled with the *ḥāl* that makes actual vision possible is not assailed by feelings of grief at separation, for what he has felt *and* seen in that state, of the Multiplicity becoming Unity and of the Unity again becoming Multiplicity only to revert to its original Unity, gives him certain knowledge of his essential reality in God. This is the profound meaning in

---

229 See *Kashf al-Maḥjūb*, p. 368.

the inner sense of Dhū al-Nūn's words, in that there is no need to grieve for what is lost to existence, for that being-lost to existence is in fact a reminder that one *is* existent, otherwise there would be no loss of existence—that one has *essential reality* to partake of existence, and in that knowledge he gains subsistence (*baqā'*) in God. His condition is characterized by 'steadfastness' (*tamkīn*), that stage of spiritual perfection which is the highest; there is no further stage, no change, no doubt nor vacillation in his condition, and although he has now returned to the stage of the 'second separation', God has erased from his consciousness all thought of what is other than He so that he sees everywhere God and His modes and aspects in verification of what is said in the Holy Qur'ān: "Wheresoever ye turn *there* is the Aspect of God.[230]

Those who have experienced the intuition of existence are of two types. The first are those who have experienced a *partial* intuition of existence, in which they directly apprehend only the first of the second aspect of the reality of the world as we have stated above. Because their experience has left them the apprehension only of the Absolute Existence, *in which particular and individual existences, including their own, subjective consciousness, have all perished,* they become prone, when they regain their individual consciousness, to the denial of the reality of particular and individual existences and the affirmation of the oneness of Absolute Existence alone. But in spite of this, however, they *know* that their intuition of existence is only a partial one, and therefore incomplete, and their denial of particular and individual existences is only personal to them, and is not meant to be understood as corresponding to the actual nature of reality. The second type are those who have experienced a *complete* intuition of existence, in which they directly apprehend

---

230 *Al-Baqarah* (2): 115.

both the two aspects of the second aspect of the reality of the world. In the duration of their intuitive experience, they have been given a fuller glimpse of the Reality. They witness the Absolute Existence *in the process of Its dynamic movement,* in which Its inner articulations are revealed to them. These articulations are the appearance and disappearance and reappearance of the modes and aspects of Absolute Existence out of the inner depths of Its oneness without that oneness being in any way affected by any change in its nature or unity. They see with the eye of the heart as if it were by ocular vision, the One individuating Itself into the Many while yet being One; and the disappearing Many being made to reappear, some in their original and others in similar forms. They who experience this vision have passed away from their human, subjective condition and have gained higher selfhood: they are at the level of their realities in the realm of the archetypes.

It is from the experience of the second type of intuition, which includes and is a stage beyond the first type, that the nature of reality as an integrated 'system' is formulated by those who have experienced it. They affirm the existence and reality both of the Absolute Existence (God) and Its modes and aspects (the world), and distinguish the one from the other.

The second type of the intuition of existence reveals that the nature of reality is twofold, characterized by complementary opposites involved in dynamic, existential movement. In metaphysical terms, it is the dynamic movement of Existence, described in terms of expansion and contraction or 'descent' and 'ascent', involving the One and the Many; the Absolute and the Determinate; the Eternal and the Non-eternal. Between the two complementary opposites is a third category between being and non-being which is neither Eternal nor Non-eternal, and this is the realm of the Archetypal Realities. In connection with the dynamic, existential movement of descent and ascent, or expansion and contraction, that gives rise to the ever-new creation and the origination of serial time, the nature of serial time is also subjective; and we said above that the man who experiences the intuition of existence is at the level of the archetypal realities. Now the loss of the subjective, human condition in the intuitive experience must also involve the loss of serial time; and the finding of the higher selfhood in the second type of intuitive experience involves coming to be in a time without past or future, a time which we said is something of the nature of eternity. To this refers the definition of intuition of this type when Abū Sa'īd al-Kharrāz, who experienced it, said: "It is a coincidence between the two opposites" (*al-jam' bayn al-ḍiddayn*).

When they say that the Truth, which is one of the Names of God, is the reality of existence, they are speaking in metaphysical terms referring to the Absolute as It manifests Itself in all the planes of existence. They are not implying thereby that God has no individuality, or that He is a vast, vague, pervasive and dynamic Being, contrary to the theological God of religion. On the contrary, they affirm individuality of God; for it is not inconsistent for the Absolute to have an individuation as God in the way that He has described Himself according to His Beautiful Names and Sublime Attributes. This individuation is at the plane of the Divine Oneness (*al-wāḥidiyyah*), whose self-revealing aspect is characterized by the names and attributes of divinity (*al-ilāhiyyah*).

The foregoing summary of the salient features of the intuition of existence, upon which is based the position of the men of discernment on the nature of reality, can be traced back in its basic form of expression to the school of al-Junayd. This school presented the vision of reality as they envisaged it based on the second type of the intuition of existence. They affirmed the transcendent unity of existence (*waḥdat al-wujūd*). Among the notable early representatives of this school after al-Junayd were Abū Naṣr al-Sarrāj, 'Alī al-Ḥujwīrī, Abū al-Qāsim al-Qushayrī and 'Abd Allāh al-Anṣārī. To this school also belonged al-Ghazālī. But their chief exponent was ibn 'Arabī, who first formulated what was originally given in the intuition of existence into an integrated metaphysics expressed in rational and intellectual terms. Among his erudite commentators were Ṣadr al-Dīn al-Qunyawī, 'Abd al-Razzāq al-Qāshānī, Dāwūd al-Qayṣarī, 'Abd al-Raḥmān al-Jāmī; and his doctrine of the Perfect Man (*al-Insān al-Kāmil*) was developed by 'Abd al-Karīm al-Jīlī. The philosophical expression of the transcendent unity of existence was formulated by Ṣadr al-Dīn al-Shīrāzī, called Mullā Ṣadrā, whose metaphysics bears marked traces of the thoughts of ibn Sīnā, al-Ghazālī, ibn 'Arabī and al-Suhrawardī.

VI

ON QUIDDITY AND ESSENCE

In our epistemology we affirm the possibility of knowledge and the reality of things, and establish sense perception and observation, reason, true report based on authority, and intuition as sources and methods of knowledge.[231] With regard to the problems connected with the nature of existence in its relation to reality as known by means of rational analysis and demonstration, we maintain that, according to the level of knowledge based upon sense perception and reason—which we consider to be valid criteria for the verification of truths, and which we ourselves apply in our own investigations—existence is a single, general and abstract *concept* common to all existences. This single, general and abstract concept common to all existences becomes multiple, we said,[232] due to a rational division into 'portions' corresponding to things in the course of its being attributed to quiddities. The meaning of 'reality', in the sense of there being in the external world something actual to which it corresponds, pertains only either to the *existence* or the *quiddity* of a thing,[233] one of them being a secondary intelligible, that is, a purely conceptual entity to which nothing in the external world corresponds. Existence *in this sense,* and in this

---

231 See al-Taftāzānī's commentary on the *'Aqā'id* of al-Nasafi, Cairo, 1335A.H., pp. 24, fol. It was al-Nasafi who wrote the first statement in concise form and well-knit phrasing of the creed of Islām to appear among the Muslims.

232 See chapter III, above, pp. 126–127.

233 The reason for this either/or situation is explained below, pp. 232–233.

sense only, is the mental entity having no corresponding reality in the external world.[234]

But we also affirm, in addition to existence understood in the above sense, and as based upon true report and intuition founded upon the authority of the Holy Qur'ān and the Tradition as well as upon reason and experience, that there is another entity corresponding to the purely conceptual notion of existence which is not mental but real. This other entity is the *reality* of existence, which produces in the mind the notion of existence as a pure concept, as well as the notion of 'things' and their 'quiddities' to which portions of existence as a conceptual entity are correspondingly attributed. We have given a gist of this already,[235] identifying this *reality* of existence, which is also the Absolute Existence, with the Aspect of God referred to in the Holy Qur'ān as That which encompasses everything in a pervasive sort of way and which remains after the perishing of created things.

Our notion of a thing as it is immediately perceived—in this case a man, for example—is simply that of a real, concrete existent (*mawjūd*) having a particular individuality to which a word—for example, 'man'—is applied to denote it, and which word when mentioned will bring to mind the object which it denotes. This, in brief, describes our primary notion of a thing, a physical object of the senses. The mind, when contemplating the thing which demands its definition, and in answer to its own inner question about the thing: "What is it?", proceeds to analyse it; to judge, discriminate, clarify and classify it until it arrives at a definition of the thing, that is, 'rational animal' in the case of 'man'. In

---

[234] This is agreed by the Muslim philosophers, theologians and Ṣūfī metaphysicians representing the Islamic intellectual and religious tradition.

[235] In chapter III pp. 126–127.

this concept–forming process the mind is able to abstract the thing's 'whatness' from its existence, existence here being considered as something which is attributed to the thing itself, as if it were a property of the thing that is superadded to it. This 'whatness' is quiddity (*māhiyyah*) .[236] In this way a mental division and distinction is made between quiddity and existence, quiddity being considered as the reality of a thing whereas existence is that which qualifies it.

From this we distinguish two stages of understanding. The primary stage of understanding refers to the objects of physics, to concrete things, such as indicated by the word 'animal' with respect to 'man', to which apply the ten Aristotelian categories of substance, or the stuff of which a physical thing is made, quantity, quality, relation, place, time, posture, possession, action, and passivity or being acted upon.[237] Things as such are the original stuff from

---

[236] The Latin term *quidditas* refers to the distinctive nature or peculiarity of a thing. It is a direct Latin translation from the Arabic text: *māhiyyah,* which in Arabic is derived from a combination of two words: *mā huwa* or *mā hiya,* meaning 'what is it?' *Māhiyyah* is that which answers the question *'mā hiya?'* Likewise in Latin *quidditas* is formed from the question *'quid est?'* As to the Arabic term *māhiyyah,* the early Muslim philosophers were the first to coin it. In my view, it could have been inspired by a *ḥadīth* of the Holy Prophet: *Allāhumma arinā al ashyā' ka mā hiya:* "O God! Show me things as they are in themselves", *i.e.* as the things are in their individual 'whatness'. This *ḥadīth* is reported in Fakhr al-Dīn al-Rāzī's commentary on the Holy Qur'ān (see note 250 below), vol. 21, pp. 37; 39–40. On the Latin *quidditas* being a direct translation from the Arabic, see further A.M. Goichon: *La Philosophie D'Avicenne et son Influence en Europe Médiévale,* Paris, 1951, p. 101.

[237] The reference here is to the Ten Categories (*al-ma'qūlāt al-'asharah*): substance (*ousīa: jawhar*); quantity (*posōn: kammiyyah*); quality (*poiōn: kayfiyyah*); relation (*prosti: iḍāfah*): place (*pou: ayna*); time (*pote: matā*); posture (*keīsthai: waḍ'*);

which are derived primary ideas apprehended by the intellect called primary intelligibles (*al-ma'qūlāt al-ūlā*). They (the things) are the concretely existent objects of the external world that correspond to the concepts derived from them which we call primary intelligibles. The secondary stage of understanding, however, refers not to the objects of physics, but rather to those of logic. It pertains to a highly abstract mental process; a rational elaboration of concepts arrived at and established according to the rules of logic and the logical divisions of genus, species, and difference. Thus at this stage the mind reflects upon itself, upon its own contents, as it were, and the way it understands the ideas it formulates. These ideas or concepts do not correspond with anything in the external world, as they are not concepts that are derived from concrete objects, but are concepts of concepts like the concept of 'rational animal' as derived from another concept 'man'. Concepts such as these are called secondary intelligibles (*al-ma'qūlāt al-thāniyah*). It is clear from the foregoing explanation that the reality of a thing, as understood according to the rules of logic and the logical divisions of genus, species, and difference, refers to quiddity as *opposed* to existence, in the sense that the quiddity is regarded as the reality which is distinct from, and is qualified conceptually by existence; the relation between quiddity and existence being respectively like that of subject and predicate. This perspective involves the understanding of the nature of existence as a secondary intelligible to which nothing in the external world corresponds.

But there is another sense in which quiddity is under-

---

possession (*échein: milk*); action (*poieîn: an yaf'al, fi'il*); passion (*pāschein: an yanfa'il, infi'āl*), See Jurjānī, *Ta'rīfāt*, p. 243; Tahānawī, *Kashshāf*, V, 1211. See further, Soheil Muhsin Afnan, *Wāzhah Nāmah Falsafī* (*Qāmūs Falsafī Fārisī-'Arabī*): A philosophical lexicon in Persian and Arabic, Bayrūt, Dār al-Mashriq, 1969, p. 246, cols. 1 & 2.

stood. In contrast to quiddity as logically understood to be what is defined in the reply to the question: "what is it?"—that is, 'rational animal' with reference to 'man', quiddity may also be ontologically understood to be 'that by which a thing is what it is'. The distinction between these two meanings of quiddity is that in the former case it refers only to genus in relation to species, for 'rational animal' is the genus by which the species 'man' is defined; whereas in the latter case it refers always to a particular existent, like the individual thing to which applies the ten categories, such as to a *particular* man.

When we consider the quiddity of a thing, we conceive it either in the thing itself as it exists in the external world, or as it exists in the mind. The nature of quiddity as conceived by the intellect has three aspects:[238]

1. as pure abstraction (*mujarradah*), unrelated to any thing or to any mind.[239] Quiddity in this aspect is completely independent in itself and cannot be related to any other concept. The concept of 'animal' as it is in itself, for example, is nothing but pure 'animal' and cannot be predicated of the concept 'man' because 'man' signifies

---

[238] The nature of quiddity as understood by reason was first systematically analysed and formulated by ibn Sīnā. See his *al-Shifā, al-Manṭiq, al-Madkhal,* eds. G. Qanawati, Mahmud al-Khudayri, and Fu'ad al-Ahwani, Cairo, 1953, pp. 15, 34; also pp. 65–72. An elaboration of the relation between the quiddity and its constituent elements as set forth by ibn Sīnā, who conceived it as having three aspects, is here given in outline. See also Sabzawārī's *Sharḥ Ghurar al-Farā'id,* eds. M. Mohaghegh and T. Izutsu, Teheran, 1969, pp. 131 fol.; and *The Metaphysics of Sabzawārī,* trs. M. Mohaghegh and T. Izutsu, New York, 1977, XXXI, pp. 144–146.

[239] 'Unrelated to any mind' here means that there is no specific object in the mind—the mind here is not attending to any particular object.

something more than pure 'animal'. In such a condition of pure abstraction, no other concept can be combined with it to form a meaningful unity. If the concept 'rational' were added to 'animal' in this case, it would not produce a coherent combination, since 'animal' as pure 'animal' cannot be qualified by rationality.

2. as absolute indeterminate (*muṭlaqah*), unrestricted by unrelatedness to any thing and free to engage itself in individual things. The concept of 'animal', in the case of quiddity in this aspect, is no longer restricted to itself as pure 'animal', but is indeterminate and has the potentiality of being predicated of other concepts in a coherent combination. When the concept 'rational' is predicated of 'animal' here, it produces the composite in the form of the concept 'man'. 'Animal' in this case can be predicated of 'man', since animality and rationality are constituent parts of man;

3. same as in (2) above, and present in the mind[240] where it receives various accidents such as predication, universality, particularity, and the like whereby the aspect of quiddity here is mixed (*makhlūṭah*), as when the concept of 'animal' refers to what is already actualized in the external world as something specified as 'rational'. 'Animal' thus specified refers to an object of the external world, to a particular man.

The same quiddity as considered by the intellect under the guise of these three aspects is called, in the first case, 'conditioned by unrelatedness to anything' (*bi sharṭ lā shay'*); in the second case, 'not conditioned by unrelatedness

240 'Present in the mind' means that the mind is here actually attending to a particular object.

to anything' (*lā bi sharṭ shay'*); and in the third case, 'conditioned by something' (*bi sharṭ shay'*) .[241] The first refers to quiddity in relation to prime matter (*māddah*); the second to genus (*jins*); and the third to species (*naw'*).[242]

The combination of the two senses of the meaning of quiddity (*i.e.* the logical and the ontological) in a specific quiddity (*al-māhiyyah al-naw'iyyah*)[243] is nothing but the very thing itself (*nafs al-shay'*).[244] It is this combined meaning of the two senses of *māhiyyah* that is meant when it is said that the reality of a thing is the thing itself. We in fact concur with al-Taftāzānī when he said that:

---

241 See ibn Sīnā *Al-Ishārāt wa al-Tanbīhāt* with the commentary by Nasīr al-Dīn al-Êūsī (ed. by Sulayman Dunya, 2nd ed., Dār al-Ma'ārif bi Miṣr, Cairo, 1971, 4V.), vol. I, pp. 184–185. See also the *Al-Mawāqif fī 'Ilm al-Kalām* of 'Adud al-dīn 'Abd al-Raḥmān ibn Aḥmad al-Ijī (published by 'Ālam al-Kutub, Bayrūt [n.d.]; distributed by Maktabah al-Mutanabbī, Cairo, and Maktabah Sa'd al-Dīn, Damascus) *al-marṣad al-thānī* containing twelve *maqāṣid,* pp. 59–68. On the quiddity as having three aspects as outlined above, see *al-maqṣid al-thānī,* p. 60. The same information on the subject as found in the *Mawāqif* is also found in *Kashshāf,* V, p. 1314.

242 *Al-Ishārāt wa al-Tanbīhāt,* vol. I, p. 184. The term *māddah* signifies prime matter as also signified by another term: *hayūlā* from Greek *hylê.* But *māddah* tends more to refer to elemental matter that receives generation and corruption.

243 Such as in the case of the third aspect of quiddity explained above, which is combined with the second aspect; hence it is 'mixed' (*makhlūṭah*).

244 On the *mahīyyah* of the logicians, it refers to *māhiyyah* in the particular, logical sense, and is the same as the mentally posited quiddity (*al-māhiyyah al-i'tibāriyyah*). The specific quiddity has equal singulars, in that what is necessary for one singular is the same as what is necessary for the other; like 'man', for example, necessitates in Zayd what is necessitated in 'Amr, in contrast to the generic quiddity (*al-māhiyyah al-jinsiyyah*)

The reality of a thing (*ḥaqīqat al-shay'*) and its quiddity (*māhiyyah*) are that by which a thing is what it is (*mā bihi al-shay' huwa huwa*), like 'rational animal' with reference to 'man' in contrast to 'laughing animal' and 'writing animal', since it is possible to conceive of 'man' without reference to them (*i.e.* laughing and writing) in as much as they are among the (category of) accidents (*al-'awāriḍ*). And it may be said further that, that by which a thing is what it is, when considered (*bi i'tibār*) as being realized externally (*taḥaqqaqa*), is a reality (*ḥaqīqah*); as being individualized (*tashakhkhuṣ*), *is* an ipseity (*huwiyyah*); and when considered independently without considering them (*i.e.* its being realized and its being individualized), it is a quiddity. A 'thing' (*al-shay'*) according to us, is the existent (*al-mawjūd*); and subsistence (*al-thubūt*); realization (*al-taḥaqquq*); existence (*al-wujūd*); and coming-into-being (*al-kawn*) are synonymous terms, and the meaning of them is self evident.[245]

In the above passage appearing at the beginning of the commentary on al-Nasafī's *'Aqā'id,* al-Taftāzānī combined reality (*ḥaqīqah*) and quiddity (*māhiyyah*) as together constituting that by which a thing is what it is. For quiddity in the particular, logical sense is merely a mental entity belonging to a class of secondary intelligibles to which nothing in the external world corresponds; whereas the theologians were concerned primarily not with mental entities, but with extramental realities such as immediately perceived as

---

whose singulars are not equal, for 'animal' as necessitated in man is associated with 'rational' and is not necessitated in this way in other animals. See *al-Ta'rīfāt,* pp. 205–206; *Kashshāf;* V, p. 1313.

245 *Sharḥ al-'Aqā'id,* pp. 16–17. My translation.

at the stage of the primary notion of things. Thus they defined reality (*ḥaqīqah*) as something realized externally (*taḥaqqaqa*), and the combination of reality and quiddity in the particular, logical sense becomes the equivalent of quiddity in the general, ontological sense, which refers to real essence having as its referent or correspondent a concrete, external object, an existent (*mawjūd*), a thing (*shay'*) . They meant by this combination, therefore, to indicate a concept that directly signifies an extramental reality, and which belongs to the class of primary intelligibles.

It is to the third aspect of quiddity according to ibn Sīnā's scheme that al-Taftāzānī referred in his commentary on al-Nasafī's statement that the realities of things are established, that is, subsistent (*ḥaqā'iq al-ashya' thābitah*) .[246] What he meant when he said that the reality of a thing and its quiddity are 'that by which a thing is what it is' refers, in the context of logic, to that by which a thing is located in its genus or species. 'Animal' alone is not 'man'; it is, rather, the nature of a being without determination of its special form.[247] Similarly, 'rational' alone is not 'man"; it is, when predicated of 'animal', its special form which is a principle of difference by which the species 'man' is defined. The combination of 'rational' plus 'animal' defines 'man', but 'man' in his quiddity is not that combination. Man is man.[248] Humanity or being-man (*insāniyyah*) when considered in itself is not some kind of entity that is common to, and can be received by, recipients of existence such as man. Being-man in itself is something negative (or something that is

---

[246] *'Aqā'id,* p. 16.

[247] *I.e.* as in the case of the second aspect in which a quiddity can be conceived: not conditioned by unrelatedness to anything (*lā bi sharṭ shay'*)

[248] See al-Isfarā'inī's supercommentary on al-Taftāzānī's commentary on the *'Aqā'id,* pp. 16–17. This is also derived from ibn Sīnā.

conditioned by unrelatedness to anything: *bi sharṭ lā shay'*); only when it is referred to as something of Zayd, in the same manner that it can be referred to as something of 'Amr, that it refers to a single, concretely existent individual. In itself, being-man or humanity is neither what is in Zayd, nor what is not in him, for the humanity in Zayd and that which is not in Zayd are mentally posited, determined entities attached to Zayd on the one hand, and not attached to him on the other, only *after* Zayd is being related to it in either case.[249] In the context of reality, that is, from the point of view of what is already actualized, where things are without exception particular and individual, the quiddity of a man is that by which the man is that *particular* man, thereby indicating the reality of an entity which, when considered together with the man, is that by which the man comes to be *that* man. Now, nothing establishes the identity of a man—neither the part (*al-juz'*), like 'rational', for example, nor what is accidental (*'āriḍ*) to him, like 'laughing', for example—except his very self (*nafs*). This entity, when considered together with the man of which it is the man's identity or very self, is other than the man. When we say, for example, that man is composed of soul (*nafs*) and body (*badan*) we are saying that man is neither soul nor body, but that out of these two there is constituted a third entity. To this refers the interpretation of Fakhr al-Dīn al-Rāzī when he said that primary knowledge (*al-'ilm al-ḍarūrī*) is arrived at because of the existence of something which is indicated by every human being when he says 'I'. This something is either a body (*jism*), or an accident (*'araḍ*), or a combination of both, or something different from both; or it is a composite (*murakkab*) formed of them as of two things from which is constituted a third entity.[250] From this it is clear that the quiddity of a composite is

---

[249] See the *Mawāqif;* 2nd, *marṣad,* 1st *maqṣid,* pp. 59–60.

[250] See his commentary on *Sūrah Banī Isrā'īl* (*17*), *āyah,* 85, in his

not the composite itself, though the quiddity itself is a composite, as illustrated by the following diagram.[251]

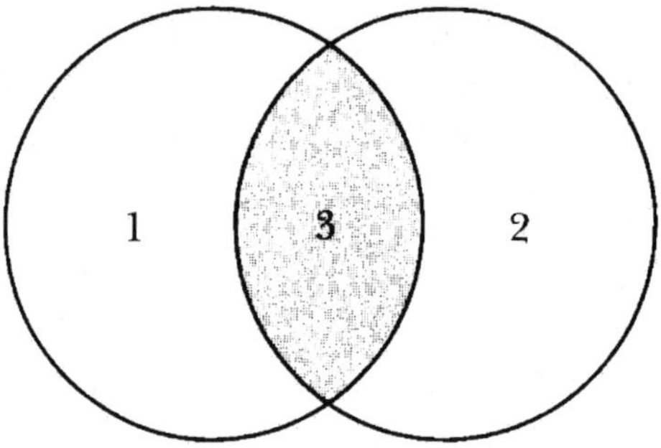

The above illustration is only meant to simplify visually what we mean. If circle 1 represents the genus (*jins*) 'animal' and circle 2 represents the difference (*faṣl*) 'rational', then 3 would represent the species (*naw'*) 'man'. Similarly, if circle 1 represents the substratum matter (*māddah*) and circle 2 represents the substantial form (*ṣūrah*), then 3 would represent the substance 'body' (*jism*). Then again, and as

---

great commentary on the Holy Qur'ān, the *Al-Tafsīr al-Kabīr,* Cairo, 1934, 32V., vol. 21, pp. 39–40. Al-Rāzī's statement on the identity of man is ultimately derived from ibn Sīnā. See ibn Sīnā's *Aḥwāl al-Nafs,* ed. F. al-Ahwani, Cairo, 1952, ch. I. An explanation of the terms *jism,* and *murakkab* in the context of our interpretation referred to above is found in *Kashshāf,* I, pp. 75–78, under the heading *al-insān.* On this third entity as the quiddity of a thing, see further *Al-Mawāqif;* p. 13.

251 In this simplified illustration, the circles 1 and 2 represent parts of the composite; 3, which is itself a composite formed of 1 and 2, is not the composite 1 and 2 but a separate entity. Even if the two circles were to be drawn as overlapping one another, it would not affect the constitution of the third entity which is not the composite of the two circles, but is a separate composite in itself. This is ibn Sīnā's conclusion.

related to man—both logically as in the former case, and ontologically as in the latter case—if circle 1 represents a composite body (*jism*) individuated in human form (*badan*)[252], and circle 2 represents a sensitive and rational soul (*nafs*), then 3 would represent a human being. The reality of a human being is his very self, neither body nor soul; nor matter nor form; nor animal nor rational.

Now in the definition of reality as 'that by which a thing is what it is' (*mā bihi al-shay' huwa huwa*), which can also be formulated as *mā bihi huwa huwa:* 'that by which it is it', what is signified by the letter *bā'* of *bihi* (*i.e.* the word *by* in the definition) is causality (*sababiyyah*), which for the thing underlies its innermost being. This meaning points to something as the cause (*sabab* or *'illah*) by which a thing is *the* thing, such as the efficient cause (*al-'illah al-fā'iliyyah*) and the agent (*al-fā'il*). But in objection to this view, it may be said that the agent is in reality that by which the thing is *existent,* not that by which the thing is *that* thing; for that by which the thing is that *particular* thing is what makes the thing to be *different* from others, not what makes it to be existent, which is common to every thing[253]. Thus because of the ambiguous nature of reality itself, the cause of a thing (*'illah al-shay'*), in order for it to be the reality of a thing (*ḥaqīqah al-shay'*), must include both the cause of existence (*'illah al-wujūd*) and the cause of quiddity (*'illah al-māhiyyah*); and this becomes apparent from the two personal pronouns

---

[252] The distinction between *jism* and *badan* is that in the case of the former, it is a material substance having a three dimensional nature which is capable of division without losing its identity as body; and in the latter case, which is also referred to as *jasad,* it is a body having complete members not capable of division without losing its identity as a whole. The former is a body referring to the genus of quantity, whereas the latter refers to a body in the genus of animal.

[253] See further, *Kashshāf,* II, art. *al-ḥaqīqah,* pp. 331–332.

(*ḍamīrān*) : *huwa huwa* (*it is it*), each of the two indicates the cause of existence and the cause of quiddity, both of which constitute the cause of a thing.

Both existence and quiddity refer to one and the same existent thing, to its actual subsistence and to its essential nature. The cause of a thing is that on which the thing is dependent for its being-a-thing. This is of two logical divisions: (1) that by which the quiddity, as from a combination of its parts, is constituted, and this is the cause of quiddity; (2) that on which the quiddity, which is constituted by its parts, is dependent for its qualification by external existence, and this is the cause of existence[254]. Insofar as its mental existence is concerned, the causes of quiddity are genus (*jins*) and specific difference (*faṣl*), and insofar as its external existence is concerned, they are matter (*māddah*) and form (*ṣūrah*), from which are derived the material cause (*al-'illah al-māddiyyah*) and the formal cause (*al-'illah al-ṣūriyyah*). As for the causes of existence, they are the active agent (*al-fā'il*), the final purpose (*al-ghāyah*), and the substratum (*al-mawḍū'*); the first two pointing to the efficient cause (*al-'illah al-fā'iliyyah*) and the final cause (*al-'illah al-ghā'iyyah*) respectively[255]. The cause of a thing as outlined

---

254 See *Al-Ta'rīfāt,* p. 160, under the heading *'illah al-shay'*.

255 See *Al-Ishārāt wa al-Tanbīhāt,* vol. I, pp. 154–155; also *Metaphysica,* tr. P. Morewedge, New York, 1973, ch. 15, pp. 41–44; also ch. 20, pp. 50–53. Matter (*māddah*) is the substratum or receptacle whose existence is actualized by receiving a substance such as form (*ṣūrah*). The latter is the substantial aspect of an entity and its essence. The material cause is the constituent element (*e.g.* wood) of an entity (*e.g.* chair) which has the potentiality to receive the form (*e.g.* shape) of that entity. The formal cause is what realizes the substance and makes it complete, as illustrated by the shape of a chair which is attributed to wood (*Metaphysica,* p. 41). The efficient cause is the initiator of actions leading to the realization of an entity,

on page 227 may be illustrated as follows:

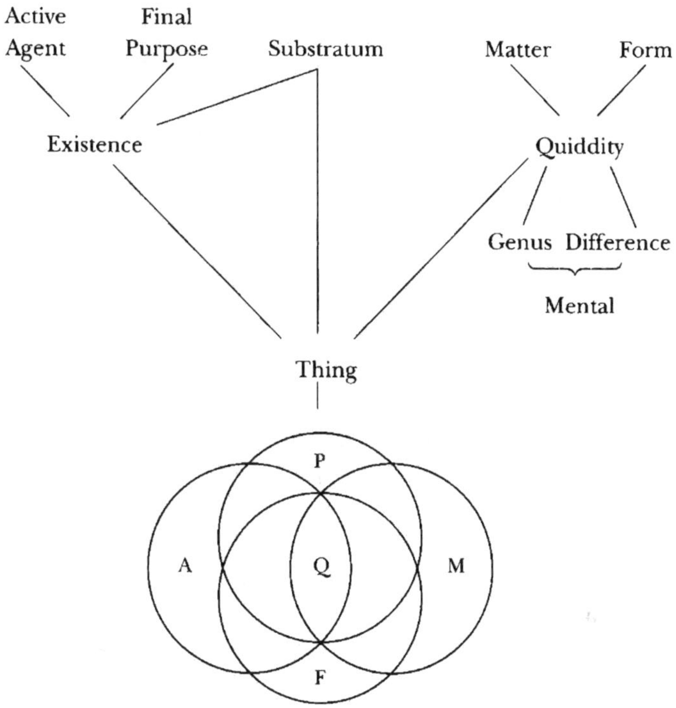

A = Active Agent
P = Final Purpose
Q = Quiddity
M = Matter
F = Form

---

as illustrated by the builder who builds a house. If the final form or purpose of the house were not envisioned by the builder, he would not become a builder of the house, the form of the house would not be actualized, and the house would not be made of its various elements (*Metaphysica,* p. 42) . See further the *Mawāqif* (2nd *mawqif;* 5th *marṣad* and 1st *maqṣid*), p. 85; for the whole section on the cause and the caused, see pp. 85–95; *Kashshāf,* IV, pp. 1039–1040. The cause of a thing as outlined above refers to the direct or proximate (*qarībah*) cause, not the indirect or ultimate (*ba'īdah*) cause. For a discussion and explanation of the problem of the two personal

The above outline represents the conceptual structure of an actual thing at the level of intellection (*al-ta'aqqul*) . At this level, the cause of a thing, as indicated by the *bā'* of casuality, necessitates a duality (*ithnayniyyah*) of quiddity and existence. At the level of actual existence, however, there is only one single and identical concrete thing, which becomes a composite of quiddity and existence when the duality at the conceptual level is projected onto it. In the definition: *mā bihi al-shay' huwa huwa:* 'that by which a thing is what it is', or 'that by which it is it', the two personal pronouns (*huwa huwa: it is it*) refer, in the first case, to an entity because of which the thing is that thing (*al-amr al-ladhī bi sababihi al-shay' dhālika al-shay'*), and in the second case, to an entity because of which the thing is that entity (*al-amr al-ladhī bi sababihi al-shay' huwa dhālika al-amr*)[256]; to its being itself in the first case, and to its being actualized in the second case. Its being actualized refers to its existence, which is common to all other existents; its being itself refers to its quiddity, which distinguishes it from all other existents. According to al-Khayālī, one of the pronouns refers back to the relative pronoun (*al-mawṣūl*),[257] and al-Tahānawī identified the pronoun as the one in the second case above[258], which refers to existence and which, since it indicates the same thing (*al-shay'*), is considered additional (*zā'id*)[259] to

---

pronouns, see the supercommentaries on al-Taftāzānī's *Sharḥ al-'Aqā'id* by Ibrāhīm al-Isfarā'inī and al-Khayālī, *ibid.* pp. 16–17. The data furnished by al-Isfarā'inī and al-Khayālī on this issue is also used by al-Tahānawī is his *Kashshāf,* II, pp. 331–333 under the heading *al-ḥaqīqah.*

256 *Kashshāf,* II, p. 331

257 That is, to what is signified by the word *mā* (*that*), to which the *hā'* of *bihi* (the *which* of *by which*) is bound in meaning *Sharḥ al-'Aqa'id,* p. 16.

258 *Kashshāf,* II, p. 332.

259 See both al-Isfarā'inī and al-Khayālī in *Sharḥ al-'Aqā'id,* p. 16.

what is defined, so that it would be sufficient to construe the definition without it, such as *mā bihi al-shay' huwa*[260], meaning *mā bihi al shay' huwa al-shay*[261]: 'that by which the thing is *that* thing'. Seen according to this perspective the duality of quiddity and existence is resolved, in that it is not really true; it is only apparently so at the suggestion of the mind.

But the matter is not as simple as to be resolved by a mere quibbling with words. If it were only a matter of logic, then perhaps the solution to the problem of duality in the formulation of the above definition is valid insofar as it pertains to a refinement of the definition in line with the position taken— the position taken being that quiddity is the reality that is being qualified by a conceptual entity called existence. Existence and quiddity are two different entities, whether considered logically or ontologically[262], and yet they refer at the same time to a single, actually existent thing. The fact that these two, as predicates, can be attributed to one and the same thing is clear enough evidence that the thing itself has two aspects corresponding to them, to one of which only does the meaning of 'reality' applies. For it is not possible that they both be real at the same time, since if they were then the thing would lose its unity and identity as one single thing and would be two different things; nor is it possible that they both be not real at the same time, since if that were the case the thing would lose its reality altogether. Either one of them, existence or quiddity, is the thing itself; and this being so, either one of them must

260 *Kashshaf;* II, p. 333; and V, p. 1313.

261 *Ibid., V,* p. 1313; *Sharḥ al-'Aqā'id,* p. 16.

262 This agrees with the positions taken by the theologians, the Ṣūfis and the philosophers, with the exception of the Ash'arīs, who held that quiddity and existence are indistinguishable, and that the duality of quiddity and existence is merely a mental affair. See my *Commentary on the Ḥujjat al-Ṣiddiq of Nūr al-Dīn al-Rānīrī,* Kuala Lumpur, 1986, pp. 303–305, 340–341.

be additional (*zā'id*) to the other, that is, either one of them must be something additional as construed by the mind, having no corresponding reality in the external world; a secondary intelligible. Whereas the one to which the meaning of 'reality' applies would be the one that has a corresponding reality, or actual object, in the external world, such as what is termed a primary intelligible.

Now for everything there is a reality by which the thing is what it is, and this reality establishes for the thing its *being-a-thing* and at the same time its *essential difference* which distinguishes it from what is not it. Reality in this sense is identical with *essence.* When we speak about the 'essence' of a thing, we do not simply mean to refer to its quiddity because quiddity itself, as we have already indicated, is ambiguous in that it can mean to refer either to a logical or to an ontological entity. Moreover, this ambiguity has led to the general problem of confusion in the understanding of the meaning of essence and its relation to existence, since the logical quiddity has generally been confused with the ontological. Finally, quiddity, by its very nature, can only be the principle of difference in things, whereas the reality that we designate as essence, despite its being also the principle of difference in things is at the same time the principle of identity in the thingness of things. Since essence, in order to denote something real and not only something mental having no corresponding reality in the external world, must denote what makes a thing an individual entity having its own identity which is different from that of other similar things, *as well as* what constitutes the very substance of that entity, it must pertain only to quiddity in the ontological sense. It must be borne in mind that the division of quiddity and existence is a mental affair; that in the extramental world no such division occurs since there quiddity and existence together indicate one and the same reality. In this we are not in fact saying that quiddity and existence are really identical, and that it is only the mind that considers them as two different entities. We maintain that quiddity and existence, whether in the mind or externally, are indeed two different entities, but that the ontological quiddity, unlike the logical quiddity, is *not opposed* to existence because *its very substance is existence,* and not something mental having no corresponding reality in the external world. Existence is common to all in a general sense in a way in which quiddity is not. For quiddity is common to everything only in the sense that everything has a quiddity that is not common in every other thing. Thus quiddity is common to everything in a *particular* sense. This applies to both the logical and the ontological quiddity. Since, however, the ontological quiddity is essentially of the nature of existence in a certain respect, its being common to every thing conveys a *general* sense also in a way in which the logical quiddity does not. Quiddity in this general sense is what we mean by essence.

Our position is that it is existence, and not quiddity, that is the reality that is being qualified by a conceptual entity called quiddity.[263] The basic problem that confronts those who believe in the fundamental reality of quiddity as opposed to existence is that if quiddity is fundamentally real and existence is only its property which the mind conjures up, as it were, then this would mean that quiddity somehow exists before being qualified by existence—a somewhat absurd conclusion. They may, however, object to this by saying that if the qualification by existence is something that happens in the mind, then it follows that the multiplicity of existents is also in the mind only, but the being-in-existence of a particular existent is not in the mind. In this sense quiddity is not being really qualified by existence. In this line of argument, what they assert is that existence does not exist in reality. To this we answer that such a conclusion does not solve the problem of the quiddity existing before being qualified by existence when we mean by existence not merely

[263] That is, quiddity in the particular, logical sense.

something that is conceptual in nature, but also that it is something that exists as a real entity independent of the mind. For we say that existence must exist in reality, since if it did not exist in reality then nothing would exist at all. In this syllogism it is demonstrated that since the consequent (that nothing exists at all) is false, it follows that the antecedent (that existence does not exist in reality) is also false. Moreover, their position in that line of argument does not solve the problem of the essential nature of quiddity, if it is something other than existence—in a certain respect. On the other hand, since our position is that existence is the fundamental reality and that true quiddities are in reality modes of existence, the problem of quiddities existing before being qualified by existence does not arise, for quiddities *as modes of existence* can exist *in the interior condition of Being* before being qualified by *external* existence.

That existence and quiddity are distinct from one another in the mind is clear enough, but at the level of external reality it would at first appear as though we have identified existence with quiddity since we say that quiddity in the particular, logical sense is in itself really nothing but a conceptual entity, and that in the general, ontological sense it is only a limitation of existence. Therefore, quiddity is in reality existence as it determines itself into a particular mode, which limitation is interpreted by the mind as quiddity. But this apparent identification of existence with quiddity is not really the case, for even though what the mind 'ontologizes' as quiddity is in reality only a mode, a determined or limited existence, it does not follow that this determined or limited existence is identical with existence as it is in its undertermined or unlimited aspect. Thus what the mind conceives as quiddity is in reality a *determining limit* and a *differentiating principle* of existence as it unfolds itself in existential movement; creating out of such determining limits the multiple and diverse realities of the external world. According to this perspective, just as it is at the conceptual level so also at the level of external reality existence and quiddity are not identical.[264]

The essence (*dhāt*) of a thing is the being-existent (*mawjūd*) of the entity (*'ayn*) which is the individuality (*huwiyyah*), the quiddity (*māhiyyah*), or the very self (*nafs*) of a thing; and these terms in their combined meanings altogether constitute the reality (*ḥaqiqah*) of a thing. Our definition of essence as formulated above contains two distinct elements: one refers to the primary stuff of which things are made, as indicated by our reference to the 'being-existent' of things, and this primary stuff is existence (*wujūd*); the other refers to that which makes things to be different from one another, or to their differentia,[265] and that is quiddity. Thus, our understanding of the meaning of essence based on this definition is that essence is more general in contrast with quiddity. It includes not only the difference, but the substance of a thing; whereas quiddity denotes only the difference. Essence is then existence plus quiddity. Because of the element of existence present in our definition of essence, essence includes the permanent aspect of being in contrast to the changing, or perishing, phenomenal aspect which does not include permanence.

The being-existent (*mawjūd*) of things may be understood in two different senses:

1. as exterior (*ẓāhir*), that is, as extrinsic to existence, in

---

[264] See further, *The Metaphysics of Sabzawārī*, translated from the Arabic by Mehdi Mohaghegh and Toshihiko Izutsu, New York, 1977. Mullā Hādī Sabzawārī was the great commentator of Mullā Ṣadrā. Perhaps the best and most analytic treatment of Islamic metaphysics to appear in English is in our estimation the profound writings of Professor. T. Izutsu, in particular *The Concept and Reality of Existence*, Tokyo, 1971. See also my *Commentary* on the *Ḥujjah*, pp. 336 fol. and the references in notes 479–485, pp. 336–338.

[265] By 'differentia' we mean not the logical differentia, but the ontological principle of difference in things.

which case it refers to the things of the external world of sense and sensible experience, the world of empirical things. Even so, the sense in which being-existent is meant here is not only the basic, physical and static one of concrete existence, but it also already alludes to the relational, metaphysical and dynamic one of existential movement (*mawjūdiyyah*) underlying it, which creates out of itself the things which constitute a world of continuous annihilation and renewal; a world which when viewed *in itself* as world is something imaginary, since as itself it is continually perishing and therefore does not exist except in the sensitive imagination; and yet when viewed as something dependent upon its underlying metaphysical Source, which is manifested by it and which continually renews it, it is real. Being-existent thus refers not only to the existent things that make up the multiple and diverse world of sense and sensible experience, but also to their continual renewal by the underlying dynamic and creative flow of Existence that produces the things existent;

2. as interior (*bāṭin*) that is, as intrinsic to existence, in which case it refers to the permanent and transcendent dynamic principle underlying (1) above, which itself has two aspects: (i), as act and (ii), as mode; and this points to that metaphysical Source which we have identified as the Reality-Truth (*al-ḥaqq*) .

We have recurrently pointed out that the Reality-Truth is the Aspect (*wajh*) of God which remains (*yabqā, i.e. baqā'*) after the perishing (*fanā'*) of created things. It is also the Absolute Existence (*al-wujūd al-muṭlaq*). The term 'absolute' (*muṭlaq*), in the way we mean, refers to a state of pure indetermination. It does not refer to a concept, but to a reality. A degree higher than this state of pure indetermination is that of God, not in that particular guise of His Aspect, but as He is in Himself which is that of His Essence; and this degree refers to a state of being that is in reality transcendent even from being qualified by absoluteness (*iṭlāq*), for such qualification is in fact already a condition that limits existence to a particular determination as an entity (*i.e. ta'ayyun*), and is as such a limitedness (*taqyīd*) among the states of being limited that is mentally posited (*i'tibārī*) in the various degrees of intelligible and sensible existence. In other words, this aspect of God as the Absolute Existence is like the first aspect of quiddity mentioned earlier (*bi sharṭ lā shay'*), sometimes also called by ibn Sīnā a 'natural universal' (*al-kullī al-ṭabī'ī*),[266] only that it is not something mental but real, not

---

[266] A natural universal is defined as an intelligible in its pure abstraction, not conditioned by being related to anything at all. It is therefore neither conceived as being existent nor nonexistent, nor universal nor particular, as these imply some sort of relation. It is quiddity as it is in itself (*min ḥayth hiya hiya*), that is, *qua* nature (*ṭabī'ah*) and conditioned by being unrelated to anything (*bi sharṭ lā shay'*). See al-Jurjānī, *Al-Ta'rīfāt,* Cairo, 1357 A.H., p. 205, under the heading *māhiyyah al-shay'.* The notion of the natural universal was first formulated by ibn Sīnā as referring to one of the three aspects of quiddity (see above, pp. 219–220, the first aspect). Metaphysicians and commentators of ibn 'Arabī, such as Ṣadr al-Dīn al-Qūnyawī, Dāwūd al-Qayṣarī, 'Abd al-Razzāq al-Kāshānī and Nūr al-Dīn al-Jāmī made use of ibn Sīnā's conception of the three aspects of quiddity, but applied it to existence rather than to quiddity. They, however, further affirmed that in so far as existence is concerned there is another aspect prior to the first aspect of quiddity which is not conditioned by any condition whatsoever (*i.e. lā bi sharṭ*) and this aspect of existence pertains to that of the Necessary Being whose essence is at once identical with His existence (see al-Kāshānī, *Sharḥ Fuṣūṣ,* p. 4). Thus for the Ṣūfī metaphysicians there are four aspects of existence, the first being unconditioned by any condition, which they identified as that of the Divine Essence in His self-concealing aspect. This aspect is consequently unknown and unknowable except to Himself. See below, p. 260, the schema of ontological descent of Absolute Being, and note 287.

something static but dynamic. The absolute indeterminacy that we mean cannot be conceived as a static state of being—indeed, there *is* no static state of being - for the nature of God, in Whom essence and existence are identical, is dynamic; He is "always in act" (*Al-Raḥmān* (55): 29), "untouched by weariness nor by slumber" (*Al-Baqarah* (2): 255) . This dynamic activity is described by way of analogy, as 'breathing out' and 'breathing in' which refers to the articulation of the creative word of God, in terms of expansion (*basṭ*) and contraction (*qabḍ*); the expansion expressing the act of bringing into existence, the contraction expressing the act of returning to non-existence. This creative activity is an eternal process, although the contents of the process are non-eternal. When we consider the contents of the process at the level of intellection, their evolvement from non-existence to existence (and back to non-existence) is described in terms of the 'descent' (*tanazzul*) of the Absolute from the degree of non-determination to those of determination, particularization, and individuation.

As it 'descends' from its absoluteness to the realms of contingency, existence determines, modifies and particularizes itself into separate entities presenting the spectacle of myriad, diverse and variegated forms that comprise the world together with all its parts, and is, as such, a veil (*ḥijāb*) unto itself. It is a veil unto itself precisely because it presents itself to our cognition and volition in the guise of multiple and diverse limitations of itself, which we naturally perceive and conceive as separate self-subsistent objects, and which our minds 'ontologize' as quiddities. The quiddities, in their real nature independent of the mind, are in fact intrinsic limitations and modes of the very act of existence; and because our cognition and volition by nature operate only on the limitations and modes of the act of existence, existence itself *qua* existence, being completely veiled by them, forever eludes our rational and intellectual grasp. The determinations, modifications, particularizations and individuations of existence describe a movement that is discontinuous in its existing, although the movement itself of existence is continuous. For existence is always in act, existentiating its intrinsic limitations and modes, annihilating them and replacing them in new yet similar forms such that it never appears for two consecutive durations in the same guises, but that it is continually actualizing existential potentialities inherent in it in accordance with the unfolding forms of their future states. The quiddities in their real nature independent of the mind, which are the intrinsic limitations and modes of the act of existence appearing at the level of sense and sensible experience, are therefore discontinuous in their existence, for they do not endure two durations. The quiddities are then in reality, and in terms of the *Categories,* 'accidents' qualifying existence; and since they do not, as accidents, endure two moments of time, so the things of the empirical world which they constitute are in a perpetual state of ontological annihilation (*fanā'*) . At the moment when the world together with all its parts is annihilated, another similar to it takes its place; and that other suffers the same fate, and so on repeatedly in this way everlastingly. This is the perpetual creation. From moment to moment a new world, a new creation (*khalq jadīd*) takes its rise; and because of the continuous process involved, and our inability to penetrate the fineness of the veil before us, we are led by the imagination and the estimation to believe in one and the same world of separate, individual and particular things in their multiplicity and diversity that endures in existence. Thus what really appears to our vision is not the world at its moment-of-itself, as that eludes our vision, but the series of similar worlds following rapidly upon one another giving to our perception and imagination a vision of the world taking on a semblance of singleness and sameness and continuance in existence.

But there is another aspect of the world that partakes of reality, and this is that aspect of the world *qua* mode of existence, which at each moment-of-itself has real existence because its very substance is existence.

The Absolute Existence, as we have earlier described, is perpetually involved in a dynamic, existential movement of expansion; a pervasive, all encompassing expression of ontological evolvement from the less determinate to the more determinate, limiting Itself without impairing Its essential oneness, in the forms of Its own inner articulations which appear as multiple and diverse particularizations and individuations at the level of particular existence. Their appearance with being is simultaneous with their disappearance with non-being, and their disappearance is simultaneous with the appearance of new others like them. Their appearance and disappearance and their simultaneous replacement by new others like them describes a continuous, perpetual, creative existential process of the evolvement of Absolute Existence called the 'expansion of existence' (*inbisāṭ al-wujūd*), which from another perspective is none other than the perpetual process of the new creation (*al-khalq al-jadīd*)[267].

At the level of particular existence, then, reality is 'that by which a thing is what it is' (*mā bihi al-shay' huwa huwa*). Now a 'thing' at this level, and according to the perspective of the new creation, only *appears* to be one and the same thing all the time it exists, but in reality the 'thing' is every moment-of-itself not one and the same thing with the 'thing' that appears to take its place at the next moment of existence. From moment to moment there is not one and the same thing appearing and disappearing and appearing

[267] Even though at a very early date the Ash'ariyyah theologians had already formulated their metaphysics of atoms and accidents to explain the nature of the universe, their theory pertains more to the renewal of accidents, and not to that of substance as well. It was ibn 'Arabī who formulated the theory of the perpetual process of the new creation based on Quranic sources (see *e.g. Fuṣūṣ*, pp. 125–126). The Quranic expression *khalq jadīd, i.e.* 'new creation', is found in *sūrah Qaf* (50): 15.

again; from moment to moment there are *two* different things, but because of their consecutive, rapid appearances in similar forms, and our unawareness of the real situation, they are *imagined* and *thought* to be one and the same thing. Yet, in spite of the thing in reality being many different things, the thing continues to maintain and to preserve from loss its original unity and identity. The truth is that the thing's continuance in its original unity and identity is due not to itself—seeing that in itself as such it is infinitely ephemeral nay, it is a perishing thing!—but is due to its fixed essence or permanent archetype (*'ayn thābit*).[268] Now even though *that* essence too undergoes the process of simultaneous appearance and disappearance and reappearance in the intelligible world of the archetypes such that it is involved in discontinuance in its existence, that, however, appears again always in its *original form and identity,* so that it is ever regaining continuance in its existence (*baqā'*); and this original form and identity contains within itself all its future states, so that at every moment of its rehabilitation, a potential form inherent in it, and consequent upon its

---

268 The word *'ayn* has many meanings. Some lexicographers say more than one hundred. The Holy Qur'ān mentions seventeen. In the context we are discussing, it means the 'original source', the 'individuating' of a thing, the 'distinguishing feature' of an 'entity', the 'very essence', 'self', and 'innermost nature' of a thing. *Thābit* refers to something 'firmly fixed', 'not movable', or 'transferable' from its position, 'established', 'secured permanently'. In the sense we mean *'ayn thābit* conveys a meaning similar to 'fixed essence', or 'permanent archetype'. As for 'archetype' (from Greek *archē* + *typon*), it refers in early Greek philosophy to 'that which was in the beginning', to 'the first principle'; later it came to refer to 'substance', or to 'primal element'; and in Aristotle to the 'actualizing principle' or 'cause'. In the general sense it means the original model from which things are made.

antecedent form, is actualized. Thus, whatever inherent potentialities (*isti'dādāt*) it may possess that are actualized in the world of sense and sensible experience in the guise of many different things, it always maintains its unity and preserves its identity as one and the same thing. This is why the essence in the archetypal state is an established and permanent entity, something fixed in its original identity. 'That by which a thing is what it is' can only refer to something original in its identity, something permanent in the midst of change and, this *that*, which is the reality of a thing, or its real and true quiddity (*māhiyyah*), is its permanent archetype.

In saying earlier that essence is quiddity plus existence, we mean then that this quiddity is in reality existence-in-act delimiting itself into a specific form. Now this act of self-delimitation into a specific form that is existentiated by existence is discontinuous in its existing, but is continually being replaced by similars. The similars are the concomitant repercussions issuing from the inherent potentialities in the archetypal realities that are being actualized in a systematic order of precedence, such that as they go on being recurrently actualized they describe a gradual unfolding of their future states.

From the exposition that we have set forth thus far, two things become apparent pertaining to the nature of essence. At the level of empirical things, the essence that we call quiddity, although real is its durational appearance, yet does not endure two durations and is therefore accidental in nature. But at the level of the original realities in the realm of the archetypes, even though there too the quiddity that we call essence is still of the nature of accident in relation to the Absolute Existence, it is yet continually renewed in its original form and identity. Thus essence, or the ontological quiddity, has two aspects corresponding to its *fanā'-baqā'* structure: it is on the one hand something evanescent, and on the other hand something permanent. The former aspect manifests and is manifested by the latter. What becomes apparent as *change* emerges in the durations between the *fanā'* and the *baqā'* process in which the realities are involved. Indeed, this *fanā'-baqā'* existential structure pervades the entire domain of the realities and owes its origin to the double nature of the Divine Names.[269]

While we say that existence is the underlying reality common to all things, we do acknowledge that there is an aspect of difference between a thing and its reality, and between the realities of things among themselves, and we also acknowledge that between them and among them all there is an aspect of identity as well; for the reality of existence is that by which things differ from one another, and at the same time it is that by which they are united in identity.

Existence as a reality, and not as a concept, is as we have said not static, but is involved in a dynamic and perpetual process of self-unfolding. When we regard the unfolding of existence in its variegated modes of self-diversification, existence presents itself in analogical grades by virtue of its expansion from the degree of non-manifestation and non-determination to the various degrees of manifestation and determination until it reaches the degree of sense and sensible experience, that is, the world of empirical things. Since everything in the various degrees of manifestation and determination of existence is accidental to it, everything is forever 'lost' to existence. Rather, that which is lost to existence loses itself in the succeeding 'breath' of existence, which reconstitutes itself into another, similar yet not identical thing, which is but another, similar mode of existence. The exception to this perpetual process of rehabilitation of similars is the fixed essences or permanent archetypes, whose original identities are perpetually reconstituted; so that while they are noneternal in the sense that their existence is discontinuous, but because their original identities

---

[269] *Fuṣūṣ*, pp. 104; 79. See futher below, pp. 251 fol.

are renewed they yet are perpetually gaining subsistence, for as Ideas in the Divine mind they cannot be subject to evanescence. Because of the various degrees of manifestation and determination through which existence expands, and the manifold intermediary grades of ontological expression that it undergoes, its manifestation in one degree and in each mode in that degree is stronger in the preceding degree and weaker in the succeeding one; is more perfect in the preceding degree and less perfect in the succeeding one; is prior in the preceding degree and posterior in the succeeding one,[270] and so on in a descending order. The multiplicity of existents that results is not in the one reality of existence, but in the manifold aspects of the recipients of existence in the various degrees, each according to its strength or weakness, perfection or imperfection, and priority or posteriority. Thus the multiplicity of existents does not impair the unity of existence, for each existent is a mode of existence and does not have a separate ontological status. In presenting itself in analogical grades in the manner we have attempted to convey, existence is then also systematically ambiguous. This analogical gradation and systematic ambiguity is called *tashkīk*.[271] *Tashkīk* basically means the causing

---

270 That is 'prior' and 'posterior' in a non-temporal sense, for example like the hand and the ring on the finger.

271 See *Ta'rīfāt,* pp. 60–61, where al-Jurjānī gives definitions of *tashkīk* in terms of priority, strength, and perfection with reference to the systematic ambiguity of existence. The roots of the metaphysics of existence have been traced back to the Holy Qur'ān and the Ḥadīth. Its basic form of expression belonged to the School of al-Junayd of Baghdad. They presented the vision of the nature of reality as they envisaged it based on the intuition of existence, from which their transcendent theosophy was gradually developed. Among the notable early members of this School after al-Junayd were Abū Naṣr al-Sarrāj, 'Alī al-Ḥujwīrī, Abū al-Qāsim al-Qushayrī, and

of doubt or perplexity by someone or something. In the case of existence here, the causing of perplexity is due to its ambiguity which pervades everything in a systematic way; for existence, in its manifold aspect as variegated modes of itself, is that by which all things differ from one another; at the same time existence, in its absoluteness, is also that by which all things are unified. It is the principle at once both of unity and diversity, of identity and difference. Thus we see here, and within the context of *tashkīk,* that the distinction between the concept and the reality of existence is not merely the static nature of the concept of existence as compared with the dynamic nature of the reality of existence. There is also a clear difference between the absolute existence and the particular and determinate existence in terms of strength and weakness and priority and posteriority, which cannot be established in the case of existence as a concept. Moreover in the case of general existence understood as a concept, it can only be conceived of as the principle of unity in things and not also the principle of diversity. The distinction between the concept and the reality of existence may be schematized in the following diagram:

'Abd Allāh al-Anṣārī. To this School also belonged al-Ghazālī. But their chief exponent was ibn 'Arabī, who first formulated what was originally given in illuminative intuition into an integrated metaphysics expressed in rational and intellectual terms. Among his erudite commentators were Ṣūfī metaphysicians such as Ṣadr al-Dīn al-Qunyawī, Dāwūd al-Qaysarī, 'Abd al-Razzāq al-Kāshānī, and 'Abd al-Rahmān al-Jāmī. The philosophical expression of this transcendent theosophy and its further development as a genuine Islamic metaphysics was formulated by Ṣadr al-Dīn Shīrāzī, called Mullā Ṣadrā who combined his own original ideas with influences from ibn Sīnā, al-Ghazālī, ibn 'Arabī, and Suhrawardī. See also, note 266 above.

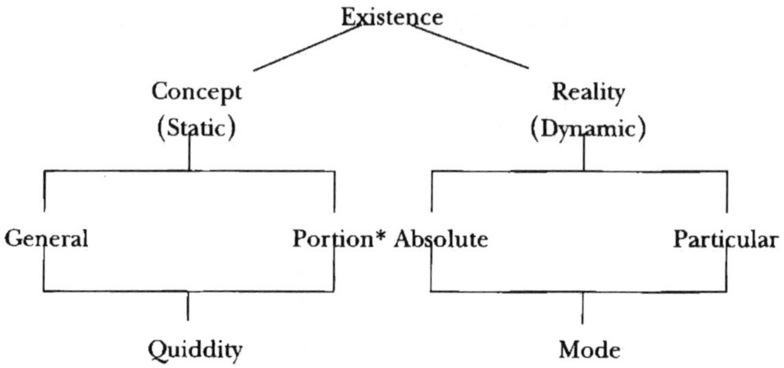

* On 'portion', see page 217, above.

Existence, as it unfolds and expands and limits itself into multiple and diverse determinations without affecting its original oneness, and in accordance with the requirements of the inner potentialities inherent in it, is that whereby all things (*i.e.* the actualization of the concomitants (*lawāzim*) in the potentialities) are united in identity; at the same time existence, as individuated into particular modes in the guise of essences or real quiddities of things as actualized (*i.e.* the concomitants and their effects (*āthār*) in the state of actualization), is that whereby things differ from one another. So according to our perspective, the reality of a thing is the determination of Absolute Existence individuated into a particular mode, as required by the archetype, by which the thing is *what* it is. The word *is,* in the expression 'what it *is*', refers to the thing in the state of actualization; the act by which the thing is actualized is the act of existence. These two aspects of existence *together* (*i.e.* the act and the mode) constitute what we have called real quiddity (*māhiyyah*) or essence (*'ayn* or *dhāt*), which is the reality of a thing and which points to none other that its archetype, whose nature is established in the interior condition (*buṭūn*) of Being.

We say it *points* to the archetype, as if the thing's being in the state of actualization, and the act of existence by which it is actualized, is something else other than the archetype itself. Indeed, the thing's actualization, and the act by which it is actualized, is not the same as the archetype itself, seeing that the archetype never leaves its interior condition, "never smells the odour of external existence".[272] What is actualized or externalized are the forces or controlling powers conforming to the nature of the archetype (*aḥkām*), its concomitants and effects (*lawāzim* and *āthār*) inherent in the potentialities (*isti'dādāt*) in the archetype. The Reality-Truth, or the Absolute Existence, manifests Himself in accordance with the requirements of the nature of the archetype,[273] and since the potentialities inherent in the archetype are multiple and diverse, His manifestations in their forms are never repeated in the same guise, but always appear in harmony with the multiplicity and diversity of the forms. Nevertheless, the multiple and diverse forms in which He is manifested is determined by the permanently abiding archetype, so that in spite of their multiplicity and diversity, they always retain their original unity and identity. In this sense, and speaking in terms of the metaphysics of substance and accident, the archetype is the substantial, antecedent reality (*matbū'*), while its repercussions that appear as a thing in the external world is its accidental, consequent reality (*tābi'*). The reality of a thing, then, is its archetype.

We have said that the term 'quiddity' is to be understood as conveying two senses corresponding to *māhiyyah* which it translates. In *māhiyyah,* the two senses in which the term is meant is (1), in the particular sense as an individual existent (*mawjūd*), which refers to the logical 'quiddity' that is derived from the answer to the question: "what is it?"; and (2), in the general sense to the ontological 'quiddity' as that

---

272 Ibn 'Arabī's expression: *mā shammat rā'iḥatan min al-wujūd, Fuṣūṣ,* p. 76.

273 See *Fuṣūṣ,* p. 103.

by which a thing is what it is (*mā bihi al-shay' huwa-huwa*), which pertains to the 'real essence' (*'ayn*) or the 'reality' (*ḥaqīqah*) of a thing.[274] In this second sense *māhiyyah* is identified as 'existence' (*wujūd*) . 'Existence' here is also understood as presenting itself in a twofold aspect: (1), as the very act itself of existence by which the quiddity is actualized; (2), as the quiddity in the state of actualization (*mawjūd*).[275] The first aspect refers to the dynamic principle whose intrinsic articulations bring to actualization the separate things that comprise the world; the second aspect refers to the separate things as they exist (*mawjūd*) .[276] The diagram below illustrates the general (*māhiyyah I*) and the particular (*māhiyyah II*) senses in which the concept of *māhiyyah* is understood.

---

274 See *Kashshāf,* V, p. 1313 article *al-māhiyyah); and* *Tā'rīfāt,* under the same heading (p. 205).

275 See above, pp. 242–245. Modern Western existentialist interpreters of the metaphysics of Thomas Aquinas will no doubt agree with us that the first aspect of existence explained above is equivalent to the Latin *esse* in the thought of Aquinas, and the second aspect to his *ens.* See Maurer's introduction to Thomas Aquinas, *De Ente et Essentia,* trans. A. Maurer (*On Being and Essence*), second revised edition, the Pontifical Institute of Mediaeval Studies, Toronto, 1968, pp. 13–19. *Esse* generally means 'to be ', *i.e.* 'be-ing' or actual being, and this is equivalent to 'essence' in the sense of quiddity. When *esse is* conceived in the mind it is esse *intentionale,* as it exists externally it is *esse in re* or *in actu. Ens* or *entia* generally means 'entity', which is real being, whether in act or as an object of thought of which predications can be made. It is something existent (*mawjūd*). Thomas Aquinas has given these terms a special, technical meaning in his metaphysics through the influence exerted upon his thought by Muslim metaphysicians.

276 This refers back to what we stated above in page 237, (1) and (2); the first aspect here refers to (2) and the second to (1).

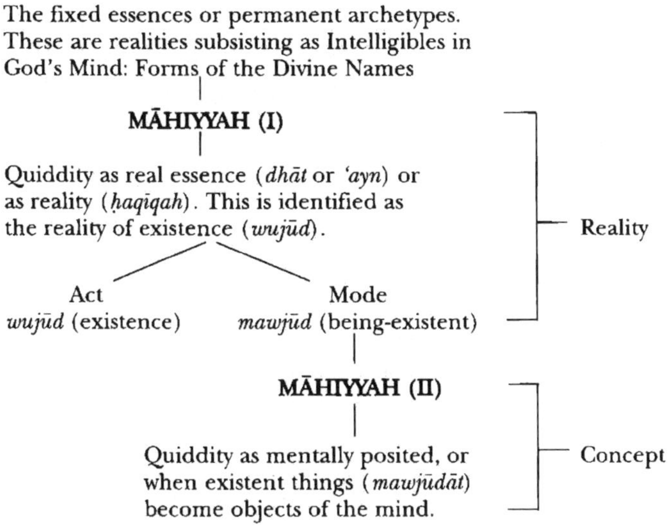
The fixed essences or permanent archetypes. These are realities subsisting as Intelligibles in God's Mind: Forms of the Divine Names
MĀHIYYAH (I)
Quiddity as real essence (*dhāt* or *'ayn*) or as reality (*ḥaqīqah*). This is identified as the reality of existence (*wujūd*).
Act
wujūd (existence)
Mode
mawjūd (being-existent)
Reality
MĀHIYYAH (II)
Quiddity as mentally posited, or when existent things (*mawjūdāt*) become objects of the mind.
Concept

Thus when we refer to the quiddities as being in reality the intrinsic limitations of the act of existence, we mean by *intrinsic* precisely what alludes to the actualization of the potentialities in the forms of their repercussions and necessary effects (*i.e.* to the act and to the mode), and not to the archetypes themselves.

As to the nature of the permanent archetypes, they are the realities of things (*ḥaqā'iq al-ashyā'*) in the intelligible or cognitive presence (*al-ḥaḍrah al-'ilmiyyah*). The term *ḥaḍrah,* meaning 'presence', refers to an ontological state in the world of intelligibles. These are subjective to God, or present to Him in His knowledge as 'ideal realities (*ma'ānī*). The realities of things are in that context not 'existent' (*mawjūdah*), but remain in a state of being 'non-existent' (*ma'dūmah*) in the consciousness and knowledge of the Truth. The reference to their being not 'existent' means their being not 'caused to emerge' (*i.q... abraza*) to a state of exterior manifestation (*ẓāhir*) in the forms of concrete, individual existence (*al-wujūd al-'aynī*); however, they nevertheless possess ontological reality and subsist (*bāqiyah*) in the interior condition (*buṭūn*) of Being. They are 'affairs', or 'states of activity', or 'predispositions' (*shu'ūn*) inherent in the Divine Unity (*al-waḥdah*), and being in the interior condition is their essential state. That which evolve from them, becoming outwardly manifest as 'exterior essences' (*al-a'yān al-khārijiyyah*), are their 'controlling powers' conforming with their natures (*aḥkām*), and 'effects' (*āthār*), and 'necessary repercussions' or 'concomitants' (*lawāzim*) resulting from causes that have their Source in the Very Being of the Truth, since there is no existent there other than the Truth. By virtue of their subsistence in a state of being non-existent, and of their potential role in the ontological evolvement to follow, the realities of things are also called 'possible things' (*mumkināt*).

The known in God's knowledge, which are in a state of non-existence (*'adam*)—that is, they have no external, concrete existence, but exist only as intelligibles in the consciousness of God—receive the 'overflowing' (*fayḍ*) or 'effusion' of the Truth[277] as He manifests Himself by means of what in the next stage only become known as Attributes (*ṣifāt*), which are inherent in the interior aspect of Absolute Oneness which remains forever unknown and unknowable except to the Essence. Every such thing, which is a particular facet of Himself, and which presents Him in a particular mode or individuation, subsequently becoming known as an Attribute - one among an infinite number—is called after the Quranic expression 'an affair', 'a mode of 'being', 'a predisposition' (*sha'n,* pl. of mult: *shu'ūn*) [278] of the Essence; and each is different from the other by means of which the Absolute Being manifests Himself yet again in a different form. The form manifested by this particular facet and par-

---

277 This refers to the expansion of existence as we have briefly described above, pp. 237–241.

278 *Al-Raḥmān* (55):29.

ticular mode, describing Him in that guise, is an Attribute, and it is distinct from the Being of God. For it to be 'distinct' from the Being of God does not mean that it is something that has an independent being or reality apart from God. It means rather that it is neither the same as nor different from the Being of God. It is something that has a double structure which when viewed in relation to God is identical with God, and when viewed in relation to its own, intrinsic structure is not identical with God, nor with each of the infinite number of Attributes. Viewed in this *second* manner, it has its own peculiarity; its own distinguishing features; its own essential property which makes it distinct from each other and from the Being of God. The explanation for this lies in the double nature of the Divine Names (*al-asmā'*) .

All the Divine Names, notwithstanding the fact that some are contraries of others, are identical with the Very Essence (*al-dhāt*) Itself when they refer to the Essence. But since each of the Divine Names is in reality naming a special aspect or particular form of the Essence in the variety and multiplicity of Its manifestations at the level of Its self-revealing aspect, each when pointing to its own, intrinsic meaning is describing only that special aspect or particular form, and not the Essence as It is in Itself, and is not then identical with It, and each is not identical with the rest of the infinite number of Divine Names. Thus every Divine Name, while being on the one hand identical with God and so with the other Divine Names is, on the other hand, an independent meaning in itself.[279]

When considered by itself independently of the Essence, in the manner described in the latter case, a Divine Name is regarded as an Attribute. When it is stated that the Essence, or the Absolute Being in His self-revealing, outward aspect, manifests Himself in different forms, and that the

---

279 *Fuṣūṣ*, pp. 79–80, 104.

forms manifested are His particular facets and modes describing Him, as Attributes of the Essence, each distinct from the other and from His Being, we mean by 'distinct', therefore, the *difference* that emerges out of the different aspect of each of the Attributes. In this manner and by each self-manifestation, and by virtue of the essential property of distinctness inherent in each Attribute, *a reality* from among the realities of the Divine Names becomes manifest (*ẓāhir*) and exists in the Divine knowledge. This is why we said elsewhere that the fundamental nature of reality is *difference.*[280] The form of each reality is called 'quiddity' (*māhiyyah*),[281] or a 'fixed and permanent entity or essence' (*'ayn thābit*). A reality, then, is a form of a Divine Name naming a special aspect of the Essence, which form is manifested in the Divine consciousness.

The effusion referred to above, which we identify as the expansion of existence, is called 'the most holy effusion' (*al-fayḍ al-aqdas*). Love (*ḥubb*) is the principle of ontological movement having its source in the Essence; it is the medium by means of which is activated this first and most holy effusion.[282] The contents of the effusion are known as the 'primordial potentialities' (*isti'dādāt aṣliyyah*), which constitute the inherent, essential properties of the fixed and permanent essences or archetypes indwelling in the Divine knowledge. The term *isti'dādāt,* which we have here translated as 'potentialities', means more precisely 'preparednesses'; for they refer to distinct essential properties pertaining to their future states, states that determine the ultimate nature and destiny of a reality or thing in which they inhere, so that the reality or thing will actualize in itself, as it unfolds from non-

---

280 See chapter III, p. 131.

281 This is the real quiddity, not the mentally posited quiddity.

282 The Holy Tradition: "I was a hidden treasure and I loved to be known, so I created the Creation that I might be known." See also Jāmī, *Naqd al-Nuṣūṣ,* p. 42; *Ta'rifāt* p. 176–177.

existence to existence, what the determining essential properties have prepared for it to actualize. The primordial preparedness, effused into each archetype or fixed essence, determines the ultimate nature and destiny of the archetype in such wise that it will actualize, in the stages of ontological evolvement that follow, what has already been prepared for it to actualize. Seen from the point of view of the realities themselves, and in relation to what is antecedent to them, that is, to the 'most holy effusion' of the Absolute Being, the permanent archetypes are so infinitely many *passive recipients* (sing. *qābil*) of their own determined natures and destinies; and since this decisive event occurs in the interior condition of nonexistence as we have explained, and the actualization of their ultimate natures and destinies in the exterior condition of existence is not yet then a realized event, we see this aspect of the permanent archetypes as so infinitely many *potentialities* and *possibilities* of exterior being and existence. However, when seen from the point of view of what is consequent to them, that is, of their separate evolvement as exterior archetypes or essences (*al-a'yān al-khārijiyyah*) that unfold themselves in the following stages of ontological descent into more and more concrete forms—that is, when seen from the point of view of their actualized natures and destinies—the permanent archetypes or fixed essences are indeed so infinitely many *active determinants* (sing. *fā'il*) of the nature and destiny of each and every thing in existence. They are here no longer seen as potentialities and possibilities, but are the *actualities* and *necessities* of being and existence. From this point of view, seen from 'below', as it were, in their active, actual and necessary aspects, the permanent archetypes project a further effusion of the Absolute Being called 'the holy effusion' (*al-fayḍ al-muqaddas*), whose contents, corresponding to the demands of the primordial preparednesses or potentialities contained in the higher, 'most holy effusion', are the inseparable and necessary consequences, concomitants or effects (*lawāzim*) and attendant repercussions (*tawābi'*) that follow from the primordial preparedness inherent in each of the archetypes.[283]

The archetypes, as we have pointed out, never leave their condition of being interior; they remain in the plane of the Unseen (*al-ghayb*) as intelligibles existing eternally *a parte ante* (*qadīm*) in the Divine consciousness.[284] As real quiddities they are the universal forms of the Divine Names, and through them the first 'most holy effusion' is effected as the first self-manifestation (*tajallī*) of Absolute Being. They are therefore also the 'loci' or the 'theatres of self-manifestation' (sing. *maẓhar*) which receive the first effusion, and which the Absolute Being effects through the Names, *al-awwal,* 'the First', and *al-bāṭin,* 'the Inwardly Hidden'. Correspondingly, and in the lower stages of ontological descent of Absolute Being towards determination and individuation into ever more concrete forms, the exterior archetypes (*al-a'yān al-khārijiyyah*) become the loci or theatres of self-manifestation, receiving the second 'holy effusion' (*i.e. al-fayḍ al-muqaddas*), which the Absolute Being effects through the Names *al-ākhir,* 'the Last', and *al-ẓāhir,* 'the Outwardly Manifest.' Thus the Names 'First' and 'Inwardly Hidden' belong to the interior world of intelligible existence; and the Names 'Last' and 'Outwardly Manifest' belong to the exterior world of concrete and individual

---

283 For a definition of the *fayḍ al-aqdas* and the *fayḍ al-muqaddas,* see *Ta'rīfat,* pp. 176–177.

284 We have already referred to them as 'ideal realities' (*ma'ānī*) in page 250 above. They are by analogy somewhat like the intelligible realities inherent in the Active Intelligence whose forms are projected by means of illumination to the human soul, but whose realities remain always in the Active Intelligence. By another analogy they are like the images in the imagination which serve the intellect as potential intelligibles, and which become actual intelligibles without being transformed or removed from their locus in the imagination. See chapter IV, p. 157.

existence.

From this brief explanation, we derive the conclusion that there are two kinds of self-manifestation of Absolute Being—two kinds of expansion of Existence; an interior and an exterior kind. The interior kind is the 'most holy effusion' which is the self-manifestation of the Essence to Its inward aspect in the world of the Unseen; the exterior kind is the 'holy effusion' which is the self-manifestation of the Essence to Its outward aspect in the forms of the permanent archetypes, which are in turn projected through the exterior archetypes in the forms of the visible world.[285]

The Divine Names are as causes whose effects are the existences in the intelligible and external worlds. Due to their double aspect, they are divided into two categories opposed to each other, the one gives impression or produces effect (*ta'thīr*), assuming the part of active agent (*fā'il*); the other receives the impression given and the effect produced, playing the role of passive recipient (*qābil*). Since the archetypes are the forms of the Divine Names (*ṣuwar al-asmā'*), they too reflect this double aspect of being on the one hand active, and on the other passive principles of existence. Considered purely as archetypes (*a'yān*), the permanent archetypes play the part of active principle in relation to the next stage of ontological 'descent' of the Absolute Being, that is, to what is 'below' them, or rather to their exterior aspect, the exterior archetypes, which assume the role of passive principle. Considered as realities (*ḥaqā'iq*), the permanent archetypes as the realities of things (*ḥaqā'iq al-ashyā'*) are the active principle in relation to the realities of the exterior archetypes (*ḥaqā'iq al-a'yān al-khārijiyyah*) which are the recipients of the existential principle, that is, the 'holy effusion' (*al-fayḍ al-muqaddas*) of the Absolute Being, that issue forth through them. The permanent archetypes as

---

285 *Fuṣūṣ*, p. 120.

the essences of possible things (*a'yān al-mumkināt*) or as the possible things (*al-mumkināt*), here refer to the realities of things.

The words 'possible things' refer to one of the three modalities of being or existence which was first formulated by ibn Sīnā.[286] The first mode of existence is 'necessity' (*wujūb*), and this refers to two ontological categories: (i), to a being whose existence is necessary by itself. This is the Absolute Existence (*al-wujūd al-muṭlaq*), also referred to as the Necessary Existence (*al-wājib al-wūjud*); (ii), to a being whose existence is necessary by other than itself, and this is the concrete existence of the world of empirical things whose existence is made necessary by the existence of the Absolute. The second mode of existence is 'impossibility' (*imtinā'*), and this pertains to the purely absolute nonexistence. It refers to a logical category such as a concept which can have syntactical meaning and can be formulated by means of proper linguistive expression, but which cannot otherwise exist in actuality and even in reality, such as a simultaneous merging of two things opposed to one another in one and the same place (*i.e.* a 'round square') or an associate, rival, or partner of God (*i.e.* a *sharīk*) . Its very nature requires non-existence as it is something existentially impossible. The third mode of existence is 'possibility' (*imkān*), and this refers to entities in a state of being nonexistent externally, but whose existence in the interior condition is nonetheless admitted. It refers to realities which subsist in the interior condition, and whose essences cannot be actualized in external existence. This is somewhat like the philosopher's notion of objective possibility, except that in

---

286 See the *Ishārāt*, vol. III, p. 19; *Metaphysica*, pp. 47–48; 316. Al-Ghazālī endorsed the three modalities of being (*Tahāfut*, p. 19) and theologians before (al-Juwaynī) and after him accepted them.

the case of the philosophers, they aligned their theory of objective possibility with their theory of the eternity of the world and allied theories. The 'possible thing', when it becomes actualized as external existence, comes under the category of a being whose existence is necessary by other than itself, as in (ii) above. Moreover, unlike the philosophers who believed that God is a necessary agent, the possible things in this case become actualized not of *necessity;* it is the Divine Will that determines their actualization as external existence.

All these modes of being or existence are in fact intellectual judgements; although if there were no intellects to judge them as such, the objects of the judgement would not necessarily cease to exist, for in some cases they would still remain in existence. In the category of the impossibles (*mumtani'āt*), for example, the partner, or associate, or rival of God (*sharīk*) is a pure impossibility, for it only exists in the intellect; if there were no intellects to perceive and judge it as such, its existence would no longer be possible. It is by nature conceptual, existing in the mind and in expression only. Hence its impossibility is absolute. But there is another class of impossibles that are not merely conceptual in nature, and this class of impossibles that are not merely conceptual in nature, refers to realities, each established (*thābit*) in itself (*fī nafs al-amr*), such as those forms of the Divine Names that come under the circumspective sway of the principal Name, the Inwardly Hidden (*al-bāṭin*), which remain eternally in the Unseen (*al-ghayb*), forever concealed from outward existence in the interior condition (*bāṭinah*). They are contraries of those forms of the Divine Names that come under the circumspective sway of the principal Name, the Outwardly Manifest (*al-ẓāhir*), which are evolved into exterior manifestation in existence. Being the reverse of the exterior forms, it is not possible for the interior forms to receive the effusion—that is, in this case, the 'most holy effusion'—that would evolve them into exterior manifestation. The distinction between this class of impossibles and the class whose mode of being or existence is designated as pure non-existence, or *'adam maḥḍ,* is that the latter, being the forms of the Divine Names that come under the circumspective sway (*hayṭah*) of the principal Name, the Outwardly Manifest, can receive the 'most holy effusion' that would evolve them into exterior manifestation; whereas the forms of the former, which are by nature inwardly hidden, cannot receive the effusion that could evolve them to outward manifestation. Only the possibles (*mumkināt*), which are the forms of the Divine Names that come under the sway of the principal Name, the Outwardly Manifest, receive the effusion, both the 'most holy' and the 'holy', that evolve them to outward manifestation and external existence.

The expansion of Existence in the various degrees of being as we have explained from page 253 above up to this page may be schematized in the diagram shown on the next page.[287]

As to the essences of the possible things (*al-a'yān al-mumkināt*), they are divided into two categories; the substantial (*jawhariyyah*), and the accidental (*'araḍiyyah*). We noted earlier that the permanent archetypes or fixed essences reflect in their nature the double aspect of the Divine Names as active agent (*fā'il*) and passive recipient (*qābil*) of existence.[288] Considered as the essences of the possible things, the permanent archetypes point to their contents, which are divided categorically into substance (*jawhar*), and accident (*'araḍ*). The substances, by virtue of their independent self-

---

[287] In this schema, the Essence is at the level of existence which is absolutely unconditioned (*i.e. lā bi sharṭ*). Existence I, II and III refer respectively to levels of existence which are, I: conditioned by unrelatedness to anything (*bi sharṭ lā shay'*); II: not conditioned by unrelatedness to anything (*lā bi sharṭ shay'*); and III: conditioned by something (*bi sharṭ shay'*). See note 266 above.

[288] See pp. 253–254 above.

Schema of the Ontological Descent of Absolute Being

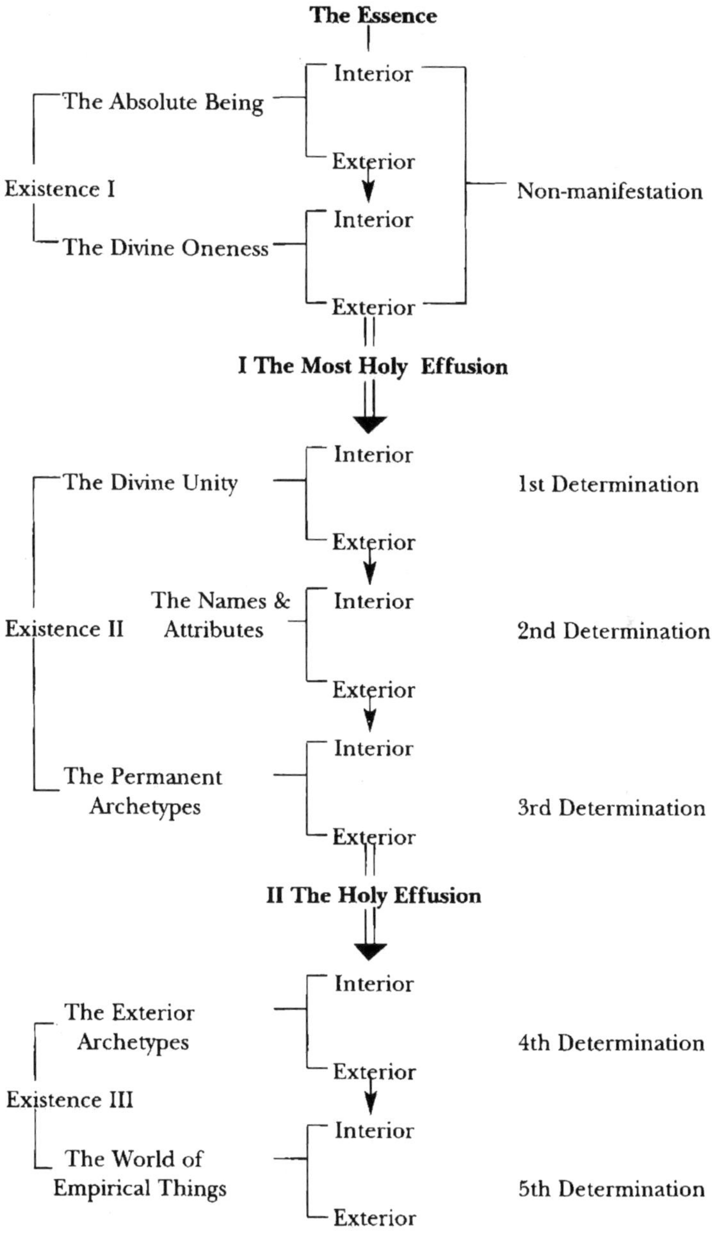

subsistence in relation to the accidents, are designated as antecedent realities (*matbū'*); whereas the accidents, by virtue of their dependence upon the substances, are correspondingly designated as consequent realities (*tābi'*). When substances exist as intelligibilia in the mode of intelligible existence (*wujūd 'ilmī*), they take the forms of pure intelligences (*'uqūl*), and pure souls (*nufūs*) – that is, intelligences and souls from which all material forms and bodily relations are subtracted (sing. *mujarrad*). When they exist as sensibilia in the mode of concrete, individual existence (*wujūd 'aynī*), they take the forms of simple bodies (*ajsām basīṭ*). When substances and accidents exist together in composite form (*murakkab*), they comprise the Three Kingdoms of Nature (*mawālīd al-thalāthah*); the animal, vegetable, and mineral worlds. Every one of the substances and accidents is deployed in such a way that together they all fall under a classification into three graded genera (*ajnās:* sing. *jins*): the lofty (*'āliyah*); the intermediate (*mutawassiṭah*); and the lowly (*sāfilah*). Every genus is further classified into various grades, each according to its capacity and requirement as a 'theatre' of manifestation (*maẓhar: i.e.* of the Absolute Being), which receives the effusions that would evolve it to actualization according to its inherent capacity and requirements, and to the sway—that is, the manifesting power that brings it into concrete, external existence—of the Divine Name which exercises circumspection over it. The Divine Names are in this respect themselves classified according to different degrees of rank corresponding to the differences in the capacities and requirements of the substances and accidents which make up the variegated and myriad things of the empirical world.[289] Thus the highest genus graded as 'lofty' comes under the circumspective sway of the principal Names ' the First' (*al-awwal*); ' the Inwardly Hidden' (*al-*

---

289 *Fuṣūṣ*, pp. 79; 152.

bāṭin); 'the Outwardly Manifest' (*al-ẓāhir*); and 'the Last' (*al-ākhir*); the genus graded as 'intermediate' comes under the circumspective sway of the Names lower in degree of rank than the principal ones above; and the lowest genus graded as 'lowly' comes under the circumspective sway of the Names even lower in degree of rank than the ones above them. In this way the Divine Names exercise their circumspective sway, according to their respective orders of rank, over the various genera of the realities; from the highest grade down to the various species at the lowest grade, while yet being influenced also by the corresponding capacities and requirements of the realities themselves, each according to its own inherent potentiality or preparedness. The ontological order of the three genera corresponds respectively to: (1) the World of the Permanent Archetypes (*'ālam al-a'yān al-thābitah*), or the World of the Divine Ideas, in which the self-manifestation of the Absolute to Itself gives rise to the forms of all possible existents making their appearance *in potentia* in the consciousness of the Absolute; (2) the World of Spirits (*'ālam al-arwāḥ*); and (3) the World of Sense and Sensible Experience (*'ālam al-shahādah*).[290]

When the theatres of manifestation belong to the species of simple bodies, for example, the Divine Names that exercise their actualizing powers over them operate in par-

---

[290] It must be noted that the general logical terms such as 'genera', 'species', 'differentia' and the like including 'universals' as we use them here are not to be understood according to their contextual meanings in the Greek philosophical tradition. We understand them not merely as names or concepts, but as realities or real entities (*ma'ānī*). The 'universals' are real entities, so that as such – even if they assume the character of universals in some respects – they are not quite the same as the Platonic Universals, for they are without exception particulars or individual essences (*a'yān*).

ticular (*khāṣṣ*) and determined (*mu'ayyan*) forms. In the case of composites, each one of the forms so composed becomes a theatre of manifestation of a combination of Divine Names acting together as a unity corresponding to the particular nature of the composite form. In the case of individuals (*ashkhāṣ*), in particular those that possess self-consciousness, the highest class being man, each is a theatre of manifestation (*maẓhar*) of a combination from among the combinations of Divine Names that operate in composite forms. In the case of man, and in particular those who are guided on the right course in true religion, each becomes a theatre of the ' subtle manifestations' (*raqā'iq* sing. *raqīqah*) that impart to him the knowledge of Divine mysteries (*asrār*) that guide him in the successive stages of his journey to the Truth. In this manner, from the loftiest heights of the ontological planes down to the lowest levels of being and existence, from the 'universals' to the particulars, the Divine Names accomplish their purpose, in actualizing all possible existences that dwell *in potentia* in the Divine consciousness, in an eternal, dynamic process.

The brief exposition on the nature of the essences of the possible things and their evolvement and actualization as the world of sense and sensible experience may be outlined in schematic form as on page 264.

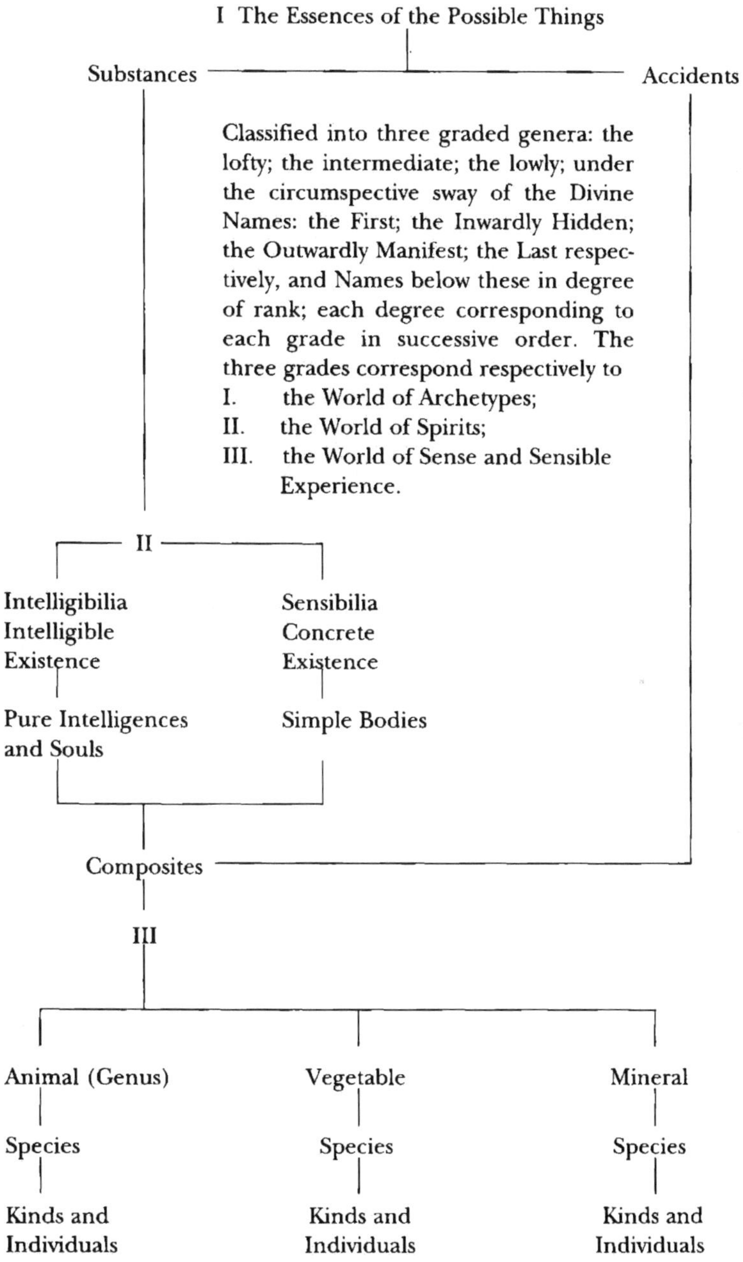
I The Essences of the Possible Things
Substances
Accidents
Classified into three graded genera: the lofty; the intermediate; the lowly; under the circumspective sway of the Divine Names: the First; the Inwardly Hidden; the Outwardly Manifest; the Last respectively, and Names below these in degree of rank; each degree corresponding to each grade in successive order. The three grades correspond respectively to
I. the World of Archetypes;
II. the World of Spirits;
III. the World of Sense and Sensible Experience.
II
Intelligibilia Intelligible Existence
Sensibilia Concrete Existence
Pure Intelligences and Souls
Simple Bodies
Composites
III
Animal (Genus)
Vegetable
Mineral
Species
Species
Species
Kinds and Individuals
Kinds and Individuals
Kinds and Individuals

To sum up, the realities are forms of the Divine Names and Attributes considered in their aspect of difference. As such they are essences that are established permanently as archetypes in the interior condition of Being. With regard to their nature within the ontological framework, they are the third metaphysical category between existence and non-existence. In the framework of the ontological planes they occupy an intermediary position between the two effusions of the Absolute Being which coincide with the interior and exterior types of the expansion of Existence. With regard to their subsistence in the ontological order, they are neither eternal nor temporal, being continually renewed in their original forms and identities, in such wise that they are, with respect to their identities, permanently established, and yet, with respect to their inherent potentialities, they evolve in change. With regard to their ontological relations with what is subsequent to them and what is antecedent to them, they are on the one hand active and on the other passive principles of concrete existence. From the point of view of scholastic philosophy, they are as 'universals' by which 'particulars' become individualized. As essences of possible things, and in terms of the *Categories,* they are on the one hand substances and on the other accidents; as substances they are the antecedent realities, and as accidents they are consequent realities. With regard to their mode of being, they are possible on the one hand and necessary on the other. In terms of being essences, they are true quiddities whose controlling powers conforming with their natures, repercussions and concomitants, and effects produce the worlds of spirits, of images, of sensible things, and of mental entities (*i.e.* imagination), all in descending order respectively. Finally, with regard to their essential nature they are identical with the reality of existence in point of substance, but differ from it and others among themselves in point of individuation.

VII

THE DEGREES OF EXISTENCE

The word 'existence' is generally understood to refer to a basic and universal concept to which no corresponding reality called 'existence' is found in the external world. What is found in the external world that are said to 'exist' are things ultimately reducible to their individual 'quiddities' or 'essences' which the mind perceives as realities independent in itself, and to which it attributes as their property the conceptual entity called 'existence'. The mind, when perceiving the things of the external world, considers the things in themselves as if their 'being-there' (*i.q. thamma*) is due to their own intrinsic nature, that is, their 'quiddities' or 'essences'. It is able to abstract what it considers to be the conceptual entity, 'existence', from the things and acts upon it performing mental divisions and delimitations into specific boundaries, apportioning each configuration of this conceptual entity called 'existence' to correspond with the individual things of the external world such that each and every one of them can be said to 'exist'. 'Existence' in this general understanding of the term is a conceptual entity that 'exists' only in the mind; it is a general, abstract concept rationally divided into portions corresponding to things and is by nature static or passive; it is a secondary intelligible.

But 'existence; may also be understood not only to refer to a conceptual entity to which there is no corresponding reality in the external world, but to an ontological reality that exists in the external world independent of the mind, and that because of its 'being-existent' externally it creates an effect in the mind which produces the concept of 'existence' by which the mind qualifies the things it perceives in the external world. We refer to this second understanding of the term 'existence', which cannot be conceptualized because it is not a universal, as the *reality* of existence to distinguish it from the *concept* of existence. Unlike its conceptual counterpart, the reality of existence is active; it is a conscious, dynamic and creative entity, articulating from within itself infinite possibilities of self expression in analogical gradations at different ontological levels in particular and individual modes that appear as separate things in the visible world as well as the invisible world. The true meaning of the word 'existence' as an objective reality pertains to this second understanding of it, and is applicable to God in this sense only.[291] In our exposition of the degrees of existence in the pages that follow, we shall concentrate on this second sense of the meaning of 'existence', that is, of existence as a real and existent entity whose effects have become manifest to our reason and our experience.

Existence as reality, and not as concept, is the very Essence of the Ultimate Reality. This Ultimate Reality is Allāh. Considered in His very Essence He is known only to Himself, for considered as He is in Himself He is unconditionally transcendent. By 'unconditionally transcendent' we wish to convey the meaning that He is in such degree of utmost isolation neither conditioned by unrelatedness to anything (*bi sharṭ lā shay'*), nor conditioned by being indeterminate in the sense of being unrestricted by unrelatedness to anything but free to engage in individual things (*lā bi sharṭ shay'*).[292] We can only

---

[291] See Nūr al-Dīn 'Abd al-Rahmān Jāmī, in his *Lawā'iḥ,* in *Majmū 'ah Mullā Jāmī,* Istanbul, 1309H., p.14; also the *Lawā'iḥ,* translated by E.H. Whinfield and Mirza Muhammad Kazvini, Royal Asiatic Societ,v, 1928, p.13: XIV. Elaborated further in his *Al-Durrah al-Fākhirah,* (in the edition of N. Heer and A. Musavi Bahbahani), Tehran, 1980, p.2:5; and Jāmī's own gloss to that passage, pp.54–55).

[292] See chapter VI; pp. 221–224, and the reference in the footnotes therein.

say that the Ultimate Reality considered in His very Essence is not conditioned by any condition whatever (*lā bi sharṭ*).[293] This means that the reality of existence at the level of the Ultimate Reality cannot even be considered as being absolute (*muṭlaq*), for existence at that level is above being qualified by absoluteness (*iṭlāq*)[294] by virtue of the fact that such qualification is already a condition that specifies existence to a certain disposition, and is as such a kind of restriction, a limitedness (*taqyīd*) among the states of being limited that is mentally posited in the various degrees of intelligible and sensible existence. In view of this the nature of the Ultimate Reality as not conditioned by any condition whatever is, strictly speaking, not conditioned even by transcendence, and can never be accessible to our knowledge and cognition, and remains eternally unknown and unknowable except to Himself. We refer to this first and highest degree of existence as the self-concealing aspect of the Ultimate Reality, as His inmost Self and very Essence (*al-dhāt*) alluded to in the sacred tradition as the 'Dark Mist' (*al-'amā'*) and the 'Hidden Treasure' (*kanz makhfiyy*).[295]

---

[293] See 'Abd al-Razzāq al-Qāshānī, *Sharḥ 'alā Fuṣūṣ al-Ḥikam,* Cairo 1966, p.4. What is meant by *lā bi sharṭ* here is that which is even above being conditioned by unconditionality; it is that which is *absolutely* unconditioned. See also 'Abd al-Raḥmān Jāmī, *Naqd al-Nuṣūṣ* Tehran, 1977, p.20, gloss 4.

[294] *I.e.* we mean being absolute and having an absoluteness in the sense as applied to natural universals. See further below, pp. 272–273 and notes 298 and 299.

[295] These traditions are well known. The *al-'amā'* tradition was reported by al-Tirmidhī referring to the commentary on *Sūrah* 11:1, in *Al-Jāmi al-Ṣaḥīḥ,* Cairo, 1938, vol. IV, 44, no: 5109; by ibn Majah in his *Sunan,* Cairo, 1952, vol. I, *Muqaddimah,* 13, no: 182; by ibn Ḥanbal in his *Musnad,* Cairo, 1313H., vol. IV, pp. 11 and 12. Al-Jurjānī in his *Ta'rifāt* says that *al-'amā'* refers to the degree of Oneness (*aḥadiyyah*). This reference is from the edition of Flugel, Beirut, 1969, p. 163. Al-Jīlī in his *Al-*

But the reality of existence, by virtue of being what it is, that is, by being itself manifest and bringing everything else into manifestation, must be posited as possessing degrees (*marātib*) of self-manifestation; otherwise nothing would ever be manifested as existing and, moreover, its degree of self-concealment also would never be known to be unknowable. Thus in spite of its utter concealment, there is an aspect of it that inclines towards self-manifestation. When we said, alluding to the sacred tradition: "I was a Hidden Treasure and I loved to be known, so I created the Creation that I might be known," that the 'Hidden Treasure' refers to the self-concealing aspect of the Ultimate Reality, the 'loving to be known' already implies a disposition pointing towards His self-revealing aspect. In this aspect He is already swayed, as it were, by love (*ḥubb*), which is the principle of ontological movement that becomes manifest in creation. Creation, being the verification of what is at once true and real, is the existentiating act of the self-manifesting aspect of the Ultimate Reality, and in this creative aspect He is called by the name signifying at once the Truth and the Real (*al-ḥaqq*).[296]

Insān al-Kāmil, Cairo, 1956, vol.1, p. 50, says that it is correlated with Oneness. The *al-kanz al-makhfiyy* tradition was reported by al-Baghawī as transmitted by Mujāhid. It revolves around the commentary on *āyah* 56 of *Sūrah* 51. The transmission by Mujāhid in a commentary on the Qur'ān of Abū al-Su'ūd al-'Imādī is found in the margin of al-Rāzī's *Tafsīr al-Kabīr,* vol. VII in the Beirut edition of 1324H., p. 777. Al-Rāzī in his *Tafsīr* also mentions it in the fifth question in the course of commenting upon the same *āyah* (p. 660). This tradition was reported by almost all eminent saints and sages. Al-Jurjānī (*op.cit*) says that *al-kanz al-makhfiyy* refers to the inmost Self, the absolute inwardness and utter concealment of God in the degree of Oneness (p. 197)

[296] There are many references in the Qur'ān pertaining to God's

From the brief explanation above, and as confirmed by sacred Revelation it becomes evident that the Ultimate Reality has two aspects: the inward, interior, self-concealing aspect (*al-bāṭin*), in which not even a trace of the initial stirring of any internal articulation is discernible from the point of view of human cognition even though it is the very ground of Being; and the outward, exterior, self-revealing aspect (*al-ẓāhir*), in which the inclination toward self-manifestation is initiated by the consciousness of desiring or loving to be known. Both these aspects are harmonized within the Ultimate Reality, whose inwardness is identical with his outwardness.[297] Existence here, as we have already said, is existence in the first degree, having two aspects which correspond to the interior, self-concealing 'Dark Mist' of sacred tradition, sometimes also referred to as the very Essence itself of the Ultimate Reality (*al-dhāt*) characterized by an utterly absolute Oneness (*aḥadiyyah muṭlaqah*); and the exterior, self-revealing 'Hidden Treasure' of the same tradition, which is predisposed towards self-manifestation in the realm of the Unseen (*al-ghayb*) and which, even though it is still considered to be in the abstract Oneness of *aḥadiyyah,* is not quite the same as the utterly absolute Oneness of the previously mentioned *aḥadiyyah muṭlaqah.* This is because it is in this second aspect already pregnant with infinite possibilities of determinations in various unlimited forms. Now this latter aspect is itself characterized by interiority and exteriority similar to the former aspect. When we regard this latter, abstract Oneness in its exterior, self-revealing aspect, it is called the Absolute Existence (*al-wujūd al-muṭlaq*). Its mode in this exterior aspect is still that of not being conditioned by anything whatever (*lā bi sharṭ*), in the sense that it is not

---

creating in which the act of creation is accomplished 'by the truth' (*bi al-ḥaqq*). See for example *Al-An'ām* (6):73; and *Ibrāhīm* (14):19.

297 *Al-Ḥadīd* (57):3.

involved in any determination, but is ready to manifest itself in determination. This exterior aspect of the first degree of existence is the center of infinite possibilities of determinations; it is the source of creative activity and the principlee of diversity. The term 'absolute', in the sense we mean here, refers to a mode of pure abstraction, somewhat like the first aspect of quiddity in ibn Sīnā's scheme, which he sometimes called a 'natural universal' (*kullī ṭabī'ī*);[298] except that here we are referring to existence, not to quiddity, and to existence that is not something conceptual or mental but real, that is not static or passive by dynamic or active. So when we liken this degree of Absolute Existence to the first aspect of quiddity in ibn Sīnā's scheme, we do not thereby mean that Absolute Existence, in virtue of its absoluteness, is *identical* with the natural universal. This is because the nature of the natural universal, as understood by theologians and philosophers generally, and whether it is applied to quiddity or to existence, is held to be something mental having no corresponding reality in the external world (theologians), or it is something both mental as well as real and having a corresponding reality in the external world (philosophers), in the sense that the words 'real' and 'reality' here refer essentially to quiddities considered as dissimilar realities, and not to existence.[299] We do not concede that the Absolute Existence, in virtue of its absoluteness, is identical with the natural universal in the above-mentioned sense. This is because we are not here speaking of existence as a conceptual entity, whose characteristics are governed by mental considerations pertaining to universals. Since we are speaking of existence as an objective and active reality indepen-

---

[298] See chapter VI, p. 237, note 266.

[299] For the arguments of the theologians against the philosophers and the Ṣūfīs, see for example, al-Taftāzānī's *Sharḥ al-Maqāṣid*, 'Ālam al-Kutub, Beirut, 1989, 5 vols.; vol.1, pp. 335–341.

dent of the mind, what is meant by the 'absoluteness' of Absolute Existence is that it does not have a determination (*ta'ayyun*) or individuation (*tashakhkhuṣ*) that is not consistent with the determinations or individuations in which it is involved in the guise of essences that occur in the various ontological levels and degrees. This means that it does not have an individuation in accordance with the characteristics of any individual essence that precludes it from simultaneously being also individuated in accordance with the characteristics of other individual essences without any multiplicity or change occuring in its own essence. Such absoluteness, which is impossible in the case of the natural universal considered as a mental entity, does not make it impossible for the Absolute Existence to be individuated in itself, in a manner of individuation that is free from the notion of universality, such as its individuation as God, for example.[300]

Now the Absolute Existence in its exterior aspect is in turn the interior aspect of the stage of ontological evolvement that immediately follows, namely that of a general determination (*ta'ayyun jāmi'*), sometimes also called 'general existence' (*wujūd 'āmm*),[301] containing within itself all the active, necessary, and divine manifestations as well as all the passive, contingent, and creaturely manifestations. This stage of ontological evolvement is effected by means of the most holy effusion of existence (*al-fayḍ al-aqdas*), which is a single expansion of existence in a general manner containing within itself manifestations of pairs of opposites of all

---

[300] Jāmī's answer to the arguments of the theologians stated in note 299 above is found, for example, in a short treatise entitled *Risālah fī al-Wujūd,* which has been edited by N. Heer in *Islamic Philosophical Theology,* ed. Parviz Morewedge, SUNY, Albany, 1979, pp.223–256. For the Arabic text, see pp. 248–256. With reference to what we have stated above, see p. 250(14). See also the references in note 291, above.

[301] See Jāmī, *Naqd al-Nuṣūṣ,* p.35, gloss 27.

possible existents in the invisible as well as the visible worlds, such as the active, necessary and divine manifestations as well as the passive, contingent and creaturely manifestations. This is the second degree of existence and it is the first of all the manifestations of the reality of existence, so that it is called the stage of the first determination of existence (*ta'ayyun awwal*).[302] We may schematize the foregoing explanation with the following diagram:

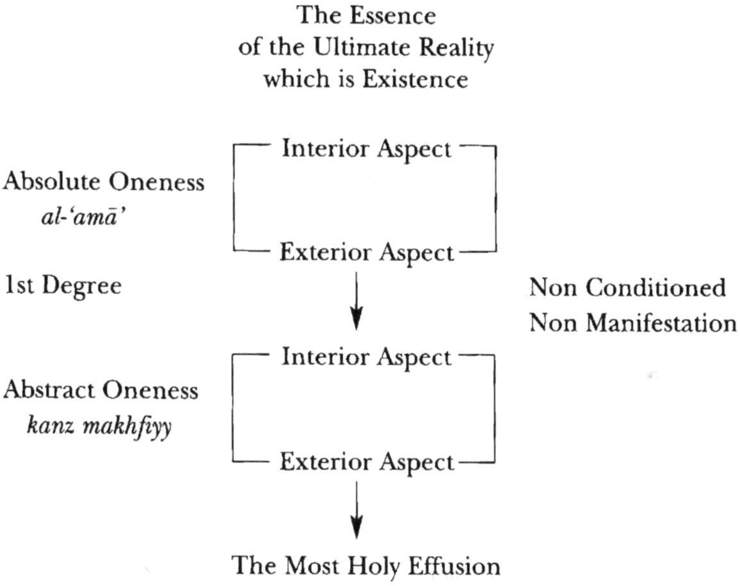

In the language of metaphor we say that when the Ultimate Reality desired to behold His resplendent Beauty (*jamāl*), He revealed Himself to Himself in His Essence (*i.e. tajallī dhātī*) and beheld therein as in a miraculous mirror His essential perfections (*kamālāt dhātiyyah*) in their eternal

---

[302] The word *'ayn* means 'entity'. *Ta'ayyun* is strictly speaking an 'entification', hence it is a determination as an entity. The pairs of opposites are comprised in the Divine Names and

and everlasting beauty. This first mirror, by which He gazed at Himself in contemplation reflects His Most Beautiful Names (*al-asmā' al-ḥusnā*) and Sublime Attributes (*al-ṣifāt al-'ulyā*). This first self-revelation and self-contemplation of the Ultimate Reality refers to the first and second degrees of the Absolute Existence, the second of which is at the ontological level of the first determination.

This level, which arises as a result of the most holy effusion containing the forms of pairs of opposites comprising all the active, necessary, and divine manifestations, as well as all the passive, contingent, and creaturely manifestations, marks the 'descent' (*tanazzul*) of the Ultimate Reality from the degree of Oneness (*waḥdah*), wherein nothing else is manifested even though it marks the first step towards manifestation, to the degree of Unity (*wāḥidiyyah*), wherein the inner articulations that are comprised in the Unity are discernible to Him as the forms of potential multiplicity. In the degree of Oneness prior to that of Unity, the particular forms that must already reside therein in a state of ontological commotion are yet negated by the Oneness, like "the lights of myriad stars that vanish in the presence of light radiating from the sun."[303] The Oneness is still here turned towards its interior aspect, which negates all manifestations and remains always in the absolute Oneness of the Essence. Only when the Oneness turns towards its exterior aspect does it resolve itself into pairs opposed to each other, such as the active and the passive, the necessary and the contingent, the divine and the creaturely, in order to become reunited in a determination that carries particularization

---

Attributes in their aspects of difference from Him. They are in continuous operation and no cessation is possible for any of them. For the meaning of *'ayn*, see further chapter VI, p. 242, note 268.

303 See 'Abd al-Karīm al-Jīlī, *Al-Insān al-Kāmil.*, Cairo, 1956, 2 vols; vol. 1 p.51.

(*takhaṣṣuṣ*) a stage further. This further stage is that of Unity, and it corresponds to the mode of existence as conditioned by being indeterminate, in the sense of not being conditioned by any particularization or individuation, but free to engage itself in particularization and individuation (*lā bi sharṭ shay'*). Then in His further evolvement to the levels of the second and third determinations the Ultimate Reality, in His aspect as the Absolute Existence, causes to arise within His consciousness the active, efficient and divine manifestations corresponding to the degree of Divinity (*ilāhiyyah*). Only at this stage is the Absolute Existence accessible to human cognition as 'God' (*ilāh*), and is described in the manner He has revealed Himself by His Names and Attributes of divinity. The 'descent' of the Absolute Existence to the second and third determinations, which correspond to the third and fourth degrees of existence, represent the outward aspect of the Ultimate Reality which is also called that of the Necessary Existence (*al-wājib al-wujūd*), because necessity is the invariable condition.[304]

---

[304] By the term 'necessity' (*wujūb*) we refer to one of the three categories of existence; the other two being 'impossibility' (*imtinā'*) and 'possibility' (*imkān*). These categories may be understood in the logical as well as ontological senses. Here we do not only mean 'necessity' in the logical sense (*i.e. wujūb; istiḥālah; jawāz*), as if the object to which it refers is merely an intellectual judgement which may have no corresponding reality in existence outside the mind. We mean by it also the ontological sense, and necessity in that sense pertains to two kinds of reality, the one dependent upon the other for its existence. In the first case it pertains to a reality whose existence is necessary by itself, such as the Absolute Existence identified by Quranic expression as the Truth (*al-ḥaqq*). It is the reality whose existence is not preceded by non-existence; it is self-subsistent by virtue of its own essence (*qā' im bi nafsih*) and this description points to the Divine name *al-qayyūm*. In the second case it pertains to a reality whose existence is necessary by

Again in the language of metaphor we say that the Ultimate Reality, after having contemplated Himself in that first mirror wherein are reflected His essential perfections, and desiring to see the essences (*al-a'yān*) of His infinite Names and Attributes, revealed Himself to Himself yet again *in their forms* and beheld, as in another miraculous mirror, the realities (*ḥaqā'iq*) inherent in them.[305] The forms of the Names and Attributes are the established essences or the permanent archetypes (*al-a'yān al-thābitah*). Thus when the Absolute Existence, in His self-manifesting, exterior aspect of Oneness at the ontological level of the first determination contemplates Himself, He is conscious of His own essential perfections, which are the essential forms of the Divine Names discernible in the Divine consciousness. They are, as it were, 'ideas' or 'intelligibles' in the Divine knowledge, and are qualified by being permanently established and fixed (*thābitah*) because they subsist permanently (*i.e. baqā'*) in the Divine consciousness and knowledge. They remain therein unaltered in their nature and unmoved from their interior,

---

other than itself, such as the concrete existence of the world of empirical things, whose existence is preceded by non-existence, and *is made* necessary by the existence of the Absolute Existence. Existence in the first case abides from and to all eternity, whereas existence in the second case is non-eternal. See further ibn Sīnā, *Al-Ishārāt wa al-Tanbīhāt,* with the commentary by Nasir al-Dīn al-Êūsī, ed. Sulaymān Dunyā, 4 pts. in 3V., Cairo, 1958 (2nd.ed. 1971), vol.3, p. 19; also his *Dānish Nāma-i 'Alā'ī* (*The Metaphysica of Avicenna*), trans. and comm. Parviz Morewedge, New York, 1973, pp.4748; 316; ch.24 and 25); al-Ghazālī, *Tahāfut al-Falāsifah,* ed. Khwājah Zādah, Cairo, 1321, p.19; al-Rāzī, *Lawāmi' al-Bayyināt Sharḥ Asmā' Allāh wa al-Ṣifāt,* ed. Êāhā 'Abd al-Ra'ūf Sa'd, Maktabat al-Kulliyat al-Azhariyyah, Cairo, 1400/1980,p.356.

305 On the nature of the realities, see chapter VI, pp 253–254, and p. 265.

intelligible condition. Moreover, because of their being distinct from each other and of their continuance (*baqā'*) as such in the Divine consciousness they are *realities,* to be sure, original realities of things whose future states are to be actualized at the lower degrees of the ontological levels.

Now the Absolute Existence in the highest degree of absoluteness does not require anything, being sufficient unto Himself and needing no 'other' whatever. But His Names and Attributes, which become apparent to Him at the lower degrees of the ontological levels, require their realities to be realized in their respective manifestation-forms (*maẓāhir,* sing. *maẓhar*), whether such manifestation-forms pertain to the invisible world or to the visible world, for without their manifestation-forms the realities will never be able to actualize their positive nature.[306] The realities of the Names and Attributes can only become positive by being actualized in their manifestation-forms. This actualization is effected by the self-revelations (sing. *tajallī*), determinations and individuations (sing. *ta'ayyun*) of the Absolute Existence in them (*i.e.* in their forms). Because every one of the realities is distinct from the other, and each one of them contains all its future states to be manifested in sequential order, His self-revelations in them are never repeated in the same forms. This further manifestation of the Absolute Existence in the lower degrees of the ontological levels takes place by means of another effusion of His existence called the holy effusion (*al-fayḍ al-muqaddas*) .

Thus far we have summarized in brief the ontological levels of the first to the third determinations of the Absolute Existence, which correspond to the second, third, and fourth degrees of existence. These are the degrees of Unity,

---

[306] Some realities have a negative nature; they have no manifestation-forms that can actualize them into external existence. See chapter VI, pp. 258–259.

of the Names and Attributes, and of the Permanent Archetypes. Each of these degrees, like the first prior to them, is characterized by having aspects of interiority and exteriority. It is at the stage of the exterior aspect of the fourth degree, that of the archetypes, that the holy effusion takes place. The following diagram follows in sequence the one shown on page 274 above:

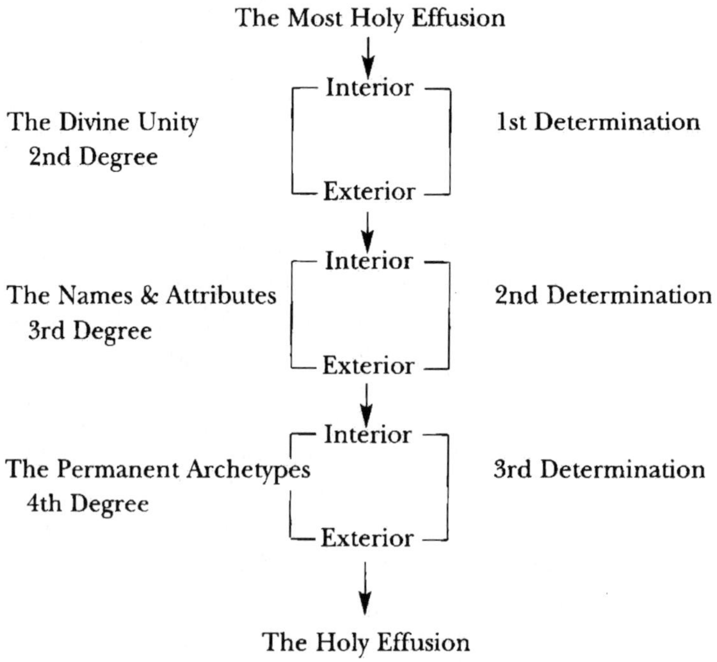

The contents of this holy effusion of existence at the stage of the exterior aspect of the archetypes, and in relation to the interior aspect, are the passive recipients of all potentialities inherent in the permanent archetypes, whose future states are consecutively being actualized through the mediacy of the exterior aspect of the archetypes (*al-a'yān al-khārijiyyah*). Since the interior aspect of the permanent archetypes are active determinants of all possible existents in relation to what is consequent to them, the corresponding exterior aspect of the archetypes, which are passive recipients of what is antecedent to them, contains all the passive, contingent, and creaturely manifestations of the Absolute Existence. In relation to what is consequent to them, however, the exterior aspect of the archetypes are active evolvers of the actualization of the potentialities inherent in the permanent archetypes in accordance with the requirements of all their future states, each actualization following upon another in consecutive order such that each one is something similar, something different, something new from the one preceding it. [307] This level marks the fourth determination of the Absolute Existence, which corresponds to the fifth degree of existence. The sixth and last degree of existence is the level of the fifth determination of the Absolute Existence. It is the manifestation in detail of the preceding degree and is the realm of the empirical world, the world of sense and sensible experience wherein contingency (*imkān*) is the invariable condition.[308] The diagram below follows in sequence the one on page 279 above.

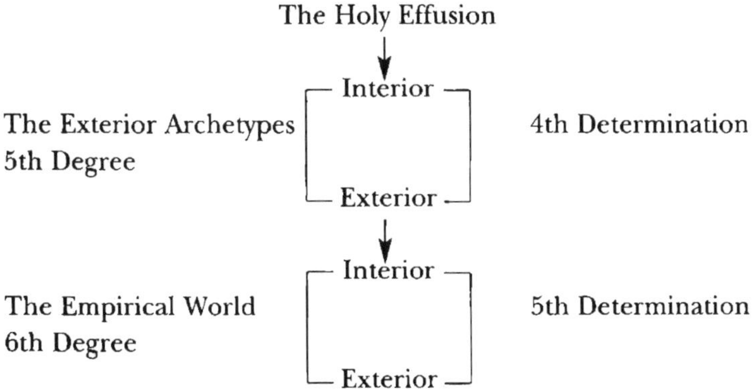

[307] See chapter VI, pp. 254–255.

[308] See also Jāmī, *Naqd al-Nuṣūṣ,* pp.29-30, and the Persian text on pp. 3031. On 'contingency', see the elaboration of its meaning in our interpretation of *majāz,* below, pp. 292–295.

We said earlier that the Names and Attributes of divinity require their realities to be realized in their respective manifestation-forms (*maẓāhir,* sing: *maẓhar*).[309] From the linguistic point of view *maẓhar* means 'locus of manifestation, not of the thing manifested'; it is like a mirror which is the locus of the image, not of the possessor of the image. Thus the manifested thing is not contained in the locus of manifestation. From the metaphysical point of view *maẓhar* refers to the form (*ṣūrah*) of a thing, whether it be in the intelligible or sensible realms of existence. The intelligible and the sensible refer to the realms of the permanent archetypes and the exterior archetypes respectively. In this sense, and with reference to the forms of the intelligible world, the permanent archetypes are the manifestation-forms in which are reflected the essential perfections of the Ultimate Reality that are being projected by the most holy effusion of existence in His first self-revelation (*tajallī dhātī*) . These essential perfections are encompassed in His Names, whose reflections appear as 'images' in the forms of the permanent archetypes. Similarly, the exterior archetypes are the manifestation-forms of the permanent interior archetypes, through which are further projected, by means of the holy effusion of existence in His second self-revelation (*tajallī shuhūdī*), the concomitants arising out of the forms of His Names. Their necessary effects become the visible world. Just as the two types of manifestation-form correspond to the two forms of His self-manifestation,[310] so they also correspond, in their existential evolvement, to the causal effects of His principal Names ' the interior' (*al-bāṭin*) and 'the exterior' (*al-ẓāhir*), 'the first' (*al-awwal*) and 'the last' (*al-*

---

309 See above, pp.278–279.

310 *I.e.* the manifestation in the invisible, the realm of the Essence (*tajallī dhātī*)*;* and the manifestation in the visible world of concrete existential entities (*tajallī shuhūdī,* or *tajallī wujūdī*).

ākhir).[311] On the analogy of the mirror, we see that what becomes manifest in the locus of manifestation (*maẓhar*) *is* the *form,* not the *essence* or the thing itself. However, the case of the Absolute Existence is different in that all whose manifestations are identical with the loci wherein they are manifested, and in all such loci, He is manifested in His own Essence.[312] Here *maẓhar is* not a real separate *locus* in union (*ittiḥād*), as it were, with the Absolute Existence manifested by it; nor is the Absolute Existence immanent (*ḥulūl*) in it, for the *maẓhar* does not *in itself* exist separately for Him to be in union with it, or to be immanent in it. The *maẓhar* in itself is something in the interior condition of Being (*i.e. bāṭin*); it is essentially non-existent (*ma'dūm bi al-dhāt*) . So the *maẓhar is* in reality the quality of the 'being-manifest' (*ẓuhūr*), it is not a real and separate 'theatre' or 'place' of manifestation. Now the becoming manifest (*iẓhār*) of a thing is its becoming distinct from another, or its becoming a *differentia.* As we said earlier with reference to realities, it is due to the essential property of *distinctness* inherent in each Divine Attribute that a reality from among the infinite realities of the Divine Names becomes manifest. The *maẓhar,* then, is constituted by the Divine Attributes.[313] In the same way that the attributes are identical with the Essence in reality, but superadded to it in thought,[314] so that the *maẓhar* constituted by the

---

311 See chapter VI, pp. 259–264.

312 *Lawā'iḥ, op.cit.* p.36. By 'loci' is meant the permanent archetypes.

313 The realities or essences subsisting in God's mind (*i.e.* the possibles, the permanent archetypes) are in reality God's Attributes (*e.g.* knowledge, will, power, *etc.*) and Names (*e.g.* knowing, willing, powerful, *etc.*). Although the Attributes are not existent in the concrete sense, they nonetheless subsist in the Divine consciousness as realities and are subjective to Him, while the Names become the modes of existence.

314 We do not mean, by the expression: 'superadded to it in

Attributes is in reality also constituted by the Essence in a certain respect, usually referred to here as the Truth (*al-ḥaqq*), in that way too is the Truth, as Absolute Existence, what constitutes His modes of existence, for the modes do not have separate, independent existences seeing that He is their real existences and their real essences. The Truth, in virtue of His infinite Names and Attributes, sees Himself as though in infinite and different mirrors, each reflecting a different aspect of His Being, thus producing a variegated multiplicity of images without impairing the absolute Oneness of His Being.[315] Our reference to the 'different aspects of His Being' as analogous to the many mirrors with their differing potentialities is an allusion to the real and individual essences in the interior, intelligible world of the archetypes, whence they are projected and evolved in the exterior, sensible archetypes to become the world of concrete things. Now, in the case of the mirror, it is the form, not the essence of the beholder, that is reflected; but in the case of the *maẓhar* of the Truth, He is Himself the manifestation-form by which He is manifested in His own Essence - He is Himself, as it were, at once the mirror and the face. The Truth appears in each and every individual essence in accordance with the nature of that essence, so that while it is true the He is manifested by that essence, yet that essence, by virtue of its inherent potentiality, limits the Truth according to its own nature.[316] So each and every manifestation-form is the Truth as manifested according to that form, not the Truth as He is in His absoluteness. Thus, while the Truth is identical with His manifestation-form the latter is not identical with Him, for it cannot be said that there is

---

thought', what the philosophers understand by the same expression which they also use. For a clarification of this see below, pp.310–312.

315 See Jāmī, *Al-Durrah al-Fākhirah,* pp. 10–11:24.

316 See *Al-Durrah al-Fākhirah,* pp.30–31:58.

absolutely no distinction whatever in the ontological condition of the Truth and His multiple and variegated individuations. There is, first, the distinction of essential priority and posteriority between the Truth and His manifestations and individuations. His being the Truth in His absoluteness is prior to His being His manifestation and individuation, and thus existence in reality pertains to what is prior. Secondly, there is the distinction of absoluteness and limitedness between them respectively.[317] Similarly, the distinction between the interior, intelligible *maẓhar* and the exterior, sensible *maẓhar* is in terms of the former being absolute (*muṭlaq*) and the latter limited (*muqayyad*), and indeed also in terms of the priority-posteriority relationship such as we have described in the case of *tashkīk*.[318] So the Truth is revealed in the manifested existence, and His manifestation-forms that reveal Him are His qualities. Said in another way, He is the One 'substance' (*'ayn wāḥid*), his manifestation-forms are the 'accidents' accessory to Him. Taken in relation to their Source they have reflected upon them the light of existence. The metaphor of light brings to mind the attendant shadow.

That which is 'other' than God in His aspect as the Absolute Existence, by which is meant the world of created things, is in relation to God analogous to shadow in relation to a person, so that in this sense the world is as it were the shadow of God.[319] For there to be a shadow there must be three things: a person who casts the shadow; a place or locus where the shadow is cast; and light whereby the shadow is cast. The person here symbolizes the Truth; the place or locus symbolizes the possible essences (*al-a'yān al-mumkināt*) or the permanent archetypes (*al-a'yān al-thābitah*); and the

---

317 *Sharḥ Fuṣūṣ,* p.141.

318 Chapter VI, pp.245–246.

319 *Fuṣūṣ al-Ḥikam,* ed. Abū al- 'Alā 'Afīfī, Cairo, 1365/1946, 2 parts bound in 1 , pt. 1 , p. 101 .

light symbolizes the Divine Name 'the manifest' (*al-ẓāhir*).[320] Light, as al-Ghazālī says,[321] is by itself visible and makes other things visible. Indeed, God is the Real Light, the Source of all the grades of lights which are, in relation to His Light, metaphorical in nature.[322] The Divine Name 'the light' (*al-nūr*) points in fact to the Divine Name 'the manifest', for like light God is by Himself manifest and brings others into manifestation (*al-ẓāhir fī nafsihi al-muẓhir li ghayrihi*).[323] Now the 'others' that are brought into manifestation are the possible essences (*mumkināt*) which are in themselves mere potentialities having no actual existence, and which are essentially in the darkness of non-existence (*ẓulmah 'adamiyyah*), but which are nonetheless established as intelligibles in the Divine knowledge.[324] The term 'darkness' (*ẓulmah*) alludes to the nature of the shadow, for all shadows are dark and nothing could be darker than the darkness of non-existence. Just as in the case of a phenomenal shadow, if there were no light to project it and no place where it can be cast, the shadow would remain in non-existence; it would remain a potentiality inherent in the phenomenal being or thing and would never emerge into actuality. So in like manner,.the possible essences in their darkness of non-existence, which in this case also means their being enveloped in mystery, are

---

[320] *Sharḥ Fuṣūṣ,* p. 138.

[321] *Mishkāt al-Anwār,* ed. Abū al- 'Alā 'Afīfī, Dār alQawmiyyah li al-Tibā 'ah wa al-Nashr, Cairo, 1383/1964, pp.4–5.

[322] *Ibid,* pp.16–18; on the various grades of lights see pp.4–16.

[323] See al-Ghazālī, *Al-Maqṣad al-Asnā fī sharḥ ma'ānī Asmā' Allāh al-Ḥusnā,* ed. Fadlou Shehadi, Dār al-Mashriq, Beirut, 1971, p.157; his commentary on the Divine Name *al-nūr* (pp.157–158); also his commentary on the Divine Names *al-ẓāhir al-bāṭin,* pp.147–150. *Sharḥ Fuṣūṣ,* p.133. Also al-Rāzī on Names in his *Lawāmi' al-Bayyināt sharḥ Asmā' Allāh wa al-Ṣifāt,* pp. 1 8–26; 347.

[324] *Fuṣūṣ,* pp.101–102.

potentialities established in the Divine consciousness. They are the essential perfections (*kamālāt dhātiyyah*) that constitute the Divine Names and Attributes. Only when the light of His Essence is projected upon them that the shadows they cast constitute the permanent archetypes, so that the archetypes represent the 'place' or manifestation-form (*maẓhar*) of the shadow of the Essence. Then through the permanent archetypes the essential light is further projected on the forces inherent in their nature (*aḥkām*), their necessary repercussions (*lawāzim*) and concomitants (*tawābi'*) casting as their effects (*āthār*) the *second* shadow that we call the world. The shadow of the Essence is called 'relative light' (*nūr iḍāfī*).[325] Now the possible essences are in themselves not luminous because they possess no being. Without the essential light, the possible essences do not become essences.[326] When the Essence manifests itself in the possible essences its shadow becomes manifest. The possible essences are like transparent glass, so that the shadow of the Essence projected through them retains its light-nature. Only when this shadow of light is further projected to the exterior archetypes (*al-a'yān al-khārijiyyah*) to appear as the world does it acquire its dark coloration due to the 'distance' from the Source of Light. The light itself is pure and colourless, but becomes coloured by the colour of the glasses through which it shines forth.[327] This is why the first shadow is called 'relative light', which is but another name for 'relative existence ' (*wujūd iḍāfī*), for in the terminology of the Ṣūfī metaphysicians light is identical with existence.[328]

---

325 See al-Qāshānī, *Sharḥ Fuṣūṣ*, p.144; *Fuṣūṣ*, p.104.

326 Please note that the relation of the human intellect to the rational imagination, and that the Active Intelligence to the human soul, is in a certain respect analogous to this. See further chapter IV, pp. 157; 164–165.

327 *Fuṣūṣ*, pp.102–103.

328 See *Mishkāt*, p.55; *Maqṣad*, p.157; *Fuṣūṣ*, p.102. The relative

Thus the world is called 'shadow' for two main reasons which demonstrate the analogous nature of their reality, namely: (1) the shadow has no independent reality; its movement is due to its possessor and it has no efficacy to bring into existence or to cause nonexistence; it is essentially non-existence, for its real essence is not itself but its possessor; (ii) the reality of the shadow is existential privation of light; it does not possess prior existence to which one can refer as its reality other than sheer possibility, and it comes into existence due to the light that casts it. Its reality, then, is other than itself.

It is clear from what we have explained that there are two aspects to the shadow of the Ultimate Reality: the first is the essential shadow which becomes manifest to Him as He reveals Himself to Himself, and this corresponds to the self-manifestation of the Ultimate Reality to His own Essence (*tajallī dhātī*). The shadow is projected on the interior archetypes (*al-a'yān al-thābitah*) which are the forms of the Divine Names and Attributes. This projection corresponds to the first effulgence of His light, which is the most holy effusion (*al-fayḍ al-aqdas*). The self-revelations (*tajalliyāt*) and self-determinations (*ta'ayyunāt*) of the Absolute Existence are here of an interior nature subjective to Him, and they refer to the ontological planes of the first and second determinations respectively. This aspect of the shadow of the Absolute Existence is variously called 'relative existence' (*wujūd iḍāfī*), 'general existence' (*wujūd 'āmm*), and the 'breath of the Merciful' (*nafas al-raḥmān*) in the degree of essential Oneness (*al-waḥdah*) in the ontological plane of the first determination; and it is called the first shadow, and the per-

---

existence (*wujūd idāfī*) *is* identical with the 'breath of the Merciful' (*nafas al-raḥmān*). See also *Kashshāf Iṣṭilāḥāt al-Funūn* of al-Tahānawī, Khayyāt, Beirut, 1966, 6v.,1V, p.938 under *al-ẓill.*

manent archetypes (*al-a'yan al-thābitah*) in the degree of Unity (*al-wāḥidiyyah*) in the ontological plane of the second determination. The second aspect of the shadow of the Absolute Existence is what is called the exterior shadow, which is the *maẓhar* or manifestation-form of the second determination. This shadow is a reflection of the first shadow as it is projected in the forms of the interior archetypes, and it corresponds to the second effulgence of His light, which is the holy effusion (*al-fayḍ al-muqaddas*), and to the self-revelations of the Absolute Existence as He goes on determinating Himself into ever more concrete forms in variety and multiplicity through the exterior archetypes (*al-a'yān al-khārijiyyah*) until finally it assumes the forms of the visible world (*tajallī shuhūdī* or *tajallī wujūdī*). This second shadow, being a reflected shadow of the first, is variously called the First Intellect (*al-'aql al-awwal:*), the World of Spirits (*'ālam al-arwāḥ*), the Perfect Man (*al-insān al-kāmil*) and that which is 'other' than God (*mā siwa Allāh*).

We have briefly outlined in the foregoing pages the six degrees of existence in descending order from the highest to the lowest. It must be always kept in mind, when we speak of the 'descent' of the Ultimate Reality from the degree of pure absoluteness and utter concealment to those of manifestation in the lower degrees of the ontological levels, that there is no temporal sequence involved, no distance measurable in terms of time between the highest and the lowest as may be suggested by the mind. Time as we know it only arises together with the empirical world of sense and sensible experience. The whole creative process of determination involved in the varying degrees occurs all at once and continuously, for the self-manifesting aspect of the Ultimate Reality is perpetually involved in self-revelations and individuations in different guises in the different degrees and in gradations at the various ontological levels, all the while remaining always as He was, maintaining His pure and absolute Oneness. Thus in spite of His evolvement in the different ontological modes of His existence, which are modes of being conditioned, first by unrelatedness to anything (*bi sharṭ lā shay'*); then by being indeterminate but free to relate to something (*lā bi sharṭ shay'*); then by being something (*bi sharṭ shay'*), His existence itself is free from being conditioned by division into absolute existence on the one hand and relative existence on the other, even when He is in His very Essence and source of such division. By way of analogy, and to borrow al-Ghazālī's similitude on the various grades of light (*Mishkāt*, p.53), the similitude of the expansion of existence in ambiguous gradations in the various ontological levels can be apprehended by one who sees the light of the moon shining through the window of a house, falling on a mirror fixed upon the wall, which reflects the light on to another wall facing it, then which in turn is reflected on to the floor which becomes illuminated by the light. Here we have four grades of light from the lowest to the highest: the light upon the floor is consequent on that upon the wall; the light on the wall follows from the reflected light in the mirror; the light in the mirror shines from the radiance of the moon; the light radiating from the moon comes from the effulgences of the hidden sun. The modes of existence may be summarized into four stages:

(I) The stage of the very Essence itself of the Ultimate Reality, which is Existence as it is in itself, exempt from all conditions, including that of unconditionality, and all relations. Theologically, this is the stage of God as He is in Himself, enveloped in utter concealment which remains eternally unknown and unknowable except to Himself.

(II) The stage of 'general existence' (*wujūd 'āmm*), which is that of the Absolute Existence identified by Quranic expression as the Truth. This is the stage of God in His self-revealing aspect, which is the exterior aspect of (I) above. It encompasses the second degree of existence as it expands and unfolds itself in initial manifestation through the mediacy of the most holy effusion to the first determination, containing within itself manifestations of forms opposed to each other of all possible existents in the invisible as well as the visible worlds. These are the active, necessary, and divine manifestations as well as the passive, contingent, and creaturely manifestations. It is the manifestation of the Essence to itself (*tajallī dhātī*), that is, it is subjective to God, in which His essential perfections (*kamālāt dhātiyyah*) and predispositions (*shu'ūn*) become manifest to Him.

(III) The stage of 'relative existence' (*wujūd iḍāfī*), which is a further articulation of (II) above. Here the Absolute Existence is conditioned by being indeterminate but free to relate itself to something. It is the stage of Oneness that is already pregnant with infinite possibilities of self-diversification; the stage of the Unity of the Many (*wāḥidiyyah*), wherein the Ultimate Reality is qualified by Names and Attributes whose forms are the permanent archetypes established in His consciousness. This stage encompasses the ontological levels of the second and third determinations corresponding to the third and fourth degrees of existence. It is also identified as the stage of the 'unfolded existence' (*wujūd munbasit*) sometimes also called the 'breath of the Merciful' (*nafas al-raḥmān*) and the 'relative light' (*nūr iḍāfī*). The metaphor of Light (*nūr*), which is often used to describe stage (II) above, is here reflected as images in innumerable and different mirrors (*i.e.* the permanent archetypes) which in turn are reflected in corresponding mirrors in the lower degrees of the ontological levels (*i.e* the exterior archetypes). The expansion of existence from the level of the permanent archetypes to that of the exterior archetypes is effected through the mediacy of the second effusion of existence, the holy effusion.

(IV) The stage of 'comprehensive existence' (*wujūd jāmi'*), which is the stage of the empirical world, the world of sense and sensible experience. Here the reality of existence is diversified into particular and individual entities, or into its manifold and variegated modes. This stage encompasses the fourth and fifth determinations of the Absolute Existence corresponding to the fifth and sixth degrees of existence.

The ontological status of that which is 'other' than God (*mā siwa Allāh*), that is, both the invisible as well as the visible worlds, consists of existential relations arising from their 'moments' of being 'related to' the effusion of existence. The existence of each such thing is then discontinuous and momentary. Indeed its existence is simultaneous with its non-existence; and our recognizing it as having an 'essence' and as a specific, individual 'thing' having apparent continuance in existence is in reality attributed to its quiddity which exists only in the mind when the mind considers it (*i.e. i'tibārī*). Its discontinuous nature means that it in each 'moment-of-itself' has no existence in the real sense —that is, in the sense that it endures in some sort of duration in each moment-of itself. But the fact that it has no real existence does not mean that it is something illusory. Indeed its momentary existence has an ontological status, the more so when the semblance of existential continuity is attained by its continuous renewal. It is then something non-eternal (*muḥdath*), something that was new, that existed newly, for the first time, not having been before, something recently originated, so that it is 'ever-new'. At each moment of its renewal, it is not the same thing as the one that precedes it, but a new thing at its every appearance and disappearance and reappearance in an eternal process. The *process* itself may be described as the *same* throughout, but the *contents* of the process—that is, the worlds in which the process involves and by which the process is involved—are not the same: every one of the things at each consecutive moment of its renewal is similar to the preceding other, and since every single manifestation in the process is new, every manifestation is *different* from the other.

In this way, and due to the fact that all are involved in the continuous process of renewal, there is no real existence to anything but to God alone. Thus only His Aspect remains.[329] The annihilation and renewal creative process involves all things; not only the universe together with all its parts, but even the world of spirits and the archetypal realities are continually annihilated and renewed, continually appearing and disappearing. But there is a decisive distinction between the annihilation and renewal, the appearing and disappearing of the realities (*ḥaqā'iq*) and that of the worlds that they project. Whereas in the case of the worlds they are new every moment, and each new world is a different though similar one in relation to the one preceding it in such wise that the worlds are ever perishing, the realities are reconstituted, reformulated and made to reappear always in the *same* forms.[330] That is why they are referred to as 'fixed' or 'permanent' (*thābitah*); for it is only because they are thus permanently established in the Divine consciousness that they can become intelligibles in the Divine knowledge; and it is only because of their permanent nature that they can be defined as 'realities', for in relation to the world that they project they are more real than the world. It is in this sense that the realities may be considered as 'substances' in relation to the world of 'accidents'. The ontological status of that which is 'other' than God is that moment of being 'related-to' the Absolute Existence; its real existence is therefore that moment of 'being-existent', that moment of being 'related-to' existence, corresponding to stage III above of the Absolute Existence called 'relative existence', and it is called 'metaphorical existence' (*wujūd majāzī*).

---

[329] Qur'ān, *Al-Qaṣaṣ* (28): 28.

[330] Ibn 'Arabī, *Fuṣūṣ al-Ḥikam,* Cairo, 1946, vol.1, p.124. See also al-Qāshānī *Sharḥ Fuṣūṣ, op.cit.,* p. 237; and ibn 'Arabī, *Futūḥāt al-Makkiyyah,* Cairo, 1972, vol. l, pp.204:290A.

Now *ḥawādith* (pl. of *ḥādith*) denotes 'originated things'; things that were new, not having been before. The root of the term (*i.e. ḥadatha*) expresses the contrary of something prior that has always been (*i.e. qaduma*), so that the term in its metaphysical sense expresses the contrary of what is eternal (*qaduma*) . Literally *ḥawādith* means 'renewed things'; things that are ever-new in their occurrence such that their existence, taken individually, is discontinuous. The existence that we predicate of them as being ever-new refers both to their temporal (*zamānī*) as well as their essential (*dhātī*) existence; that is, they have a beginning in time and their essences are not self-subsistent. So because they are ever-new temporally and essentially, their individual existences taken collectively as a series is a 'happening' that takes place and then ceases to take place. Then their renewal by similars occurs and is repeated perpetually so that we see their existence *as a whole* as continuous. Indeed, existence must by nature be continuous in its existing; but existence in that real sense belongs only to the Ultimate Reality. In the case of the originated things, however, their existence is discontinuous even though we perceive the contrary due to the perpetual process of the renewal of similars. So what we see is in reality 'metaphorical' existence (*wujūd majāzī*).

A semantic analysis of the concept of *majāz* will clarify further what is meant by 'metaphor' when it is applied to existence as it is here. The root *jāza* refers to something 'allowable', and hence, in the metaphysical or theological context to a thing *in potentia* or to a 'possible' thing; and its infinitive noun, *jawāz* to 'possibility'. What is meant by 'allowable' or 'possible' here is depicted in the mind when a thing passed across from one place (*e.g.* a path, a road) to another (*e.g.* the other side of the path or road) because it has become allowable or possible for the thing to actualize the passing at the specific time. The active participial noun of *jāza: jā'iz,* is the actual passing taking place. When we transfer this meaning to the metaphysical context we immediately perceive the idea that a thing that was possible has, due to the actual creative connection with God effected by Him through His Attributes of power and will combined, passed over from the stage of potentiality to the stage of actuality: from non-existence, into existence. *Majāz* then refers to the occurrence of contingency, or the taking place of the contingent, that is, the world of contingent being. The actualization of what was once potential, even though it *is* an actualization, does not subsist in its actualization; it simply passed from non-existence into existence and back to non-existence. The actual passing taking place—that is, the actualization—is what is termed as *jā'iz,* so that when the theologians refer to *jā'iz al-wujūd* they mean precisely this sort of transient existence.

Now the meaning of *majāz* as metaphor is brought to mind when something passes beyond the meaning to which it is originally applied, such as for example, to transfer the meaning of 'lion', originally applied to a beast, beyond the beast to a man, calling the brave or courageous man a 'lion', because of the analogy or connection between the two senses of the meaning of 'lion'. The man in reality is not a lion, but only *like* a lion in bravery or courage.[331] When we transfer the meaning of *majāz* as metaphor to the metaphysical context, what is meant by it is that we have transferred the meaning of existence, originally applied to something eternal and self-subsistent (i.e. to 'real existence', *wujūd ḥaqīqī*), beyond that to something non-eternal and dependent (i.e. to the world of created things), predicating of the existent world 'existence' because of the analogy or connection between the two senses of the meaning of 'existence'. The world in itself does not possess real existence (i.e. eternal

[331] See al-Fīrūzābādī, *Al-Qāmūs al-Muḥīṭ,* Cairo, 1319AH. 4 vols., vol.2, pp.176–77; see also al-Tahānawī, *Kashshāf Iṣṭilāḥāt al-Funūn,* Beirut, 1966, 6 vols., vol.1, pp.208–209; 213–217 and under *al-majāz al-lughawī: isti'ārah,* pp.214–217; al-Jurjānī in his *Ta'rīfāt,* pp.20;214.

and self-subsistent existence), but it only looks as if it has existence because of its apparent continuance in existence. We say 'looks as if' and 'apparent' because, as already explained, the actual connection of God with the world through His Attributes of power and will combined is discontinuous, and yet it is a process repeated continuously in an everlasting sort of way which permits the renewal of similars in the created things, giving them a sense of continuance in existence. Thus the existence of the world *qua* world is metaphorical (*wujūd majāzī*), creating in our minds a semblance of real existence (*wujūd ḥaqīqī*).

Metaphorical existence is a property, possession, or condition (*milk*) of real existence. The term *milk* in Muslim philosophy is the equivalent of one of the Ten Aristotelian Categories (*al-maqūlāt al-'ashr*),[332] specifically that of condition (*ēchein*). Condition here refers to a state of existence, a state of existence in possession of a certain mode of existing. The way in which the theologians apply the term *milk*, however, is that it is a relationship of possession a body has to the covering it has over the whole part of its extension, or over a part of it, like the clothing one has on and which one carries about wherever one goes, in contrast with the house one has which one does not so carry about, and which does not cover one all the time the way clothing does. In that sense, when metaphorical existence is said to be a *milk* of real existence, the meaning is that the coming-into-existence (*kawn*) of contingent things is a property of real existence; and property refers to a passing mode of existence which is called *mawjūdiyyah*. *Mawjūdiyyah* means among others: (1) condition or state of affairs (*ḥālah*); (2) coming-into-existence (*kawn*); (3) a series of coming-into-existence (*akwān*); (4) 'is'-ness (*kā'in*); (5) the being-existent (*mawjūd*). It also means—with reference to the Ṣūfī metaphysicians' perspec-

---

[332] See chapter VI, p. 219, note 237.

tive in this matter rather than with that of the philosophers and the theologians—the actualized determinations, limitations, particularizations or individuations of real existence at the level of sense and sensible experience. We have said that the *process* of actualization of the possible things is continuous as formulated in a series of renewals, while the *actualization* itself of the things is discontinuous. So the actualized things—the determinations, limitations, particularizations and individuations of real existence—are all the time passing away and being replaced continuously by their similars giving them in their every part and as a whole a semblance of real existence. When we regard the things-in-themselves in their moments of actualization at their specific times, then we are regarding their moments of 'being-existent', which are modes of existence; when we regard them in their continuance in existence in the aspect of the continuous renewal of their similars, then we are regarding the existentiating act of real existence, the condition or state of real existence which is formulated in terms of a necessary relationship with metaphorical existence. This necessary relationship is one of connection and possession. While the necessary connection of the two is mutual, the possession is on the side of real existence only. Similarly, despite the mutual, necessary connection, the need or dependence for existence is on the side of metaphorical existence only. With respect to the concept of *milk* metaphorical existence is like the clothing of real existence. Now the two senses in which being-existent is meant reveals that although the same word signifies two referents, its meaning in each case is not the same because the two referents are not the same: the one refers to an eternal, self-subsistent essence, the other to a temporal, non-self-subsistent essence. In this lies the basic difference between real existence and metaphorical existence. Indeed this constitutes a real difference between the two, and this difference is further emphasized by the possession exercised on the side of the former and which gives the latter existence, and by the dependence on the side of the latter for that existence. Thus because existence, which is equivocally applied to God as well as to the world, is conceived as their common element, a temporal as well as essential difference must obtain between real existence and metaphorical existence, that is, between Necessary Existence and Contingent Existence or between the Being of God and the being of the world, otherwise they would necessarily be identical, or there would be another existence duplicating God's existence, both of which are impossible.

The position of the Muslim philosophers (*ḥukamā'*) and the theologians (*mutakallimūn*) regarding the nature of existence and its relation to things, that is, to realities existing in the external world independent of the mind, is that existence is a general, abstract concept common to all existences in the sense generally understood as explained at the beginning of this chapter.[333] According to their perspective existence is not something that exists objectively, but is merely something posited in the mind when externally existent things become objects of the mind (*i.e. i'tibārī*). Existence for them is therefore a conceptual entity to which nothing in the external world corresponds; it is a secondary intelligible.

Some of the early theologians among the Ash'ariyyah and the Mu'tazilah maintained that the existence of everything, including the existence of God, is identical with its essence (*dhāt*) both in the mind and in the external world independent of the mind. They did not mean by 'identical' (*'ayn*) a combination of two entities becoming one and the same, as they did not recognize any distinction between existence and quiddity or essence. They meant by 'identity' 'indistinguishability', whether in the mind or externally; that is, that existence and quiddity or essence is in fact one and the same thing viewed sometimes as existence and

---

[333] See above p.267.

sometimes as quiddity. Therefore, according to their perspective, there is not in the external world something which is the quiddity, and something else subsisting in it which is existence; rather, in the external world, *and* in the mind, there is only the same 'something' viewed differently at different times, sometimes named by the word 'existence', sometimes named by the word 'quiddity' or 'essence'.[334] We have already pointed out that the above-mentioned position of the early theologians with regard to the nature of existence and its relation to quiddity is untenable.[335] The later theologians, however, affirmed a distinction between existence and quiddity or essence maintaining that existence is a conceptual entity rationally divided into portions that are superadded to externally existent objects whose quiddities are real entities. In our present brief summary of the position of the theologians regarding the nature of existence and its relation to quiddity, we refer here to that of the later theologians.

The position of the philosophers, insofar as it concerns existence being a single, general and abstract concept common to all existences, is the same as that of the theologians; but they differed with the theologians concerning existence at the level of external reality. They maintained that at the level of external reality existence is not something rationally divided into portions corresponding to quiddities which are the really existent entities as the theologians maintained, but that there is a real multiplicity of existences, not through specific difference, but through being in themselves multiple. Thus according to them existences differ from one another essentially, each being an independent entity. They are dissimilar realities (*ḥaqā'iq mukhtalifah*) existing in the external world independent of the mind, and

---

334 *Al-Durrah al-Fākhirah,* pp.2–3; para 5 and 6.

335 See chapter VI, p. 232, and note 262.

which the mind posits as portions of the general, abstract concept of existence due to its being rationally multiplied and divided as such (*i.e.* as portions) solely because of their being ascribed to the quiddities which are their substrata. In reality, then, the portions of existence are superadded in the mind to the existences with dissimilar realities and are therefore external to them.[336] The existence of God, the Necessary Existence, which is identical with His essence, is one of these dissimilar realities.[337]

The positions of the theologians and the philosophers as outlined so far may be represented thus:

1. Theologians

(a) Single concept of existence common to all existences;

(b) Portions of

  (a) individuated through attribution to (c);

(c) Quiddities which are their substrata.

2. Philosophers

(a) Single concept of existence common to all existences;

(b) Portions of

  (a) individuated through attribution to quiddities(c);

(d) Particular existences as dissimilar realities.

From the foregoing gist of the positions of the theologians and the philosophers regarding the nature of existence and its relation to quiddities we derive three things: (1) the general, abstract concept of existence common to all existences; (2) its portions individuated through its attribution to quiddities; (3) particular existences which are dissimilar realities. Existence as in (1) above is essential to and inherent in (2), but both (1) and (2) are external to (3). Particular existence is identical with the essence in the case

---

336 *Al-Durrah al-Fākhirah,* pp.2–4; para 6.

337 See Jāmī's *Ḥawāshī* on the *Durrah, ibid;* pp.54–55; para.5(1).

of God, the Necessary Existence, but superadded and external in the case of everything else.[338] As regards the position of the Ash'arī theologians, they maintained a complete identity of existence and essence or quiddity at all levels, that is, at the conceptual level as well as at the level of external reality. As for the later theologians, they considered (a) and (b) above to be conceptual, and (c) to be real. Similarly, the philosophers considered (a) and (b) to be conceptual, and (c) considered as (d) to be real.

With regard to the position of the Ṣūfī metaphysicians (*ṣūfiyyah*), they maintained that just as it is possible for this general, abstract concept of existence (*i.e.* (a) above) to be superadded in the mind to God and to all particular existences with dissimilar realities (d), it is also possible for it to be superadded in the mind to a single, absolute and existent Reality which is the reality of the Necessary Existence. Whereas this superadded concept would be something existing in the mind, its substratum would be an extramental, real existent which is the reality of existence.[339]

The position of the Ṣūfī metaphysicians may be represented thus:

(a) Single concept of existence common to all existences;
(b) Portions of (a) individuated through attribution to (c) considered as (d);
(e) Absolute Existence (*wujūd muṭlaq*);
(f) Particular existences (*wujūdāt khāṣṣah*) considered as modes of (e).

For the metaphysicians, then, existence at the levels of (a), (b), (c) and (d) is nothing but a mental entity having no cor-

---

338 *Al-Durrah*, p.3; para.7.
339 *Ibid.*, pp.3–4; para.8.

responding existence at the level of external reality. Only (e) and (f) are considered real. In this respect, a gloss in Jāmī's *Naqd al-Nuṣūṣ* makes their position clear:

> Existence (*al-wujūd*), according to the philosopher (*al-ḥakīm*) and the theologian (*al-mutakallim*), is accidental (*'āriḍ*)[340] to quiddities (*al-māhiyyāt*) and realities (*ḥaqā'iq*), and quiddities and realities are substrata (*ma'rūḍāt*) for existence. But according to the verifier (*al-muḥaqqiq*)[341] and the unitarian (*al-muwaḥḥid*),[342] existence is the substratum (*ma'rūḍ*), while the determined and limited existents (*al-mawjūdāt al-muqayyadah*) are accidental to it by virtue of attribution (*al-iḍāfah*) and relation (*al-nisbah*).[343] Between them[344] is a great difference (*bawn ba'īd*). In view of this, the theologians and the philosophers are led to the position that the Absolute Existence (*al-wujūd al-muṭlaq*) does not have external existence (*wujūd fī al-khārij*), but only has mental existence (*wujūd dhihnī*); it is a universal entity (*amr kullī*), a general concept (*'āmm*) which becomes existent by way of its singulars (*afrād*). The verifying knower (*al-'ārif al-muḥaqqiq*),

---

340 That is, inhering in quiddities and realities, or occuring to them from the outside.

341 The verifier is one who proves by demonstration. In this case it is one who verifies by way of the intuition of existence through revelation (*kashf*) and intuitive experience (*dhawq*).

342 That is, Ṣūfī metaphysicians of the school of the transcendent unity of existence (*waḥdat al-wujūd*) .

343 The limited or conditioned existents are the 'quiddities' and 'realities' existing extramentally. Their being-existent is due to their attribution and relation to the Absolute Existence which is their substratum, and which is also known as *wujūd iḍāfī*.

344 The theologians and the philosophers on the one hand, and the Ṣūfī metaphysicians of the school of *waḥdat al-wujūd* on the other.

however, cleaves to the position that the Absolute Existence is existent (*mawjūd*),[345] and there is in reality no other basic (*i.e.* root) existence (*wujūd aṣlan*) besides it, although it is possible to posit such a thing (*i.e.* another source of existence) in the mind (*fī al-i'tibār*). The strange thing is that the philosopher and the theologian describe the Absolute Existence saying that it is the opposite of the absolute non-existence (*al-'adam al-muṭlaq*), and that it is the apportioner (*al-muqaṣṣim*) for all existents, and that it is pure good (*khayr maḥḍ*), and that it is single (*wāḥid*) without contrary (*ḍidd*) and like (*mathal*), and yet they still say that it is non-existent (*ma'dūm*) in the external world (*fī al-khārij*).[346]

The Ṣūfī metaphysicians, then, maintained that in addition to existence at the levels of (a), (b), and (c) considered as (d), which are all mentally posited, there is some other entity because of whose association with quiddities ((c) considered as (d)) and their being clothed with it, existence at the levels of (a) and (b) comes to inhere in them. This other entity is the reality of existence.[347] It is the Absolute Existence ((e) in the foregoing) ; and the particular existences ((f)), which are modes and aspects of the Absolute Existence are, in their actualized states, realities that correspond to (c) and (d), or (c) considered as (d); whereas existence as a secondary intelligible to which nothing in the external world corresponds is one of its effects. As we pointed earlier,[348] the Ṣūfī metaphysicians maintained that there is a higher level of existence than even the Absolute Existence. The Absolute Existence, in the schema

---

345 That is, exists externally.

346 *Naqd al-Nuṣūṣ,* p.21; gloss 5. My translation.

347 *Al-Durrah, Ḥawāshī* p.55; 5(2).

348 See above, pp.268–269.

of ontological 'descent' of the Ultimate Reality, is already at the level of the first determination, whereas the higher level of existence we refer to pertains to the very essence and reality itself of existence at the level of the Essence (*al-dhāt*). This is the level of existence that is not conditioned by anything whatever, including that of unconditionality; it is transcendent from being conditioned even by transcendence, so that it is absolutely pure indetermination, and is consequently unknown and unknowable to our cognition. Their position, then, insofar as the reality of existence under discussion is concerned, involves four things: (1) Existence as absolutely nonconditioned; (2) Absolute Existence, which is a determination of (1) and is existence in reality; (3) its determinations and individuations into particular existences, which are its modes and aspects arising from the dynamic act of the Absolute Existence; and (4) as a general concept rationally divided into portions corresponding to quiddities which are also conceptual in nature. This last is inapplicable to the previous three.

Whereas most philosophers and theologians adhere to the position that the extramental world of concrete things is comprised of composites of essence and existence, out of which is formulated their corresponding metaphysics of substance and accident, the metaphysicians, on the other hand, maintain the reverse of this position: they hold that existence is the only reality, and the world of concrete things is not a composite of essence and existence at all because *essence* is in reality *existence* as it occurs in a particularized and individualized form. The reality of a thing is its very existence as determined into a particular and individual form, not its 'essence' if 'essence' is taken to be something different in substance from existence: there is not 'something' to which existence is then attributed; existence, as a particular and individual mode, is the thing itself. Essence is then a mode of existence. The extramental and dissimilar realities underlying the multiplicity of things are in fact the self-limitations and individuations of existence which create in the mind the notion of 'essences'—'quiddities' having separate ontological reality. In themselves as contemplated by the mind, however, the 'essences' or 'quiddities' are not externally existent entities—they are only something in the mind. Thus, because existence is always in act, the real substance of every individual thing is either an individuation of existence according to that particular aspect of which the thing is its external image, or it is the actual individuation itself of existence at that specific time according to the same aspect. Consequently each individual thing is either an individuation of existence, or it is existence itself as individuated momentarily in that particular form; it is either existence made manifest, or an 'accident' of existence thus manifested. The manifested 'accident' is a quality or existential mode of the manifested existence, and although mentally the quality or existential mode is posited as being distinct from the thing qualified, it is extramentally identical with it insofar as its substance is concerned. This does not necessarily mean that existence contains multiplicity, or that it is compounded of many things. For existence is not static and passive; it is in perpetual movement; a dynamic, creative and systematic process of unfolding itself in gradations from the more indeterminate to the more determinate; from the more general to the more particular until it diversifies itself into the more and more concrete. This unfolding itself of existence is what the metaphysicians call *inbisāt al-wujūd*—the expansion and pervasion of existence in diversified modes—as conceptualized in terms of their metaphysics of the degrees of ontological 'descent' (*tanazzul*), determination (*ta'ayyun*) and individuation (*tashakhkhuṣ*), and self-manifestation (*tajallī*) of Absolute Existence. When the Absolute Existence 'descends',[349] creating out of itself its myriad particulariza-

---

[349] The 'descents' of Absolute Existence are only mentally posited (*i'tibārī*). In reality the eternal process is not measured in terms of time sequence, as we have already stated.

tions and individuations, there is all the time only *one* existence, the particularizations and individuations being only its many modes. These modalities of existence cannot be regarded as having separate ontological reality because their real essence is existence. Only the mind posits the modes of existence as having separate ontological reality other than existence which it regards as 'essences' or 'quiddities'. But in reality there is only one existence.

The world *qua* world—that is, the 'essences' or 'quiddities' that comprise the world when considered in themselves as mentally abstracted from existence—is in reality nothing; it is something only in the mind. It is nothing not only because it is a mere mental construct, but because the 'essences' or 'quiddities' that comprise the world together with all its parts are, when considered in themselves in their extramental state, that is, as modes of existence, 'accidental' in their nature and, therefore, do not endure two moments of time, in such wise that they are perpetually 'lost' to existence. What the mind perceives as the world possessed of existence and continuance in existence is actually only a mental phenomenon which arises in the mind as a result of the rapid succession of similar modes of existence, yet each distinct from the other, involved in the dynamic process of the unfolding of existence, which modes are abstracted in the mind as separate, individual 'essences' having continuance in existence. In their *real* nature, however, the mental 'essences' or 'quiddities' are the effects of the extramental modes of existence. It is only when we consider the 'essences' or 'quiddities' *in themselves* as comprising the world together with all its parts that the world is nothing. Now by 'nothing' is here meant a complete negation or utter privation of existence, and this is denoted by the term *'adam maḥḍ,* or 'pure non-existence'. In this sense, the world *qua* world as perceived by the mind in terms of being composed of multiple and dissimilar quiddities is absolutely nothing; it is pure non-existence. But sometimes the term means something else, and this only when applied to refer not to the world as perceived by the imagination, but to the permanent archetypes or fixed essences (*al-a'yān al-thābitah*) considered as things known (*ma'lūmāt*) in the Divine knowledge or consciousness wherein they subsist as ontological possibilities (*mumkināt*). In that sense *'adam maḥḍ* does not refer to the sort of nothingness characterized by absolute negation or privation of existence, but rather to a mode of existence in the interior condition (*buṭūn*) of Being, which is denoted by the term *'adam,* or 'non-existence', in the sense of something not being concretely existent but whose subsistence in the interior condition of Being is nonetheless established. The qualification *maḥḍ* or 'pure', when *'adam* denotes this aspect of non-existence, means that the something real subsisting in the interior condition of Being *remains purely in the interior condition* and cannot *essentially* become existent externally or concretely actualized. What of that reality that can become existent externally or actualized concretely are its forces conforming with its nature (*aḥkām*), its concomitants (*lawāzim*) and effects (*āthār*), which become externalized and evolve into exterior existence in accordance with the inherent potentiality or preparedness (*isti'dād aṣlī*), *i.e.* the future state, of the particular reality. Thus what is in the condition of pure non-existence, as referring to this aspect of non-existence, pertains to a mode of possibility (*imkān*), and it is the same as possible existence (*wujūd mumkin*).[350] The possible things (*al-mumkināt*) are in this sense the realities (*ḥaqā'iq*) subsisting in God's mind, wherein they appear as the forms of the Divine Names that come under the circum-

---

350 The metaphysicians, unlike the theologians, mean by 'possible' existence an objective possibility; something subsisting in the interior condition of Being before being qualified by external existence. Although this seems somewhat like the philosophers' notion of objective possibility, it is in fact distinct from that of the philosophers. Cf. chapter VI, pp. 257–258.

spective sway of the principal Name *al-ẓāhir,* the outwardly manifest, and by virtue of which can receive the effulgences (sing. *fayḍ*) that evolve them, in terms of their forces, effects and concomitants, to outward manifestation and external existence. Thus when we consider the mentally posited 'essences' or 'quiddities' in their real nature—that is, not as they exist in the mind, but as they exist extramentally—as the perpetually unfolding existence presenting itself in diversified modes and in similar series, then the world that they comprise is not nothing. Indeed, that it creates in the mind the notion of innumerable, separate and dissimilar 'quiddities' demonstrates that there is something about the world *qua* itself, and independent of the mind, that is not nothing. A thing as regarded by the mind when it contemplates the thing's 'whatness' (*māhiya*) creates in the mind the notion of 'quiddity' (*māhiyyah*).[351] This 'quiddity' is, as we have recurrently said, nothing in itself but a mental phenomenon. But when the thing is considered in terms of ' that by which it is it' (*mā bihi al-shay' huwa huwa*),[352] then it is no longer considered merely as a mental phenomenon, but also as an existent reality independent of the mind.[353] This latter concept of *māhiyyah* denotes the constituent determinant of a thing, but here it does not mean 'quiddity' in the sense of something essentially other than existence to which existence is then superadded as an attribute; here it means the 'real essence' (*'ayn*), the 'very self' (*nafs*) or reality (*ḥaqīqah*) that makes the thing what it is.[354] In this latter case the thing is in reality a mode of existence. There is not, as we have said, something essentially other than existence to which existence is attributed; existence (*i.e.* as a particular

---

[351] See chapter VI, p.248 (1); and the diagram on p. 250, *Māhiyyah II.*

[352] See *ibid.*, p.248 (2).

[353] See *ibid.*, pp.241 fol., p.250, *Māhiyyah 1.*

[354] Cf. *ibid.*, pp.236; 233–234.

mode) is the very thing itself.

Muslim philosophers, theologians and metaphysicians are agreed that God, the Necessary Existence, is One in essence; no division in His Essence, whether in the imagination, in actuality, or in supposition is possible; no plurality or duality inheres in it. There is no multiplicity in Him; He is not a locus of qualities, nor a thing portioned and divisible into parts, nor is He compounded of constituent elements,[355] for such things come under the category of bodies limited by boundaries, and hence they are originated, and that is inconsistent with His being the Necessary Existence. But the theologians and the philosophers disagree on the nature of the Oneness; whether it is absolutely One in all aspects as the philosophers maintain, or whether it is One to which real attributes are superadded as the theologians affirm. On this problem the position of the metaphysicians approximates that of the theologians in a certain respect, and that of the philosophers in another, although it is not quite the same as that of either of them, seeing the existentialist basis on which the metaphysicians establish themselves as opposed to the essentialist bases on which the theologians as well as the philosophers erect their respective positions.

The theologians say that God possesses real and eternal Attributes superadded to His Essence, both in the mind and externally, so that God knows through knowledge, wills through will, and exercises power through power, and so on with the rest of the attributes. They contend, against the views of the Mu'tazilah and the philosophers, that if knowledge, will, and power are identical with the Essence, then it would follow that knowledge, will and power are also identical with one another, and that this conclusion leads to many

---

[355] That which has parts, when the parts are in composition together, is a thing compounded, when the parts are separated from one another, is a thing portioned or divided.

absurdities.[356] Neither are the Attributes to be taken merely as synonymous terms describing the Essence according to its modes or states (*aḥwāl*); they are real and eternal, distinct from one another and more so from the Essence. Their reality and eternity do not necessarily imply the existence of a plurality of eternals in the Divine Essence, for the Attributes are not separate essences 'in' God, nor do they give rise to eternal essences 'outside' of God; they subsist in God and are inseparable from Him, but they are dependent upon Him while He is not dependent upon them. The Essence must be taken together with its Attributes as one entity, and since the Essence is eternal and without any efficient cause for its existence, so are its Attributes eternal and without any efficient cause for their existence. The term 'God' could not be predicated of an essence denuded of Attributes, as it points to the essence and the attributes together. The Attributes are not God, nor are they other than God, in the sense that the word 'other' denoting the Attributes is not to be taken to mean that their existence is possible to the exclusion of the Essence in relation to them. Thus while the theologians affirm that the Divine Unity (*al-tawḥīd*) is far exalted above composition, the kind of composition that can be proved by rational methods is to be incompatible with the essence of the Necessary Existence, they yet maintain that it is not an absolute simplicity.[357]

---

356 Cf. al-Shahrastānī, *Kitāb Nihāyat al-Iqdām fī 'Ilm al-Kalām,* ed. A. Guillaume, London, 1934, ch.I, and pp. 238–267.

357 For their details and argument, see al-Ghazālī's *Al-Iqtiṣād fī al-I'tiqād.*, eds.A.Cübükcü & H.Atay, Nur Matbaasi, Ankara, 1962, pp.129–139; 139–141;142–157; *Tahāfut,* pp.40–48; 'Aḍud al-Dīn 'Abd al-Raḥmān al-Ijī, *Al-Mawāqif fī 'Ilm al-Kalām,* 'Alam al-Kutub, distributed by Maktabah al-Mutanabbī, Cairo, and Maktabah Sa'd al-Dīn, Damascus [n.d.]; pp.279–296; Sa'd al-Dīn al-Taftāzānī, *Sharḥ al-'Aqā'id.,* Dār al-Kutub al-'Arabiyyah al-Kubrā, Cairo, 1335, pp.69–77.

The philosophers, on the other hand, maintain that the Divine Unity is absolute simplicity. No duality or multiplicity inheres in Him. He is not subject to division into quantity, principle, or in definition, this last because He has no genus nor specific difference. He is knowing, willing, and powerful not by knowledge, will, and power, for His attributes are the very Essence itself. Thus His Essence, with respect to its connection with things known, is described as 'knowing'; and with respect to its connection with things willed, is described as 'willing'; and with respect to its connection with things over which He has power, is described as 'powerful'. They insist that the Essence is One in all respects, such that it can have no Attributes inhering in it. This, they contend, would involve the Essence in either a duality or a multiplicity. So they deny Attributes altogether, maintaining that Attributes exist only in the mind and not in external reality.[358]

The metaphysicians agree with the theologians that the Essence possesses real Attributes which are multiple and superadded to it, but differ from them in that the Attributes are multiple and superadded to the Essence only in intellection, or in thought, and not externally. Furthermore, they maintain that these Attributes are manifestations of His Essence in the external world appearing as separate and concrete, existential entities. Their affirmation that the Attributes are multiple and superadded to the Essence in intellection only, and not also externally as the theologians maintain, would seem to imply that the metaphysicians in fact agree with the philosophers in denying their reality. For the philosophers say that the Attributes are multiple and superadded to the Essence only in the mind, and that in

---

358 *Al-Ishārāt,* vol.III, pp.44–45; 49–50; *Metaphysica,* ch.13, 21; *Tahāfut,* pp.40 fol; *Sharḥ al-'Aqa'id,* pp.60, 69–71; *al-Mawāqif* p.279; *Kitāb al-Milal wa al-Niḥal* of al-Shahrastānī, 2nd.ed. Beirut, 1395/1975, 2V., vol.II, p.182.

reality the Attributes are the very Essence itself, not in the sense that there is an Essence having Attributes and that the two of them are united as one entity, but in the sense that the Essence has in reality no Attributes at all, the latter existing only in the mind. What they mean by 'existing in the mind' is existing only as a concept (*mafhūm*). What the metaphysicians mean by 'intellection' (*ta'aqqul*), however, is not the same. The difference between essence and attribute, with respect to concept, is that the two concepts, of essence and of attribute, refer to two different things, but that what they are true of is the same, that is, the very essence itself. For the philosophers conceive the Essence as real whereas the Attributes of the Essence are only in the mind; so what the concept of the Essence is true of is in reality the Essence itself, and what the concept of Attributes is true of—since Attributes are only in the mind—is also in reality the same Essence. But the metaphysicians mean that just as the concept of the attribute differs from that of the essence, so do what the two concepts are true of differ from one another: what the attribute is true of is not the same as what the essence is true of. What God's knowledge is true of is thus not the Essence itself, but the Essence *in a certain respect.* The Essence, as we have explained earlier,[359] is characterized by two aspects: the interior, self-concealing aspect (*al-bāṭin*), and the exterior, self-revealing aspect (*al-ẓāhir*). The first aspect is that of absolute, essential Oneness (*aḥadiyyah muṭlaqah*), transcendent in itself, unknowable except to itself. The second aspect is also that of Oneness, (*waḥdah*) but a oneness in which there is already adumbrated the latent possibilities of articulation in multiple and diverse forms. When in this second aspect God, as the Necessary Existence, contemplates Himself and is conscious of His essential perfections (*kamālāt dhātiyyah*), the first effusion of

[359] See above, pp.271 fol.

existence takes place (*i.e. al-fayḍ al-aqdas*). The contents of this effusion of existence are the forms of the Divine Names and Attributes which are, in their emergence in His act of existence, identical with Him, and yet also something different as well.[360] They are different in the sense that in this first self-contemplation, there is already adumbrated in His Essence the latent forms of His perfections that require realization in the realms of contingency. Then in a second self-contemplation, He reveals Himself to Himself in their forms such that their essences (*al-a'yān*) become manifest to Him as distinct realities (*ḥaqā'iq*). The Attributes take their rise at this level of Divine self-contemplation. This 'descent' (*tanazzul*), or effusion of His existence, from the degree of His absoluteness (*iṭlāq*) to that of determination (*taqayyud*), that is, the first determination, occurs in the interior condition of Being, that is, in God's mind. The Attributes and their realities are thus inseparable from Him, that is, they remain as intelligibles in Him, and what become separate and contingent are their forces, concomitants or effects which are actualized externally as the self-unfolding existence expands over them in a second effusion of existence (*i.e. al-fayḍ al-muqaddas*) .[361] The Attributes, then, are not the Essence itself, but the Essence in a certain respect; that is, in a certain aspect, relation, or facet of itself as it qualifies itself in their forms. The difference, therefore, exists not only in our minds, but in God's mind or consciousness at the level of God's cognitive manifestation of Himself to Himself wherein the Attributes appear as ideal realities, the permanent archetypes or fixed essences.[362] The metaphysicians, then,

---

360 They are identical in respect of existence and reality, but are different in respect of determination and individuation.

361 Here the self-unfolding existence is identified as the 'breath of the Merciful' (*nafas al-raḥmān*), *i.e.* the 'relative existence' (*wujūd iḍāfī*).

362 See *Al-Durrah al-Fākhirah,* 12:27; 13:2–29;*Ḥawāshī,* 62:19–20;

agree with the theologians that Cod possesses real Attributes superadded to His Essence; but they also agree with the philosophers that the Essence (and here the metaphysicians mean the Essence at the level of absolute Oneness where not even a trace of multiplicity is discernible) is One in all respects; and that from what is really One there can proceed only one effect. The theologians, as we have seen, affirm of Him attributes superadded to His Essence both in the mind and externally, so that even though He is asserted by them as being far exalted above composition, His Unity is not really one of absolute simplicity. Since this is their position they do not find it impossible for multiple effects to proceed from the One, as their position does not come under the principle that from what is really One only one can proceed. The metaphysicians affirm the true position in this matter—*i.e.* the principle that from what is absolutely One only one effect can proceed—to be that of the philosophers, with whom they are in agreement in this case. But they also differ in this from the philosophers; whereas the philosophers affirm an absolute Oneness in an *individuated* Essence,[363] the metaphysicians assert an absolute Oneness in an *absolute* Essence[364] that becomes individuated at the level of Divinity (*ilāhiyyah*) where, as God, He is already invested with Names and Attributes. This level, which corresponds to the level of the First Principle according to the theologians, does not represent absolute Oneness, but is characterized by Unity in Multiplicity (*wāḥidiyyah*). However, since the metaphysicians

---

Sharḥ al-Durrah, 88:28; *Lawā'ih,* 14(XV) 14–15. Indeed, they are realities because of their *difference* in God's mind. See also *Fuṣūṣ,* pp.48 fol; 101–106.

363 *I.e.* at the level of 'God', or the first determination of Absolute Existence.

364 *I.e.* at the level of the Essence in His self-concealing aspect of absolute Oneness.

affirm the sole reality of existence, the multiplicity and diversity are in their real nature nothing but the modes, the particularizations and individuations of the same reality of existence, so that there is no real multiplicity and diversity there. Moreover, again different from the philosophers, they maintain that the multiplicity and diversity in the concrete existential entities that we see and behold are in reality His Names and Attributes—or rather their concomitants, and repercussions of the concomitants—that have descended in gradations from the level of their absoluteness to that of determination and limitation. As for the philosophers, since they maintain the primacy of essence over existence, and affirm an absolute simplicity in an individuated Essence, their position on the Attributes is confused, and their solution as to how multiple effects can proceed from something absolutely simple is still subject to contradictions.[365]

Although the metaphysicians agree with the philoso-

---

[365] The Essence which according to the philosophers is identical with existence in God, but other than existence in contingents, in virtue of their position that it is an individuated Essence, is identical with an individuated existence. What the philosophers mean by existence, when they say that the Essence is identical with existence in God, but other than existence in contingents, is merely existence as a concept, not as reality, in line with the position of essentialists in general, namely that essence is the sole reality rather than existence. Among later philosophers, al-Êūsī has attempted to demonstrate how multiple effects can proceed from what is absolutely One, but al-Ghazālī's argument that what proceeds in such a case must also be simple entities seem still to hold good against its validity —as long, that is, as the matter is viewed from an essentialist position. But the matter would be different if viewed from the position of the existentialist metaphysicians. See *Al-Durrah al-Fākhirah,* 67–78, 79; *Ḥawāshī,* 98:20; *Sharḥ al-Durrah* 127–128:28.

phers on the principle that from the One only one effect can proceed, they however disagree with the philosophers on what that single first effect is. The philosophers say the single first effect from the One which they call the First Principle[366] is the First Intelligence (*al-'aql al-awwal*), which according to them is a concrete existent having no other existents in its plane. The metaphysicians, however, since they affirm the sole reality of existence, say that the single first effect from the One which is the Absolute Existence is general existence (*al-wujūd al-'āmm*) which, as the unfolded existence (*al-wujūd al-munbasiṭ*), expands as a result of God's self-contemplation in the first degree of existence to the level of the first determination (*al-ta'ayyun al-awwal*).[367] Now this first effusion of existence, as we know, is not a concrete existent, but is a relation of existence in a general way, and its expansion over the intelligible, individual essences established in His knowledge. These intelligible existents become realized as essences precisely due to the expansion of general existence over them.[368] Thus there are other existents in this plane, including the First Intelligence. It is clear from this that the Ṣūfīs make the First Principle of the philosophers to be the equivalent not of the Essence in its absolute

---

366 *I.e.* at the level of 'God', the same as the First Principle of the theologians.

367 There is a resemblance between the general existence (*al-wujūd al-'āmm*) of the Ṣūfīs and the prime matter (*al-hayūlā*) of the philosophers; only that whereas prime matter is merely receptive of form in a passive way, the general existence of the Ṣūfīs is active agent. As to the notion of emanation inherent in the concept of expansion, it must be understood that there is no 'emanation' as if the effects are separate from the source; what is termed as 'emanation' is only the *act* of the Source.

368 General existence is also identified variously as relative existence (*wujūd iḍāfī*), relative light (*nūr iḍāfī*) and the Breath of the Merciful (*nafas al-raḥmān*).

Oneness at the transcendent degree of non-determination (*i.e. aḥadiyyah muṭlaqah*), but the Essence that has descended to the degree of self-manifestation at the level of the first determination or individuation in the plane of unity in multiplicity (*i.e. wāḥidiyyah*).[369] The philosophers believe the effects of the Essence to be separate entities different from the Essence. According to the metaphysicians, however, the effects of the Essence, or God as the Absolute Existence, are its inherent modes or predispositions (*shu'ūn*) and aspects (*i'tibārāt*), or its intellection of the possibles within itself which produces the essences of things in the Divine knowledge. At the level of His essential unity these are undifferentiated, but become differentiated through the effusion of general existence which expands over them and takes place at the level of the first determination. The Essence at this latter level is according to the metaphysicians' scheme equivalent to the First Principle of the philosophers. The multiplicity of the effects of the Essence adumbrated in itself at the former level become realized at the latter level in the forms of Attributes and fixed essences through the mediacy of the first effusion of existence. Thus what first proceeds from the Essence is this single effusion. Then through the mediacy of the first effusion of existence, which effects the rise of Attributes and essences, and through the mediacy also of these Attributes and essences concomitant with the flow of existence in the second effusion as it goes on expanding, other modes and aspects arise until finally their effects appear as contingent, existential entities, some of which are actualized at the level of sense and sensible experience. In this way, then, the metaphysicians concur with the theologians who believe it possible for multiple effects to proceed from the one First Principle,[370] although they affirm with

---

369 With the theologians this is the level of God and His Attributes, which they consider to be the First Principle.

370 *I.e.* First Principle in the sense of the level of *wāḥidiyyah* in the

the philosophers the principle that from what is really One there can proceed only one effect.[371]

The foregoing gist of the positions of the philosophers, the theologians, and the metaphysicians on their understanding of the nature of God's Oneness and allied matters relating to the Divine Attributes and the problem of creation clearly reveals that their fundamental difference from which other differences followed, revolved around the basic question as to whether it is quiddity (essence) or it is existence that is primarily real. As a matter of fact, if one were to classify Muslim thought as a whole into distinct schools in the sense of adherence to certain basic principles or agreeing in typical characteristics, then it must either be that which affirmed the fundamental reality of essence, or that which affirmed the primacy of existence over essence. The philosophers and the theologians generally affirmed the former, and their perspective on the nature of God's Oneness, the Divine Attributes, the creation and allied matters is therefore essentialistic. But the Ash'ariyyah theologians were the closest to the metaphysicians in ontological outlook, because their position on the matter of essence versus existence was somewhat ambivalent. They adhered to the position that essence and existence are indistinguishable.[372] Even though we have shown that the validity of this position cannot really be defended,[373] it is however significant in showing that the position of the Ash'ariyyah as a whole *already implied* the primacy of existence and the transcendent unity of existence (*waḥdat al-wujūd*) affirmed by the metaphysicians. Moreover, apart from their similarity with the

---

metaphysicians' scheme.

[371] See *Al-Durrah al-Fākhirah,* 70/86; 87; 71/88; 89, 90, 91. *Lawā'iḥ,* pp.1618 (XVIII).

[372] See above, pp.298–299; 300.

[373] See chapter VI, pp. 232–233; 234 fol.

position of the metaphysicians in certain department of their metaphysics of atoms and accident, there were similarities also between the Ash'ariyyah and the metaphysicians in their respective statements on the creed and the articles of belief and faith, and in the affirmation of God's exclusive efficacy. Because of their preponderance towards essentialism, however, the Ash'ariyyah had to affirm God's difference from originated things (*mukhālafah li al-ḥawādith*). The metaphysicians, since they were established in their existentialism, maintained that God is different from originated things in point of determination and individuation, but not different from them in point of existence and reality; for the reality of existence can become the principle at once both of the One and the Many, without the One becoming the Many or the Many becoming the One. Again, the essentialistic position of the theologians demanded the affirmation of the doctrine of creation from nothing, denying thereby the third metaphysical category between existence and non-existence, which is the realm of possibilities, such as the archetypal realities affirmed by the metaphysicians. But since the theologians transferred infinite possibilities to God Himself they were in fact approaching the position of the metaphysicians, only that their essentialism prevented them from arriving at the same truth. Furthermore, the problem of determinism in human destiny can only find its explanation in the nature of the archetypal realities. On the Divine Unity the Ash'ariyyah affirmed of Him real Attributes superadded to the Essence both in the mind and externally. Thus, while they denied any composition in the Essence, they nevertheless denied an absolute simplicity in it, such as affirmed by the philosophers. The metaphysicians too affirmed of Him real Attributes superadded to the Essence, but not externally, nor yet only in the mind. We have already indicated this in our explanation on the double nature of the Divine Names and Attributes; and have also pointed out that for the metaphysicians the Attributes are manifestations of the Essence in the external world appearing as separate and concrete existential entities.[374] Moreover, in terms of the degrees of the 'descent' of the Absolute in analogical gradations as formulated by the metaphysicians, the Divine Unity as understood by the theologians corresponds in the metaphysicians scheme to the level of *wāḥidiyyah* in the planes of the first and second determinations and individuations, where the Absolute as God is already invested with the Names and Attributes of divinity. The metaphysicians therefore affirmed a higher, unmanifested and hence unknown level of the Divine Unity, in which the Essence is only known to itself.

From this summary statement of the significant similarities and dissimilarities in the positions of the metaphysicians and the theologians on the nature of reality and of God, the reason why most or all of the *Sunnī* metaphysicians of this school also endorsed the Ash'ariyyah theology and metaphysics should already become clear. For it is because the metaphysicians considered the interpretation of the Ash'ariyyah, *insofar as it pertains to the ordinary, albeit sophisticated, level of reason and of sense and sensible experience,* to be the one that coincided closest with the truth. The metaphysicians considered that the Ash'ariyyah interpretation is true at this level, which is the level of the generality of mankind, where everyone is an essentialist in his perception of truth in accordance with the natural disposition of the mind.

---

374 *Ibid.*, pp. 251–253; and above, pp. 310–313.

EPILOGUE

Our compendious exposition of the Six Degrees of Existence may well serve as a possible interpretation of certain difficult passages in the Holy Qur'ān pertaining to the Creation in Six Days. There it is stated that Allāh, the Ultimate Reality, "has created the Heavens and the Earth in Six Days, and is firmly established on the Throne" (*Al-A'rāf* (7):54; *Yūnus* (10):3); and "has created the Heavens and the Earth, and all between them, in Six Days, and is firmly established on the Throne" (*Al-Sajdah* (32):4; "without being touched by any sense of weariness" (*Qāf* (50):38). We interpret this to mean that He has created the entire universe—that is, the visible as well as the invisible worlds together with all their parts (*al-'ālamīn*): He declares Himself in the passages on creation as the 'Lord of all the worlds' (*rabb al-'ālamīn, Fuṣṣilat* (41) :9)—in Six Stages, since the Divine Day in our reckoning would span, we are told, "like a thousand years" (*Al-Ḥajj* (22):47), or of "the measure of fifty thousand years" (*Al-Ma'ārij* (70):4). We are also told that for God the creative act is "a single act" (*amr wāḥidah*) accomplished in "the twinkling of an eye" (*ka lamḥin bi al-baṣar*): *Al-Qamar* (54):50). In this we see, from the point of view of human cognition, and when we consider the act of creation and the creative process that follows in terms of the 'descent' of the Ultimate Reality from the degree of pure absoluteness and utter concealment to those of manifestation and determination in the lower degrees of the ontological levels, that it is the human mind that posits (*i.e. i'tibār*) a temporal sequence, a distance measureable in terms of time, from the highest to the lowest degree; whereas in reality the act of creation and the whole creative process involved in the varying degrees occurs all at once—"in the twinkling of an eye". Then in that twinkling of an eye His being all the while "firmly established on the Throne" means that in spite of His involvement in the creative process He remains always as He was, in absolute control, maintaining His absolute Oneness. The act of creation and the creative process is repeated (*Yūnus* (10):4; *Al-Naml* (27):64; *Al-'Ankabūt* (29) :19-20), in a new creation (*Qāf* (50):15; also *Al-Ra'd* (13):5; *Ibrāhīm* (14):48; *Banī Isrā'īl* (17):49, 98; *Al-Anbiyā'* (21):104; and *Fāṭir* (35) :16).

The Six Days may be divided into distinct phases of Four Days and Two Days (*Fuṣṣilat* (41):10; and 9;12). In these passages we are further informed that He brought into being (*ja'ala*) *rawāsiya* — which commentators usually interpret to mean 'mountains' — setting them high above the Earth. The basic meaning of the word *rawāsiya,* which is a plural from the root *rasā,* conveys the notion of entities that are fixed, steadfast, firmly established in a permanent sort of way that cannot be moved or transferred to another place. The interpretation of it as 'mountains' is therefore sound; for mountains are characterized by the sort of fixity that is described by *rawāsiya,* and they rise high above ground level. He also blessed the Earth, and measured in due proportion (*qaddara*) all things therein, giving them their sustenance (*aqwātaha*) "in accordance with the requirements of those who ask" (*sawā'an li al-sā'ilīn*). This phase of creation is accomplished in Four Days.

Now the interpretation of commentators of the above passages on creation and the creative process is based on the apparent meanings conveyed by them, and is explained as the creation of the Heavens and the Earth in stages from primeaval formless matter to become the physical forms that we behold, comprising the mineral, vegetable, and animal kingdoms of nature and the firmaments of the universe together with all its parts. From the point of view of human cognition, this interpretation is established upon the principles of reason and observation supported by the evidence of relevant sciences such as physics, astronomy, and geology. Without discounting the validity of that interpretation, rather in accord with it and from the metaphysical point of view which serves as a framework within which all human sciences find correspondence and coherence, we maintain that it is also possible to interpret the passages on Creation in Six Days in conformity with the Six Degrees of Existence. We have in fact already alluded to this metaphysical interpretation of the passages even at the beginning of this Epilogue; and we now continue by suggesting that the expressions 'the Heavens' (*al-samāwāt*) and the 'the Earth' (*al-arḍ*) mentioned in the passages on creation may not *always* refer to the *physical* Heavens and Earth, but at certain stages and with reference to the causal priority-posteriority relation in the creative process understood within the context of the degrees of existence, they refer to their *archetypes* (*al-a'yān al-thābitah*). In this sense we may then interpret the *rawāsiya,* which are firmly established "high above" the Earth, to mean the archetypal realities that are firmly and permanently established in fixity such that they cannot be moved or transferred from their domain in the interior condition of Being.

We said at the beginning of our exposition (cf.pp.268–278 above) that the Ultimate Reality in His Absolute Oneness in the first degree of existence is characterized by aspects of interiority and exteriority, the latter being His self-revealing aspect referred to in the sacred tradition as the 'Hidden Treasure'. This aspect, which is likewise characterized by interiority and exteriority, and which is not yet involved in any determination, is in its exterior aspect already pregnant with infinite possibilities of determination in various unlimited forms; it is the center and the source of creative activity, and the principle of diversity. In this aspect of the *first* degree of existence the Ultimate Reality is the Absolute Existence, and origination of all creation, beginning with the first effusion of existence, pertains to this aspect wherein His essential perfections (*kamālāt dhātiyyah*) and predispositions (*shu'ūn*) become manifest to His consciousness (cf.pp.289 (II) and 290 above). Creation is the existentiating act of the Ultimate Reality; it is also the verification of what is at once *true* (to the creative

Command) and *real* (potentially as well as actually). The Absolute Existence is then here identical with the Quranic 'Truth' or 'True-Real' (*al-ḥaqq*).

The first effusion of existence is the most holy effusion (*al-fayḍ al-aqdas*), which is a single expansion of existence in a general manner (*i.e. wujūd 'āmm*), containing manifestations of forms of pairs of opposites of all possible existents in the invisible as well as the visible worlds. These are all the active, necessary, and divine manifestations as well as all the passive, contingent, and creaturely manifestations. This is the first of all the manifestations of the reality of Existence and is called the first determination (*ta'ayyun awwal*), corresponding to the *second* degree of existence. The Ultimate Reality, at this level of ontological expression, is no longer to be regarded as absolutely One (*aḥadiyyah muṭlaqah*), but as Single (*fard*) by virtue of having caused to arise within His consciousness the potentiality of the 'other', Himself being Other than the otherness of the 'other'. This is the stage of the Unity of the many (*wāḥidiyyah*).

Then, as a further articulation of ontological expression and creative activity the Ultimate Reality, in His aspect as the Absolute Existence, causes to arise within His consciousness the active, necessary, and divine manifestations corresponding to the degree of Divinity (*ilāhiyyah*) in which, as ' God' (*ilāh*), He is qualified by Names (*e.g.* knowing, willing, powerful, *etc.*) and Attributes (*e.g.* knowledge, will, power, *etc.*) of divinity. These Names and Attributes are further particularizations of His predispositions and essential perfections that have become manifest to Him already in the first degree of existence. This stage marks His 'descent' to the second determination (*ta'ayyun thānī*) corresponding to the *third* degree of existence. This is the stage of the Names and Attributes.

Now the predispositions and essential perfections of the Ultimate Reality are manifest to Him as forms of the Divine Names and Attributes. These forms are essentially 'ideas' or 'intelligibles' in the Divine knowledge. Inherent in each of these forms is an aspect of 'otherness', a distinctness peculiar to itself and thus also different from Him. They are qualified by being permanently established because as 'ideas' in the Divine mind they subsist permanently (*baqā'*) in the Divine knowledge, unaltered in their nature and unmoved from their interior, intelligible condition. By virtue of their being distinct from each other and from Him, and of their continuance as such in the Divine knowledge, they are original *realities* (*ḥaqā'iq*) whose future states are to be actualized at the lower degrees of the ontological levels as the effusion of existence expands over them. Inherent in each reality are potentialities peculiar to each; each has received its measure in due proportion (cf. *qaddara*), so that each has a preparedness (*isti'dād;*) to become actualized in accordance with its own requirements. His intellection of these forms in their aspect of 'otherness' from Him, and His self-revelation (*tajallī*) in them as well as the effusion of His existence as it expands over them, brings about their positive nature as realities that can be actualized as concrete, individual existence in the external world. The realities are therefore archetypal in nature and essence and are appropriately called 'permanent archetypes' (*a'yān thābitah*), whose ontological level corresponds to the third determination (*ta'ayyun thālith*) of Absolute Existence in the *fourth* degree of existence (cf.pp. 277–278; 290 (III), above).

We said (p. 278, above) that the Absolute Existence is self-sufficient in His eternal plenitude, needing no 'other' whatever, but that His Names and Attributes which are apparent to Him at the lower degrees of the ontological levels have need of their positive realities to be actualized in their respective manifestation-forms (*maẓāhir*) in the invisible as well as the visible worlds. Their actualization pertains to the consecutive actualization of potentialities inherent in every one of them, such that it appears as an unfolding of their future states in external existence. This actualization of the positive realities is effected by means of the self-revelations, determinations, individuations of the Absolute

Existence in their respective manifestation-forms. Because every one of the realities is distinct from the other, and each one of them contains all its future states to be actualized in sequential order, His self-revelations in them are never repeated in the same forms. This further manifestation of the Absolute Existence in the lower degrees of the ontological levels takes place by means of another (*i.e.* the second) effusion of His existence called the holy effusion (*al-fayḍ al-muqaddas*), which brings us to the remaining second phase of creation in Two Days. Before coming to that, however, we continue our interpretation that His giving to all things their "measure of the means of subsistence in due proportion" (*qaddara aqwātaha*), and "in accordance with the requirements of those who ask" (*sawā'an li al-sā'ilīn*), mean in this context to refer to the potentialities inherent in the realities of things, each measured in due proportion and in accordance with the requirements of its nature. His giving them their sustenance means ultimately His giving them *existence*. Now since the realities evoke in themselves a preparedness (cf. *isti'dād*) to be recipients of existence in accordance with what is inherent in them, this condition of being in *need of actualization* is then the *asking* of "those who ask" (*al-sā'ilīn*).

The foregoing brief sketch, whose import can be properly apprehended only after having fully understood the exposition set forth in this book, is our metaphysical interpretation of the first phase of creation which is accomplished in Four Days. The creative activity of the Ultimate Reality arises, according to this interpretation, at the ontological level of the exterior aspect of His absolute Oneness that is variously called 'the Hidden Treasure', 'the Truth', 'the Absolute Existence', and then proceeds to that of the first, second, and third determinations of the Absolute Existence. These correspond to the first, second, third, and fourth degrees of existence, namely: the degree of Oneness (*al-aḥadiyyah*) that characterizes the Absolute Existence; of the Divine Unity (*al-wāḥidiyyah*); of the Names and Attributes (*al-asmā' wa al-ṣifāt*); and of the Permanent

Archetypes (*al-a'yān al-thābitah*) in their respective order. Each of these degrees is characterized by having aspects of interiority and exteriority and causal relations of priority and posteriority. Our exposition of these four degrees of existence shows that they coincide with the first phase of creation in Four Days mentioned in the Holy Qur'an, which may indeed also allude to them in reality. If so, then this means that this phase of creation occurs in the interior world of intelligibles subjective to the Ultimate Reality, which from the point of view of human cognition is the world of spiritual entities.

As for the remaining second phase of creation in Two Days, we are informed that God, "after having accomplished the previous (*i.e.* first phase of) creation, directed His design (*i.e.* His plan contrived with a definite purpose) to the Heaven" (*Fuṣṣilat* (41):11; see the various meanings of *istawā ilā* in the *Lisān al-'Arab,* XIV p.414, cols. 1&2). The Heaven that is meant, we are told, is as smoke (*dukhān*), meaning something partly physical and partly non-physical in nature. He then bade the Heaven and the Earth to come together willingly or unwillingly; and they both came together in willing obedience. Then He completed them seven firmaments in Two Days, and assigned to each heaven its duty and command. The lower heaven He adorned with lights and secured with guard (41:11–12).

Already we see here, in the Two Days mentioned to complete the creation of the universe together with all its parts, an allusion to the last two degrees of existence: the fifth and the sixth degrees, corresponding to the fourth and fifth determinations of the Absolute Existence. It may well be that at the level of ontological articulation in the fifth degree of existence (the fourth determination), the Heaven and the Earth referred to still symbolize their spiritual or intelligential aspect in their evolvement into ever more concrete forms. This is the level of the exterior archetypes (*al-a'yān al-khārijiyyah*). The exterior archetypes receive the holy effusion of existence which flows from the exterior aspect of the permanent archetypes. Now the permanent archetypes are in fact the realities of things established in the cognitive presence of the Ultimate Reality. They are 'ideal realities' subsisting permanently in God's mind, and as such they are not caused to emerge to a state of exterior manifestation in the realm of empirical things. They are in that sense not 'existent' although they possess positive ontological reality. In relation to the exterior archetypes they are active determinants of all possible existents, for they are, after all, the articulations of the Divine predispositions; they are the original, positive realities poised in readiness to activate the potentialities inherent in them, and to unfold their future states in the form of concrete, individual existences in the external world. In this respect the corresponding exterior archetypes serve as their passive recipients. The contents of the holy effusion of existence are these potentialities, whose future states are consecutively being actualized in the world of empirical things through the mediacy of the exterior archetypes as the effusion of existence expands over them. The exterior archetypes then are all the passive, contingent, and creaturely manifestations of the Absolute Existence. Since these archetypes themselves have aspects of interiority and exteriority, they become, in relation to the world of empirical things, active evolvers of the actualization of their contents through their exterior aspect as the effusion of existence continues to expand over them to the lowest degree of the ontological levels. The ontological level of the exterior archetypes is the fourth determination of the Absolute Existence which corresponds to the *fifth* degree of existence. The *sixth* and last degree of existence is the level of the fifth determination of the Absolute Existence. It is the manifestation in detail of the preceding degree and is the realm of empirical things, the world of sense and sensible experience whose nature is characterized by contingency. (cf.pp. 279–280, and 290 (III), and 290 (IV) above).

Now in the passage where God calls upon the Heaven and the Earth to come together "willingly or unwillingly" (*ṭaw'an aw karhan*) is clear indication showing that the Heaven and the Earth have consciousness of obedience and disobedience to the Divine command in spite of the reality that the command cannot be contradicted. It also indicates they possess a power or capacity to respond to the Divine word of command, for they answered: "we come in willing obedience" (*ataynā ṭā'i'īn*) . We understand from this that the creative process described occurs at the ontological level of the exterior archetypes in the fifth degree of existence. One may recall that the exterior archetypes are the recipients of all the contingent and creaturely manifestations of the Absolute Existence, and that in relation to what is consequent to them, that is, the world of empirical things in the sixth degree of existence, they are active agents of the actualization of their contents into external existence at the lowest degree of the ontological levels. Their saying "we come in willing obedience" explicitly suggests their passive nature; and the "we come" implicity points to their latent power or capacity to activate the actualization of their contents.

Then God completed their creation as seven firmaments; assigning to each heaven its duty and command, and adorning the heaven of our earth (*samā' al-dunyā*) with luminous celestial bodies and securing it with guard. According to our interpretation, it is only at this stage that the words: 'heavens' or 'firmaments' (*samāwāt*), 'heaven' (*samā*) and 'earth' (*arḍ* which in this case is referred to as *dunyā*) refer to the physical universe together with all its parts. The word *dunyā*, derived from the root *dana*, conveys the meaning of something being 'brought near'. The being 'brought near', according to us, mean 'brought near' *to the sensible and intelligible experience and consciousness of man.* That which is brought near to our sensible and intelligible experience and consciousness is the physical universe together with all its parts. The entire physical universe is being brought near to us in this way by virtue of the reality and truth that it constitutes God's *signs* and *symbols* (*āyāt*) displayed to our sensible and intelligible experience and consciousness in order that we may discern their meanings and purpose. The Holy Qur'ān declares so in many passages. If we are correct in our interpretation, it is the *last* of the Two Days that is referred to as the completion of the creation into seven firmaments; and the entire physical universe is the *last* of the seven heavens.

It is important to emphasize here, even though we have not explicity elaborated upon the matter in the foregoing pages of this book, that the creative act of the Ultimate Reality in His aspect as God, that is, the act of creation: the Divine operation that brings into existence from non-existence things 'other' than He, is not accomplished by means of the operation of His creative power and will alone. Indeed, the combined operation of His creative power (*qudrah*) and will (*irādah*) is certainly instrumental in the creative act, but without His word of command to 'be', and without the giving of His existence to what He has commanded to 'be', the thing thus commanded would never be able to come into being. The giving of His existence in terms of His self-revelations, determinations, particularizations and individuations in the guise of the thing is what we have elaborated in the present book. It is the effusion of His existence and its expansion over the realities of things in accordance with their respective requirements, and in ambiguous gradations involving causal relations of priority and posteriority in the various degrees of the ontological levels. Creation is then (i) the infusing of His existence in the forms of the things; (ii) His commanding the things to come into existence; (iii) His power bringing forth the things into external existence; and (iv) His will specifying the things to come into external existence at the time specified. Since He reveals Himself in the form of every single one of the things, what has come to 'be' is His existence actualizing one of its modes in the guise of that thing; so that creation involves also the thing's capacity or power to respond to His command, such as its thingness or otherness, its hearing, and its obedience in becoming like as what it is commanded to become—all acting together simultaneously bringing itself into external existence. The creative act, we said earlier, is one single act accomplished "in the twinkling of an eye"; but the act of creation is repeated, so that the created things evolve as a process of unfolding their future states in a perpetually new creation which undergoes ontological stages.

Finally to conclude, with respect to the Creation in Six Days as interpreted by commentators based on the apparent meanings of the relevant passages, their explanation of the six stages corresponding to the Six Days coincide only with the last degree of existence in our interpretation. This means that they have interpreted the words 'Heavens' and 'Earth' and 'what lies between them' in those passages on creation to refer only to the physical universe together with all its parts, which in our interpretation is at the ontological level of the sixth degree of existence. This is as much as we wish to convey here without going into further details. We beseech God to forgive us where we slip and err, to grant us His succour and guidance in correctly understanding His words and His signs and symbols whose ultimate meanings He alone knows best.

والله أعلم بالصواب

والحمد لله رب العالمين

والصلاة والسلام على اشرف المرسلين

وعلى آله واصحابه والتابعين

لهم باحسان الى يوم الدين

General Index

A
'Abd al-Karīm al-Jīlī 215
'Abd al-Raḥmān al-Jāmī 215
'Abd al-Razzāq al-Qāshānī 215
'Abd Allāh al-Anṣārī 214
'abd 50 , 59, 180 ,188
'ābid 50
absence 211
Absolute 178
absolute existence 210, 212, 213, 218, 237, 241 ,272
absolute indeterminate 222
absolute oneness 251, 271
absolute potency 158
absoluteness 237, 312
absorption 191
abstraction 156, 157
Abū al-Qāsim al-Qushayrī 214
Abū Naṣr al-Sarrāj 214
Abū Sa'īd al-Kharrāz 214
accident 210, 224, 304
accidental 226
accidents 182, 207, 292
acquired intellect 160, 162
action at will 148
active 149, 154
active agent 229, 256
active determinants 254
Active Intelligence 161, 162, 164, 165, 169
actual intellect 164
actual intelligibles 164
actual union 197
actual vision 211
actualities 254
actuality 294
actualization 136, 159
adab 16, 17, 18, 31
adab implies knowledge 18
adab toward art and music 18
adab toward family 17
adab toward home and furniture 18
adab toward knowledge 18
adab toward language 18
adab toward nature and environment 18
adab toward one's self 17
'adam 195, 251, 306
'adam maḥḍ 195, 259, 305, 306
'adl 31, 33, 36, 65
affirmation 165
afrād 301
agent 228
aḥadiyyah muṭlaqah 271, 311, 316, 324
aḥkām 286, 306
Ahlu 'l-Kitāb 54
aḥwāl 60, 183
'ayn 201
'ayn al-yaqīn 105
'ayn thābit 253
ajnās 261
ajsām basīṭ 261
ākhirah 21
akwān 295
al-'adam 206
al-'adam al-muṭlaq 302
al-aḥadiyyah 326
al-'ahd 144
al-ākhir 255, 262, 282
al-ākhirah 1

Cited Bibliographical References

Adler, M., *Reforming Education*, Macmillan, New York, 1988.

Afnan, Soheil Muhsin, *Wāzhah Nāmah Falsafī* (*Qāmūs Falsafī Fārisī-'Arabī*), Dār al-Mashriq, Beirut, 1969.

Āmulī, Sayyid Ḥaydar, *Jāmi' al-Asrār wa Manba' al-Anwār*, bound together with his *Naqd al-Nuqūd fī Ma'rifat al-Wujūd*, eds. Henri Corbin and Osman Yahia, Tehran, 1347/1969.

Aquinas, T., *De Ente et Essentia* (*On Being and Essence*) tr. Armand Maurer, 2nd revised edition, the Pontifical Institute of Mediaeval Studies, Toronto, 1968.

ibn 'Arabī, Muḥyī al-Dīn, *Fuṣūṣ al-Ḥikam*, ed. Abū l-'Alā 'Afīfī, Cairo, 1365/1946, 2v. bound in one; vol. I text of the *Fuṣūṣ*; vol.II 'Afīfī's *Ta'līqāt*.

———. *Al-Futūḥāt al-Makkiyyah*, 4.v, Cairo, 1911. Also the new edition by 'Uthmān Yaḥyā, Al-Majlis al-A'lā li al-Thaqāfah, 12 v., Cairo, 1988.

Arberry, A.J., *Avicenna on Theology*, Wisdom of the East Series, London, 1951.

Aristotle, *Nichomachean Ethics*, tr. Sir David Ross, Oxford University Press, London, 1963.

———. *Poetics*, tr. S.H. Butcher, London, 1911.

al-Attas, Syed Muhammad Naquib, *Islām and Secularism*, Angkatan Belia Islam Malaysia (ABIM), Kuala Lumpur, 1978.

———. *The Concept of Education in Islām*, ABIM, Kuala Lumpur, 1980.

———. *A Commentary on the Ḥujjat al-Ṣiddīq of Nūr al-Dīn al-Rānīrī*, Ministry of Culture Malaysia, Kuala Lumpur, 1986.

al-Bayḍāwī, Abū 'Abd Allāh, *Anwār al-Tanzīl wa Asrār al-Ta'wīl,* 2v. Cario, 1939.

al-Bukhārī, Muḥammad ibn Ismā'īl, *Matn al-Bukhārī,* with marginal glosses by al-Sindī, Dār al-Fikr, Beirut, 4v. [n.d.].

Cox, H., *The Secular City,* SCM Press Ltd., London, 1966

al-Fīrūzābādī, Muḥammad ibn Ya'qūb, *Al-Qāmūs al-Muḥīṭ,* 4v. with marginal commentaries, Cairo, 1319.

al-Ghazālī, Abū Ḥāmid Muḥammad, *Iḥyā' 'Ulūm al-Dīn,* Cairo, 1939, 4v; also the *Iḥyā'* of 16v. in 4 with the *Takhrīj* of al-Ḥāfiẓ al-'Irāqī, and the publisher's introduction and preface by Aḥmad Ibrāhīm al-Sarāwī and Muḥammad al-Khiḍr Ḥusayn. Dār al-Tamal li al-Nashr wa al-Tawzī', Istanbul, 1985.

———. *Ma'ārij al-Quds fī Madārij Ma'rifat al-Nafs,* from the text of Aḥmad bin Sha'bān bin Yaḥyā al-Andalusī, known as ibn 'Abd al-Azīz al-Amīr, dated 1066H. and collated with the text from Tunis dated 923H, together with two *qasīdah* by the author dated 882H. 3rd printing, Beirut, 1978.

———. *Mīzān al-'Amal,* Beirut, 1986.

———. *Mishkāt al-Anwār,* ed. Abū al 'Alā Afifī, Cairo, 1964.

———. *Tahāfut al-Falāsifah* (bound together in a single volume with the *Tahāfut* of ibn Rushd and the *Tahāfut al-Falāsifah* of Khwājah Zādah, Musṭafā al-Bābī al-Ḥalabī, Cairo, 1321.

———. *Al-Maqṣad al-Asnā fī Sharḥ Ma'ānī Asmā' Allāh al-Ḥusnā,* ed. Fadlou Shehadi, Dār al-Mashriq, Beirut, 1971.

———. *Al-Iqtiṣād fī al-I'tiqād,* ed. I.A. Çubukçu and H. Atay, Nūr Matbaasi, Ankara, 1962.

Goichon, M., *La Philosophie d' Avicenne et son influence en*

Europe Mediévalé, Paris, 1951.

ibn Ḥanbal, Aḥmad, *Musnad,* 4v. Cairo, 1313.

al-Hujwīrī, 'Alī ibn 'Uthmān, *Kashf al-Maḥjūb,* tr. R.A. Nicholson, E.J.W. Gibb Memorial Series, London, 1911, vol. XVII.

al-Ījī, 'Aḍud al-Dīn 'Abd al-Raḥmān ibn Aḥmad, *Al-Mawāqif fī 'Ilm al-Kalām,* 'Ālam al-Kutub, Beirut, distributed by Maktabah al-Mutanabbī, Cairo, and Maktabah Sa'd al-Dīn, Damascus [n.d.].

Izutsu, T., *The Concept and Reality of Existence,* Keio Institute of Cultural and Linguistic Studies, Tokyo, 1971.

Jāmī, Nūr al-Dīn 'Abd al-Raḥmān, *Naqd al-Nuṣūṣ fī sharḥ Naqsh al-Fuṣūṣ,* ed. W. Chittick, Imperial Iranian Academy, no. 17, Tehran, 1977.

———. *Majmū'ah Mullā Jāmī,* Istanbul, 1309. Containing the *Lawā'iḥ;* the *Sharḥ Rubā'iyyāt;* and the *Lawāmi': Sharḥ Khamriyyāt ibn Fāriḍ.*

———. *Lawā'iḥ fī Bayān Ma'ānī 'Irfāniyyah,* tr. E.H. Whinfield and Mirzā Muḥammad Qazwīnī, Oriental Translation Fund, New Series, vol. XVI, Royal Asiatic Society, London, 1928.

———. *Al-Durrah al-Fākhirah,* with the author's Glosses (*Ḥawāshi*), and the Arabic commentary of 'Abd al-Ghafūr al-Lārī, and Persian commentary of 'Imād al-Dawlah; eds. N. Heer and A. Musavi Behbahani, Tehran, 1980.

———. *Risalāh fī al-Wujūd,* Arabic text, trans. by N. Heer in *Islamic Philosophical Theology,* ed. P. Morewedge State University of New York Press (SUNY), Albany, 1979.

al-Jarrāḥī, Ismā'īl bin Muḥammad, *Kashf al-Khafā' li Muzīl al-Ilbās,* ed. Aḥmad Qalash, Mu'assasah al-Risālah,

Beirut, 1985, 2v. 4th. pr.

al-Jīlī, 'Abd al-Karīm, *Al-Insān al-Kāmil fī Ma'rifat al-Awā'il wa al-Awākhir*, Muṣṭafā al-Bābī al-Ḥalabī, 2nd.ed. 2v. in one, Cairo, 1375/1956.

al-Junayd, Abū al-Qāsim, *Rasā'il al-Junayd*, E.J.W. Gibb Memorial Series, New Series, XXII, Luzac, London, 1976.

al-Jurjānī, Sayyid Sharīf 'Alī, *Kitāb al-Ta'rīfāt*, Muṣṭafā al-Bābī al-Ḥalabī, Cairo, 1357; and the reprint of the first edition by G.Flugel, Leipzig, 1845, published by the Librairie du Liban, Beirut, 1969.

al-Kalābādhī, Abū Bakr Muḥammad, *Kitāb al-Ta'arruf li Madhhab Ahl al-Taṣawwuf*, ed. Êāha 'Abd al-Bāqī Surūr, 'Īsā al-Bābī al-Ḥalabī, Cairo, 1966; also the ed. by 'Abd al-Ḥalīm Maḥmūd, Beirut, 1400/1980.

Liddel, H.G., and Scott, R. *et al*, *A Greek-English Lexicon*, Oxford, 1968.

MacIntyre, A., *After Virtue*, University of Notre Dame Press, Indiana, 1984.

ibn Mājah, Abū 'Abd Allāh Muḥammad ibn Yazīd, *Kitāb al-Sunan*, Cairo, 1952.

ibn Manẓūr, Jamāl al-Dīn Muḥammad, *Lisān al-'Arab*, Dār Ṣādir and Dār Beyrut, 15v., Beirut 1388/1968.

Mohaghegh M., and Izutsu, T., *The Metaphysics of Sabzavārī*, Wisdom of Persia Series, no. X, Caravan, Delmar, New York, 1977.

Morewedge, P., *The Metaphysica of Avicenna* (a critical translation - commentary of the *Dānish Nāma-i 'Alā'ī*, and analysis of the fundamental arguments), Columbia University Press, New York, 1973.

al-Nasafī, Abū Ḥafṣ 'Umar, *Al-'Aqā'id al-Nasafiyyah*, Cairo, 1335.

Peters, F.E., *Greek Philosophical Lexicon,* New York, 1967.

al-Qāshānī, 'Abd al-Razzāq, *Sharḥ 'alā Fuṣūṣ al-Ḥikam,* Musṭafā al-Bābī al-Ḥalabī, 2nd. ed., Cairo, 1386/1966.

al-Qushayrī, Abū al-Qāsim, *Al-Risālah al-Qushayriyyah,* Dār al-Kitāb al-'Arabī, Beirut, 1957.

Rahman, Fazlur, *Avicenna's Psychology,* Oxford University Press, London, 1952.

al-Rāzī, Fakhr al-Dīn, *Al-Tafsīr al-Kabīr,* Al-Maṭba'ah al-Bāhiyyah, 32v., Cairo, 1934.

———. *Kitāb Lawāmi' al-Bayyināt Sharḥ Asmā' Allāh al-Ḥusnā,* ed. Êāha 'Abd al-Ra'ūf Sa'd, Maktabat al-Kulliyyāt al-Azhariyyah, Cairo, 1400/1980.

Sabzawārī, Mullā Ḥādī, *Sharḥ Ghurar al-Farā'id* (*Sharh-i Manẓūmah*) eds. M. Mohagehgh and T. Izutsu, Tehran, 1348/1969.

al-Sarrāj, Abū Naṣr, *Kitāb al-Luma' fī al-Taṣawwuf,* ed. R.A. Nicholson, E.J.W. Gibb Memorial Series, no. XXII, London, 1963.

Shabistarī, Sa'd al-Dīn Maḥmūd, *Gulshan-i Rāz,* Persian text with an English translation and notes from the commentary of Muḥammad ibn Yaḥyā al-Lāhijī by E.H. Whinfield, Iran-Pakistan Institute of Persian Studies, Islamic Book Foundation, Lahore, 1978 (reprint of the 1880 edition).

Shahrastānī, 'Abd al-Karīm Muḥammad, *Kitāb al-Milal wa al-Niḥal,* 2v. 2nd.ed. Beirut, 1395/1975.

———. *Kitāb Nihāyat al-Iqdām fī 'Ilm al-Kalām,* ed. A. Guillaume, Oxford University Press, London, 1934.

ibn Sīnā, Abū 'Alī al-Ḥusayn, *Kitāb al-Shifā'* (*al-Êabī'iyyāt: al-Nafs*), ed. G. Qanawātī and Sa'īd Zāyid, Al-Maktabah al-'Arabiyyah, Cairo, 1975.

———. *Kitāb al-Shifā' (al-Manṭiq: al-Madkhal)*, ed. G. Qanawātī, Maḥmūd al-Khudayrī and Fu'ād al-Ahwanī, Cairo, 1953.

———. *Kitāb al-Najāt*, ed. Muḥyī al-Dīn Ṣabrī al-Kurdī, Cairo, 1938; and also the edition of Mājid Fakhrī, Dār al-Āfāq al-Jadīdah, Beirut, 1985.

———. *Al-Ishārāt wa al-Tanbīhāt*, with the commentary by Naṣīr al-Dīn al-Êūsī, ed. Sulaymān Dunyā, 4 pts. in 3v., Dār al-Ma'ārif, Cairo, 1958; 2nd. ed., 1971.

———. *Risālah fī Ma'rifat al-Nafs al-Nāṭiqah wa Aḥwālihā*, ed. Aḥmad Fu'ād al-Ahwanī, 'Īsā al-Bābī al-Ḥalabī, Cairo, 1952.

al-Taftāzānī, Sa'd al-Dīn, *Sharḥ al-'Aqā'id* (commentary on the *'Aqā'id* of al-Nasafī with supercommentaries by Aḥmad al-Khayālī and Ibrāhīm al-Isfarā'inī 'Iṣām al-Dīn), Dār al-Kutub al-'Arabiyyah al-Kubrā, Cairo, 1335.

———. *Sharḥ al-Maqāṣid*, Istanbul, 1277, 2v., also the Beirut edition of 1988, in 5v.

al-Tahānawī, Muḥammad A'lā ibn 'Alī, *Kashshāf Iṣṭilāḥāt al-Funūn*, ed. Muḥammad Wajīh, 'Abd al-Ḥaqq, and Ghulām Qādir; A. Sprenger and W. Nassau Lees, Khayyāt, Beirut, 1966, 6v.

al-Tirmidhī, Abū 'Īsā Muḥammad ibn 'Īsā, *Al-Jāmi' al-Ṣaḥīḥ*, Cairo, 1939.

Weber, M., *Essays in Sociology*, New York, 1958.

———. *Sociology of Religion*, Boston, 1964.

Made in the USA
Columbia, SC
04 September 2024

41785072R00200